Beyond Mount Rushmore

Beyond
Mount

Edited and with

an Introduction by

MARY A. KOPCO

Rushmore

Other Black Hills Faces

SOUTH DAKOTA

STATE HISTORICAL SOCIETY

PRESS *Pierre*

The articles in this anthology originally appeared in: *South Dakota History*
South Dakota State Historical Society
900 Governors Drive, Pierre, SD 57501

This publication is funded, in part, by the Deadwood Publications Fund provided by the City of Deadwood and the Deadwood Historic Preservation Commission.

Library of Congress Cataloguing-in-Publication data
Beyond Mount Rushmore : other Black Hills faces / edited and with an introduction by Mary A. Kopco.
p. cm.
"The articles in this anthology originally appeared in South Dakota history"—T.p. verso.
Includes bibliographical references and index.
ISBN 978-0-9822749-6-5
1. Black Hills (S.D. and Wyo.)—History. 2. Black Hills (S.D. and Wyo.)—Biography. 3. Pioneers—Black Hills (S.D. and Wyo.)—Biography. 4. Frontier and pioneer life—Black Hills (S.D. and Wyo.) 5. Black Hills (S.D. and Wyo.)—Social life and customs. 6. Black Hills (S.D. and Wyo.)—Ethnic relations. I. Kopco, Mary A., 1959– II. South Dakota history.
F657.B6B45 2010
978.3'9—dc22
2010010225

Printed in the United States of America

Text and cover design by Rich Hendel

Please visit our website at www.sdshspress.com

14   13   12   11   10   1   2   3   4   5

Contents

Introduction

by Mary A. Kopco

I n 1923 Doane Robinson, secretary and superintendent of the South Dakota State Historical Society, pitched a colossal idea to his United States senator, Peter Norbeck. Robinson proposed the carving of a patriotic monument out of one of the Black Hills' granite rock formations with the goal of attracting national attention to South Dakota, thereby drawing throngs of tourists to the region. With Norbeck on board, Robinson then approached famous sculptor Gutzon Borglum. Likewise, Borglum enthusiastically embraced the idea, and by 1925, he and four hundred workers had begun carving out the faces of four American presidents on Mount Rushmore, named for nineteenth-century attorney Charles E. Rushmore. Completed in 1941, the Mount Rushmore National Memorial continues to attract millions of visitors to the Black Hills each year.

While the granite busts of Washington, Jefferson, Roosevelt, and Lincoln may be South Dakota's most identifiable faces, the region's history is replete with the stories of the many people who carved out lives here. This anthology features a selection of memoirs, biographies, and essays written by and about Black Hills personalities. The articles originally appeared in the South Dakota State Historical Society's award-winning journal *South Dakota History* during the past twenty years. The ten essays and personal reflections brought together in this volume give evidence of the colorful culture and heritage of South Dakota and provide a complex image of the Black Hills region. Common threads emerge that both demonstrate the diversity of the people who impacted the area and explain how the natural environment has shaped nearly one hundred years of human events.

Formed nearly forty million years ago, the Black Hills are a rugged and isolated mountain range rising from the Great Plains in western South Dakota and extending into Wyoming. While considered the sacred center of the earth by a number of American Indian tribes, the Black Hills failed to register on many European Americans' radar until the economic panic of 1873 sent government officials in search of new gold fields. In one of the American West's defining moments, the United States government authorized an expedition to the Black Hills in 1874 with the pretense of locating a suitable site for a future army post. In reality, officials were anxious to confirm earlier rumors of significant gold deposits in the region, completely ignoring the fact that the Fort Laramie Treaty of 1868 designated the Black Hills, part of the Great Sioux Reservation, off-limits to non-Indians. Approximately one thousand men and at least one woman spent sixty days exploring the region under the command of Lieutenant Colonel George Armstrong Custer and the United States Seventh Cavalry. The expedition did not establish a site for a fort, but it did confirm the presence of gold, a fact then broadcast coast-to-coast.[1]

Although the expedition was well documented in newspaper articles and government records, few personal accounts exist. Thus, the diary of correspondent Fred W. Power offers a rare and candid glimpse into the daily life of an expedition member. In "'Distance Lends Enchantment to the View': A Diary of the 1874 Black Hills Expedition," edited by Thomas R. Buecker, Power details the difficulties—real and imagined—faced on a march that began on 2 July from Fort Abraham Lincoln near Bismarck, Dakota Territory, and ended there on 30 August of the same year. Power's diary reveals the raw beauty of the Black Hills along with the often harsh reality of the natural environment. He also gives a human face to the expedition, recounting both humorous and tragic stories. Power's reason for joining the expedition as a correspondent appears to be little more than wanderlust, as he barely mentioned the discovery of gold in his dispatches to the *Saint Paul Daily Press*. Clearly, the rest of the country had a different reaction, for the Black Hills were soon crawling with people looking to strike it rich.

The northern Black Hills became the focus of miners' attention when major gold discoveries were made in Deadwood Gulch during the fall of 1875. Neither the army's attempts to keep non-Indians out of the region nor the constant threat of Indian attacks served to dampen the lust for gold. Up to ten thousand people had descended on the area by the summer of 1876. Unlike most of his compatriots, journalist Leander P. Richardson was attracted to the chaotic mining camp in search of a good story rather than riches. James D. McLaird's essay, "'I Know . . . Because I Was There': Reports of the Black Hills Gold Rush," which is based on Richardson's articles, offers a snapshot of the turmoil of daily life during one of the last great gold rushes. Like Fred W. Power's diary, newspaperman Richardson's narrative account details the rugged terrain and the harsh travel conditions from Fort Laramie in Wyoming Territory to the Black Hills. Although Richardson spent only five days in Deadwood, he arrived in the nick of time to meet Wild Bill Hickok just days before the gambler's death, an encounter the journalist would exploit to great advantage. The majority of Richardson's observations concentrate on the colorful characters who populated the mining camp.

One person who failed to capture Richardson's attention, however, is the focus of Todd Guenther's essay in Chapter Three. "A Black Woman in the Black Hills" is the account of Lucretia Marchbanks, a remarkable black woman who traveled to Deadwood during the summer of 1876. A former slave who garnered the respect of all who came to know her, Marchbanks rose above both gender and racial stereotypes commonly associated with mining camps. "Aunt Lou," as she was called, earned the reputation for being one of the camp's finest cooks, but she eventually ran a boarding house and owned her own hotel. In later years, she moved to Wyoming, where she lived on her own ranch until her death in 1911. Guenther's discussion of the sometimes tenuous relations between white and black populations in the region serves to make this detailed portrait of an independent black woman making her way in the world all the more impressive.

Blacks were not the only non-Europeans to journey to the gold mining camp. Approximately two hundred Chinese immigrants followed the gold rush to Deadwood, where they established a Chinatown on lower Main Street. A small percentage of Chinese pioneers worked the placer mines, but most either took on service jobs or established retail businesses. "Deadwood's Pioneer Merchant," by Edith C. Wong, Eileen French, and Rose Estep Fosha, explores in depth the life of Wong Fee Lee, a Chinese merchant who rose to prominence in Deadwood. Arriving in 1876, Wong established the Wing Tsue Bazaar, from which he sold a variety of merchandise as well as groceries. Although Wong Fee Lee's story is relatively unique by comparison to that of other Chinese pioneers in Deadwood, the narrative explores Chinese and European-American race relations and provides insight into the challenges Chinese immigrants faced. The Wong story also adds a wealth of details about the personal lives of Chinese pioneers in the American West.

The Wong history may be unique, but the challenges created by the natural environment of South Dakota were not. Fires and floods shaped Wong's endeavors in much the same way as they altered the lives of the

Bower family. In his annotated compendium of family memorabilia, "A Photograph Album of the 'Genuine Original Family Band,'" Maxwell Van Nuys gives new voice to the Bower Family Band, which performed across South Dakota in the 1880s and 1890s. Walt Disney turned Van Nuys's mother's memoirs into a fantastic musical in 1968, entitled *The One and Only Genuine Original Family Band*, but in reality their story was anything but fantasy. In 1881, a flood had destroyed their home in Vermillion on the southeastern edge of Dakota Territory. The family of talented musicians then moved to the Black Hills, where they made an indelible mark on the region. Whether playing for celebrations, political rallies, fairs, or weddings, the Bower Family Band was a popular addition to any event. While their story of self-determination is common to many of the people who made the Black Hills their home, each of the Bower family children left important individual legacies.

During the same period when the Bower family members were carving out lives for themselves, a young bookkeeper named Thomas J. Grier quickly rose to a position of power when he was appointed superintendent of the Homestake Mining Company, located in Lead, South Dakota. Susan L. Richards and Rex C. Myers's essay, "An Iron Hand in a Velvet Glove: The Management of the Homestake Mine, 1885–1914," examines how Grier's management style had a long-term impact on the region. Under his leadership, backed by mining mogul George Hearst's capital, the Homestake Mining Company would become the driving economic engine in the Black Hills and the largest single producer of gold bullion from low-grade ore in history. As superintendent, Grier consolidated the mines, foundries, stamp mills, electric plants, water system, railroad, timberlands, and sawmills into a single operation. Shrewd yet benevolent, Grier's attitude of "what's good for Homestake is good for everyone" was pervasive.

Grier ruled with an iron hand; yet, he was a beloved employer and member of the community. Journalist and prohibitionist Edward Louis Senn, on the other hand, was not so well liked. Denise Karst Pearce's account of Senn, "A Crusader on the Last Frontiers," details the life (1865–1951) of a crusader for justice and morality. A deeply religious man, Senn fought cattle rustlers while ranching in Lyman County, South Dakota, and politicians and purveyors of vice while running his newspaper in Deadwood. As he moved across the South Dakota prairie to the Black Hills, Senn built a frontier newspaper empire that served as his pulpit. Deadwood, however, was not to be tamed, and Senn endured acts of violence against himself and his newspaper. He was partially vindicated when South Dakotans voted in favor of statewide prohibition and was at the pinnacle of his anti-vice crusade during the Roaring Twenties. That all came to a halt in 1929 with the stock market crash that plummeted the nation into the Great Depression. Senn likely went into a depression of his own when the Eighteenth Amendment was repealed in 1933 and liquor again flowed legally and freely.

During the 1930s, while the rest of the state and nation suffered, many Black Hills residents fared better than most. The price of gold soared to thirty-five dollars an ounce, thus allowing the Homestake Gold Mine to expand its operations and become the major employer in the region. Elsewhere in the Hills and across the state, however, people suffered as employment dried up and crops shriveled. Under President Franklin D. Roosevelt, the federal government established various programs to put people back to work. The Civilian Conservation Corps (CCC), one such New Deal program, provided employment for thousands of young men across the nation. Claire Patterson's "A CCC Recruit Looks Back on a Black Hills Experience," edited by George A. Larson, recounts his experiences in the CCC in 1940 and 1941. The young man's reflections show the lasting impact these workers had on the Black Hills environment and the future of recreation in the region. Whether they were planting or thinning trees or building dams and reservoirs, CCC workers' efforts can still be seen throughout the area.

Recreation and tourism have been tied to the Black Hills economy since European Americans first settled in the region. The town of Deadwood, for example, quickly sought to capitalize on the legendary characters Wild Bill Hickok and Calamity Jane, who both had the misfortune of dying on visits to the Black Hills and were interred in Mount Moriah Cemetery in Deadwood. The business community had had the foresight in 1903 to bury the newly departed Calamity Jane next to Wild Bill, who had died in 1876, announcing that this placement was her dying wish.[2] Other communities such as Custer, Spearfish, and Hot Springs, on the other hand, sought to take advantage of natural resources. The construction of Sylvan Lake, of the railroad line through Spearfish Canyon, and of the mineral baths of Hot Springs are examples of boosters' attempts to attract tourists to other parts of the Black Hills.

Both the state and federal governments played significant roles in making Black Hills tourism economically viable during the first three decades of the twenty-first century, once again making the most of the area's surroundings. The federal government designated Wind Cave as a national park in 1903 and made Jewel Cave a national monument in 1908, while the state government established Custer State Park as a natural preserve. Furthermore, under the leadership of Senator Peter Norbeck, a highway was built through the Needles in the 1920s. Of course, it was also during this time period that Gutzon Borglum began carving Mount Rushmore. Dedicated in 1941, the national memorial quickly became known as America's Shrine of Democracy.[3]

To a country on the brink of entering World War II, the faces of the four presidents engendered deep feelings of patriotism on a national level. Those feelings of devotion to the memorial continued to grow as the nation concluded that war and segued into the Cold War. Taking into account Rushmore's sacrosanct status, Todd David Epp's essay "'Expedient Exaggerations' and the Filming of *North by Northwest*" examines the controversy surrounding the filming of the 1959 thriller. Legendary English filmmaker Alfred Hitchcock approached the National Park Service in 1958 about shooting the culmination of his mistaken-identity spy adventure at Mount Rushmore. Park Service officials, worried about the possible desecration of the national shrine, reluctantly agreed to the film shoot, albeit with many stipulations, including a promise that there would be no scenes of violence associated with the memorial itself.

Much to the consternation of the Park Service, Hitchcock was far more interested in making a compelling film than in honoring his agreement. Angered about the movie's potentially negative impact on the image of the shrine, the National Park Service and South Dakota's senior United States senator Karl E. Mundt exchanged a series of threatening letters with Hollywood studio executives during the summer the movie was being released. In the end, the government's worries proved unfounded. The film went on to become one of Hitchcock's masterpieces, and the ensuing controversy has long been forgotten in light of the positive publicity the film continues to garner for the memorial.

At the beginning of World War II, the Homestake Gold Mine was shut down as nonessential to the war effort, causing a mass exodus from the northern Black Hills. The establishment in 1942 of what eventually became Ellsworth Air Force Base dramatically shifted the population density to Rapid City on the east-central edge of the Hills. Between the base and the city's close proximity to Mount Rushmore, Rapid City became the major hub of the Black Hills. After the war, the federal government initiated efforts to manage the vast natural assets of the area, especially its water resources. Throughout the 1950s, the government funded the building of new dams, including one near the town of Pactola, which provided water for the air base and the growing population of Rapid City.

The government's management of water resources also aimed to control flooding in populated areas by damming rivers in and around the Hills. Sadly, this measure backfired in 1972 when a freakish amount of rain caused the Canyon Lake Dam above Rapid City to break. The flood killed at least 235 people and destroyed over $100 million worth of property.[4] Donald W. Bolin's reminiscences of the summer of 1972, "Jim Creek Journal: Remembering a Black Hills Summer," contain a personal account of what it was like in the aftermath of the devastating flood. Like so many other visitors, Bolin and his wife Christina fell in love with the Black Hills on a visit from Ohio and planned to retire there after their careers as schoolteachers. Bolin recorded in his journal their decision to purchase thirty acres of land near Nemo, northwest of Rapid City. He painted a vivid picture of a summer spent on their rustic ranch. Trout fishing, cleaning up from the flood waters, and the somewhat ironic challenge of locating a place to drill a well on the property occupied the couple's days. Bolin's reflections confirm, once again, that no matter how much humans attempt to control the natural environment, ultimately nature has the upper hand. It is a lesson that plays out year after year in the Black Hills, a land with rugged topography and a dramatic climate.

For more than a century, stories about the Black Hills have largely focused on the characters found in dime novels, in Hollywood films, or on the faces carved on mountains.[5] Behind those faces are the real people whose hard work had a lasting impact on the future of the region. Fortunately, some of these people took the time to record their stories so that modern readers can share their experiences. As the chapters in this anthology show, it is people like Fred Power, Lucretia Marchbanks, Wong Fee Lee, the Bower family, Thomas J. Grier, Edward L. Senn, Claire Patterson, and Donald Bolin who give deeper insight into the complexities involved in creating a life on one of America's last western frontiers.

NOTES

1. For an overview of Black Hills history, *see* [David A. Wolff], "The Black Hills in Transition," in *A New South Dakota History*, ed. Harry F. Thompson (Sioux Falls, S.Dak.: Center for Western Studies, Augustana College, 2005), pp. 288–317. The United States government argued that it was not in violation of the treaty and that the military had the legal right to enter the reservation on official business. Francis Paul Prucha, ed., *Documents of the United States Indian Policy* (Lincoln: University of Nebraska Press, 1975), p. 110. For a discussion of the military presence, *see* John D. McDermott, "The Military Problem and the Black Hills, 1874–1875," *South Dakota History* 31 (Fall/Winter 2001): 188–210.

2. *See* James D. McLaird, *Wild Bill Hickok & Calamity Jane: Deadwood Legends*, South Dakota Biography Series, no. 2 (Pierre: South Dakota State Historical Society Press, 2008), pp. 108–10.

3. For a history of the development of Black Hills tourism, *see* Suzanne Barta Julin, *A Marvelous Hundred Square Miles: Black Hills Tourism, 1880–1941* (Pierre: South Dakota State Historical Society Press, 2009).

4. Wolff, "Black Hills in Transition," pp. 313–14. *See also* "Rapid City Flood of 1972," *Rapid City Public Library*, www.rapidcitylibrary.org/lib_info/1972Flood/index.asp

5. In 1948, Korczak Ziolkowski began carving the image of Lakota warrior Crazy Horse out of Thunderhead Mountain, located between Custer and Hill City and approximately eight miles from Mount Rushmore. The sculpture is still in progress but, when completed, will be the largest sculpture in the world.

Fred W. Power

"DISTANCE LENDS ENCHANTMENT
TO THE VIEW" A DIARY OF THE 1874
BLACK HILLS EXPEDITION

edited by Thomas R. Buecker

INTRODUCTION

On 2 July 1874, a large military expedition of nearly one thousand soldiers, Indian scouts, teamsters, and attached civilians left Fort Abraham Lincoln, near Bismarck, Dakota Territory. During the next sixty days, this impressive cavalcade led by Lieutenant Colonel George Armstrong Custer successfully explored the Black Hills, a mysterious region that had long been the subject of rumor and speculation. Despite the large number of people who marched with the 1874 Black Hills Expedition, remarkably few left personal recordings. While the official reports and accounts of the newspaper correspondents accompanying the expedition have been widely available to researchers, few reminiscences and diaries are known to survive. One rare example is the diary of correspondent Fred W. Power. A welcome addition to the scant literature of the 1874 expedition, Power's diary offers significant insights into this monumental event of Northern Great Plains history.[1]

Although government explorers had skirted the periphery of the Black Hills, none until the 1874 expedition had penetrated the region's interior. First Lieutenant Gouverneur K. Warren of the United States Topographical Engineers conducted the first army reconnaissance

This article originally appeared in slightly different form in *South Dakota History* 27 (Winter 1997): 197–260. Additional biographical material on Power, some of which is incorporated here, appeared in *South Dakota History* 33 (Summer 2003): 180–91.

of the Black Hills in 1857. Warren's small party left Fort Laramie and scouted the western edge of the Hills before the Lakota Sioux Indians compelled them to turn back at Inyan Kara mountain. The group then traveled around the south and east sides of the Hills to Bear Butte before leaving the vicinity. Two years later, Captain William F. Raynolds explored and mapped the Belle Fourche River to the north and east of the Black Hills while on his way from Fort Pierre to the Yellowstone and Powder River country of Montana and Wyoming.[2]

By 1874, officials had determined to send a military expedition to "[clear] up the only mysterious spot of any great size" left in the United States.[3] Lieutenant General Philip H. Sheridan, commanding officer of the Military Division of the Missouri, ordered the reconnaissance to locate any hideouts of Indian raiding parties and to select a site for a future army post, something Lieutenant Warren had recommended in 1858. Although the Black Hills were situated on the Great Sioux Reservation, an area declared off-limits to non-Indians by the Fort Laramie Treaty of 1868, officials contended that the agreement permitted "officers, agents, and employees of the government" to enter the reservation to discharge their official duties. Yet another reason for the proposed expedition, although it was not officially stated, was to search for gold. Stories of its presence in the forbidden Black Hills had circulated for years, and for the gold-crazed frontiersmen waiting along the eastern boundary of the Great Sioux Reservation, the expedition was a means to confirm rumors of the region's potential wealth.[4]

Plans for the expedition moved rapidly forward. Officials selected Fort Abraham Lincoln, located on the west bank of the Missouri River across from Bismarck, as the departure point. In addition to being located near the western terminus of the Northern Pacific Railroad, the fort headquartered the Seventh United States Cavalry and its flamboyant yet capable commander, Lieutenant Colonel George A. Custer. With experience in commanding large forces in the field, Custer was the natural choice to conduct the expedition. The editor of the *Army and Navy Journal* lauded his selection, calling Custer "the luckiest of all lucky leaders" and declaring, "The choice could hardly have fallen on a better man."[5]

As preparations continued, several delegations of Lakota Sioux Indians visited Custer at the fort, threatening war if he entered the Black Hills. To counter a possible attack, Custer requested a large number of troops to guard the expedition. Ten companies of the Seventh Cav-

Lieutenant Colonel George A. Custer's experience as a field commander earned him the leadership of the 1874 Black Hills Expedition. This engraving depicts him during his years as commander of Fort Abraham Lincoln. State Archives Collection, South Dakota State Historical Society

alry, along with its band, and two companies of the Seventeenth and Twentieth United States infantries were assigned the task. The cavalry force was divided into two battalions, one of which was placed under the command of the Ninth Cavalry's Major George A. Forsyth, an aide to General Sheridan, and the other under the Seventh Cavalry's Major Joseph G. Tilford. Custer also took an artillery detachment of three Gatling guns and one Rodman ordnance rifle. To supply the large number of men and horses, a wagon train of 110 wagons driven by 115 civilian employees and teamsters carried equipment, grain, and provisions. In addition, three hundred beef cattle were driven along. Finally, to enhance security as the column moved or camped, Custer included a sizable detachment of Arikara and Santee Dakota Sioux scouts.[6]

Although the reconnaissance was to be conducted rapidly, Custer arranged for several noted scientists to accompany the expedition. This select group included Newton H. Winchell, Minnesota's state geologist and a professor of geology at the University of Minnesota, and George Bird Grinnell of Yale University's Peabody Museum, who served as the expedition's zoologist and paleontologist. Captain William Ludlow, chief engineer for the Department of Dakota, was assigned to record the region's topography, measuring distances, drawing maps, and

More than one hundred wagons carried the equipment and provisions needed to supply the Black Hills Expedition, which included nearly one thousand soldiers, scouts, and civilians. The portable darkroom of the expedition's photographer, William H. Illingworth, appears in the foreground. State Archives Collection, South Dakota State Historical Society

shooting astronomical observations when possible. Aris B. Donaldson, who had resigned his position as professor of English literature at the University of Minnesota to join the expedition, served as its botanist. To satisfy the public's curiosity, Custer allowed two practical miners to go along and conduct an unofficial search for precious metals.[7]

The last contingent of the Black Hills Expedition was a small group of young newspaper correspondents. They included William E. Curtis, a professional journalist reporting for the *Chicago Inter-Ocean* and *New York World*; Samuel J. Barrows, a correspondent for the *New York Tribune*; Nathan H. Knappen, a reporter for the *Bismarck Tribune*; and Aris Donaldson, who wrote for the *Saint Paul Daily Pioneer* in addition to his botanical research.[8] Knappen wrote of his fellow correspondents,

"As newspapermen love excitement as a duck loves water, they are reasonably happy."[9] Rounding out this group of adventurers was Fred W. Power, who covered the expedition for the *Saint Paul Daily Press* and kept a private diary for his own use.

Our diarist was a sixth-generation scion of the old-line Power family of Virginia. His father, Frederick William Power (1819–1870), was married to Caroline D. Hanes, daughter of an influential Richmond family, and the two made their home in a historic house in Yorktown, where Power had an active medical practice and also owned a plantation of several hundred acres immediately south of town. Bordered on the west by the Hampton Road, his lands contained original British earthworks from a 1781 siege. Frederick William Power, Jr., was born in 1847 in Henrico County, his mother having evidently gone to her family home for his birth. He was the second of nine children born to the couple.[10] Young Fred received his primary education in a small schoolhouse located just behind the Power home in Yorktown. By the time of the 1860 census, its teacher resided in the Power household.[11]

In the spring of 1861, the Powers' idyllic life at Yorktown came to an abrupt end. The Confederate government quickly realized that a northern army could advance up the peninsula and attack their capital at Richmond. An army under General John B. Magrauder arrived in Yorktown to build a defensive line to hold northern troops in check until the capital could be adequately defended. Consequently, Confederate forces occupied the former British earthworks and constructed new ones. In the process, the Confederate government confiscated virtually everything Frederick Power owned. All the doctor's newly planted crops were destroyed, his livestock seized, teams and wagons impressed, and all of his lands, except the house, were forfeit. His field fencing was dismantled for firewood, and materials from outbuildings and dwellings were used to build winter quarters for Confederate soldiers. The family was forced to seek refuge at the home of Caroline's parents in Richmond. Documents detailing Power's attempt to gain compensation noted that his was the first private property seized by the South for the "public good." He was never reimbursed. In the words of a close associate, "Dr. Power is a most worthy gentleman whose loyalty to the South has cost his fortune."[12]

After leaving Yorktown, the Power family took up residence at Edgewood, the three-hundred-acre estate of young Fred's maternal grandfather, Garland Hanes, a prominent Richmond businessman. Hanes, a veteran of the War of 1812, had by 1860 amassed a fortune reportedly worth three hundred fifty thousand dollars. Once the family had established its new home, young Fred was sent to attend school in Amelia County, southwest of Richmond, in 1862. Concerning this phase of his son's education, the father boasted, "His preceptor speaks in high terms of him" and "with application [he] will make a fine mathematician."[13]

In the spring of 1863, Fred Power left school to return to Richmond. Although the elder Power had lost his material wealth in 1861, he still wanted his son to be educated. He also believed young Fred was spending too much time idling in the army camps that encircled the city. Worried that his son would not "improve in mind or morals," Power decided to apply to the Virginia Military Institute (VMI) for his admission as a state cadet. The initial letter of application declared that the teenager had fine physical development, was active and energetic, and not addicted (so far as anyone knew) to any vices. Influential friends such as George W. Randolph, James Lyons, and J. B. Cary also sent letters of support. In July 1863, Frederick W. Power, Jr., received his appointment to VMI as a state cadet.[14]

Unfortunately, his term as a student there was short. Due to circumstances beyond his control, young Power could not begin his classes until 5 October 1863, a full month after the fall session began. He could not obtain textbooks for another two weeks. Because of several federal raids early that winter, the VMI Corps of Cadets was called out for active service, again interrupting Power's studies. Consequently, he could not keep up academically and was permitted to resign from the institute in January 1864 because of "deficiency in his classes." Although his father and others attempted to have him reinstated, Power's brief career at VMI was over.[15]

In March 1864, Fred Power turned seventeen and was liable for military service. Perhaps because he was not anxious to leave the area, he enlisted in the Twentieth Battalion Virginia Heavy Artillery. The Twentieth Battalion was assigned to the interior line of Richmond's defenses and was generally stationed just north of the city at Battery Nine. Besides improving the works, the Confederate artillerymen also guarded northern prisoners in Richmond. Because he had received some military training at VMI, Power was made a corporal in Company C. As the 1864–1865 sieges of Richmond and Petersburg progressed, his battalion, like the rest of Robert E. Lee's army, hunkered down in the trenches to endure the last days of the Confederacy.[16] In 1865, Power's unit became part of Colonel Stapleton Crutchfield's "Artillery Brigade," composed of four under-strength heavy artillery battalions and other reserve units. On 2 April, Richmond was evacuated; Power's unit joined Lee's forlorn retreat to the west.

Four days later along Saylor's Creek, Union forces attacked General Lee's rear guard. On the opposite side of the creek was another figure destined to play a prominent part in Power's story—Brevet General George A. Custer. Like many southern units that day, Crutchfield's Brigade, on the left side of the line, disintegrated. Power and most of his company were captured and transported to the sprawling Union prison camp at Point Lookout, situated on the southern tip of Maryland, arriving on 14 April. On 16 June, Power signed his oath of allegiance to the United States and returned to Richmond.[17]

The Power family never went back to Yorktown.[18] By the end of the war Fred Power, Sr., was a broken man, both physically and financially. At least three of his children had died of sickness during the war, and he followed on 24 February 1870 at the age of fifty-one. After his father's death, Fred W. Power resided with his mother and three sisters near the Hanes estate in Henrico County. He was working as a clerk with a life insurance company, the beginning of what later became his professional work. He was romantically infatuated with Lizzie Quarles, whom he frequently mentioned in his Black Hills Expedition diary. In those bitter days of reconstruction, however, Power was not yet ready to settle down. The loss of his mother and a sister within three weeks, coupled with Lizzie's apparent rejection, led to his decision to leave the South and seek employment elsewhere.

By November 1872, Power had left Virginia and headed west. The next year he was in Chicago, on the lookout for any opportunity. Somehow he learned of Custer's upcoming expedition to the Black Hills. On 12 June, he arrived in Saint Paul, where he applied with the *Saint Paul Daily Pioneer* to cover the expedition as a correspondent. When *Pioneer* publisher David Blakely decided to have expedition botanist Aris Donaldson write dispatches, Power turned to the *Saint Paul Daily Press*, the *Pioneer*'s Republican rival. Arrangements were quickly made for him to serve as correspondent for the *Press*, and Power checked in at Seventh Cavalry headquarters on 20 June. While awaiting the expedition's departure from Fort Abraham Lincoln, he contacted several other papers offering to write for them on commission, as well.[19]

Although he undoubtedly received some sort of stipend from the newspaper, the expedition carried Power and several other civilian members on its rolls as teamsters, paying them thirty dollars per month. In this way, civilians whose expenses were not being covered by an outside party could be provided "place and provisions" at government expense. Photographer William H. Illingworth, whose glass-plate images provide invaluable visual documentation of the expedition, benefited from the same arrangement.[20] Custer was apparently eager to ensure favorable press coverage of the expedition, for, as Power noted, "General Custer says that he will be pleased to have me go."[21]

Fred Power became the "unknown" newspaperman of the expedition. None of the other correspondents mentioned him in their lengthy dispatches from the field. As a result, his name is missing from the body of literature that grew out of the expedition. Aside from his listing on the teamster rolls, Power's name appears only in the diary of First Lieutenant James Calhoun, who lists him among the other newspaper correspondents.[22] Although slighted by the historical record, Power apparently became an accepted member of the expedition. He wrote that he found the officers sociable and at one point mentions riding in the advance party with Custer—hardly a privilege accorded to a lowly teamster.[23] He was a messmate of Second Lieutenant Benjamin H. Hodgson, one of the Seventh's well-liked junior officers, who appears in Power's diary many times. Hodgson, like many of the other men Power associated with that summer, died two years later at the Little Bighorn.[24]

As a journalist, Power kept a diary to which he referred when writing his dispatches. In many places, the diary wording strongly matches that of his published articles. He also wrote shorter articles and with less frequency than did the other correspondents. For example, he sent nothing from Fort Abraham Lincoln before the expedition's departure, even though he arrived at Bismarck nearly two weeks beforehand. Correspondents Barrows, Curtis, Donaldson, and Knappen had eight to ten datelines apiece, in contrast to Power's four. Power does not appear to have been a disciplined reporter, sometimes writing his dispatches just before sending them off. On one occasion he informed readers, "I was unfortunate enough to lose my letter, consequently had to write this up very hurriedly today."[25] The press corps had only three opportunities to send dispatches back via mounted courier: on 15 July from the expedition's camp on the Little Missouri River, on 2 August from the permanent camp in the Black Hills, and on 15 August from the camp at Bear Butte.[26]

Fred Power marked the beginning of the Black Hills Expedition portion of his diary with this fanciful script. Kirk Budd, Rushville, Nebr.

Fortunately, Power was a more dedicated diarist. Although his diary contains nothing from 2 July through 12 July, on the march from Fort Abraham Lincoln to what became known as Ludlow's Cave near the Grand River, Power began making routine entries on 13 July and thereafter recorded events of interest nearly every day. Power kept his diary in a common notebook, three and seven-eighths inches by six inches in size. Covered in brown leather, it contains 108 lined pages, of which 86 record the Black Hills trip. Because Power wrote in pencil, some passages are smudged and difficult to read. Occasionally he made errors in chronology, a common mistake of the expedition's chroniclers. "We have been out so long," correspondent Barrows told his readers, "that we have entirely forgotten the days of the week, and few men in the command could tell it at any time without considerable reckoning."[27]

Power's diary is interesting because it records his candid observations of expedition personnel and his impression of places and events along the route. It describes both humorous and serious incidents, the difficulties of the march, and the splendor of the Black Hills. Power wrote of events that other expedition members failed to mention. The 31 July champagne party documented in the famous photograph by William Illingworth is a good example. Along this same line, Power's account contains numerous references to officers drinking or becoming drunk on the expedition, amply supplied by a well-stocked trader's wagon. These observations contrast starkly with the story George Custer told his wife Elizabeth in a 15 July letter. "I am more than ever convinced of the influences a commanding officer exercises for good or ill," wrote Custer. "There has not been a single card party, not a single drunken officer, since we left Ft. Lincoln."[28]

The diary also records the personal feelings of a young man seeking adventure in the West. Power wrote about his homesickness, his longing for his sweetheart Lizzie Quarles back in Virginia, and his hopes for the future. He had some sympathy for the American Indians whose lands he was trespassing upon, but his diary contains the attitudes and language usage of the time. Power's writing style is brisk and interesting, but he tended to ignore periods, commas, and question marks, using dashes instead as universal punctuation marks. In the interest of readability, the editor has replaced most of Power's dashes with standard punctuation, except in instances where the dashes emphasize a point or indicate a closely related thought. Likewise, because Power's handwriting makes it difficult to distinguish between capital and lowercase letters, capitalization has been adjusted to conform to standard usage except in instances where capital letters were clearly indicated. Power's spellings, or misspellings, have also been preserved in order to retain the flavor of the diary, with letters or words inserted in brackets where needed to clarify the diarist's meaning or add necessary information. Finally, the ellipses at the end of the first and last entries represent the omission of lists of names and cryptic notations that appear to represent personal reminders for the diarist and are unrelated to the events recorded in the expedition portion of the diary.

The history of Power's diary itself is unclear, for no record of its owners or its whereabouts over the past century has been discovered.

However, the diary's physical condition, along with the fact that its contents closely match and often expand on Power's newspaper accounts, the official expedition reports, and the other rare diaries of expedition members point to its authenticity. Moreover, the tone of the diarist is what one would expect from an adventurous young man on a lark. Today, the diary is in the possession of Kirk Budd of Rushville, Nebraska, who purchased it at auction in 1985 and encouraged its publication. The author also wishes to thank Faye and Clyde Bryant of Red Lion, Pennsylvania, for their interest and assistance with this project.

Fred W. Power's Black Hills Expedition Diary

St Paul, Minn, June 12th 74
I reached here this A.M. from Memomonie Wis. Went around to the Pioneer Office and saw Mr Blakely, who still wants me to travel on commission, but I cant afford to do so. My expenses at the lowest calculation will am[oun]t to 75 a month. Should Mr B consent to my arrangement, that is, give me one hundred a month, why then I can stand it for the next six months or so, maybe more. . . .

Hd.Qts, Ft Lincoln, June 20th 74
The Cavalry Expedition under Genl Custer left Post to day and are at present encamped just below on the Mo [Missouri] river.[29] I am now at the Genl Hdqrs. Came over with Mr Knappen of the *Bismark Tribune*. There are several ladies—Saw Genl Dandy[30]—had quite a pleasant time. Spent most of the afternoon at his house. The conversation was principally of the past—10 years ago—and some little about the trip down to the Black Hills. They have some 1000 Cav[alry], 3 Companies of Inft [Infantry] and 4 Ps [pieces] of Art[illery].

Ft Lincoln, June 24/74
Forsyth—$7-8-7
I came over yesterday & remained over all night with Col [Robert] Wilson, P[ost] T[rader]. Enjoyed our selves very much—played the "National Game" for several hours but came out behind. Genl Custer says that he will be pleased to have me go with him—Shall I go[?] Black Hills exp st[arts] 30th. "Shall I go."—What pay correspd. *St. Louis Globe*—What pay correspd. Blk Hills Expedition—shall I go. Start 30th.

Fred W. Power : 19

Illingworth captured this view of Custer's wagons en route
to the Black Hills from a bluff above the Cannonball River.
State Archives Collection, South Dakota State Historical Society

Bismark, D.T.
The expedition will not leave here until after the 30th June. Genl Custer is fully under the impression that he has troops enough to whip the combined Indian Nation. He carries some 1000 men in—600 Cavalry, 200 Infty, 100 Artillery, bal[ance] camp attendants [illegible]. "Nappen" [of the] *Bismark Tribune* has been refused permission to accompany the expedition on account of an article in the *Tribune* of this A.M. Our friend "Knap" of the *Tribune* did not write it.[31]

July 13th, Camp G[rand] R[iver] Cave
We reached the cave day before yesterday. Camped at foot of the [Cave] hills. In the cave we found Arrows, Beads, Earrings & other trinkets given to the Great Spirit who the Indians say inhabit or dwells there.[32] Sunday 12th we left camp at the usual hour. Marched 12 miles & at night camped within 2 miles of our "cave" & now Monday morning I am setting on my saddle awaiting orders. There goes "General."[33] Now I must saddle up.

Indian scouts guided the expedition to a cave, seen here from the
mouth looking out, located between the forks of the Grand River.
Custer named the feature Ludlow's Cave in honor of his chief engineer.
State Archives Collection, South Dakota State Historical Society

15th July, Camp Little Mo, Montana Teritory
Sent dispatch to *Globe* St Louis, *Balt[imore] S[un]*, *State Journal*, *Phil[adelphia] Age*, *St Louis Globe*, *St Paul Press*. Nothing of interest transpired in our camp except the pleasure of remaining over all day, which was of it self a treat.[34] While there we saw smoke said by Bloody Knife to be an Indian signal recalling the hunting parties and giving notice to those Indians at the agency that we (the Expedition) had made its appearance.[35] We also had the pleasure of sending in let-

ters—two [Arikara] Scouts [Skunk's Head and Bull Neck] started at sunset for Lincoln. The supposition is that they have reached the cave by this time.

July 16th, 2 P.M., Little Mo River

We broke camp this A.M. at 4. Marched west so.west. Saw nothing until after 11 P.M. A few Indians were seen east of us about 2 miles and later in the day we saw a few more. After leaving camp Lieut Hod[g]son commdg B Co., 7 Cavl., went to the left accompanied by or rather as an escort to Col Ludlow [and] Profs Winchel[l] [and] Donaldson. Grant[36] went with them, also the reporters of *Tribune* N.Y. & *Inter Ocean* Chicago. Our march to day has certainly been the most disagreeable of the trip—very little water, hot sun, Cactus, Sage brush & rather rough march—several revine [ravines] that delayed the train some time. Genl Custer Escort & Scouts arrived at this place some 4 hours ahead of train. No game today—all seems to have disappeared. The country for the past 5 miles is so full of cactus that it is impossible for any thing to subsist on it. The grass all parched up by the sun. The [Little] Missouri River here is about ten yards—30 ft wide & may be 40, but certainly not over that. The water while it is very good to us would not be appreciated when better could be gotten—the only objection is that it is two muddy. The valley just here is not noted for its beauty. East of the river it extends about a [illegible]. West it varies between mile & ½ and 3 hundred yards. The bluff[s] on either side are not very grand, but more of a very rolling prarie land. West, Nature displayed more taste and the hills in some parts look quite imposing. We marched 30 miles & camped on the prarie without wood or water. Reported to night that Knappen is missing. Suppose that he will turn up all OK. The Escort with Col Ludlow came in in good time with out doing any thing worthy of relating. The Black Hills are in sight. The order is to day to make the Belle Fouche—which is 32 miles distant.[37]

July 17th

We did not march the expected distance & Knap turned up all OK.[38] The 1st few miles of its starting the road was quite fair. We then came in contact with that God forsaken (as Prof Donaldson expresses) country—only fit for rattle snakes and Indians.[39] The Government would do well to give the Indians, their hairs [heirs] & assigns a deed convey[ing] it to them for ever. We made camp about 1 P.M. after marching 18 miles.

We are encamped within 12 miles of the foot hills & would have made them by 4 P.M. but for the almost impassable Little Mo bad lands country between this place and there. Should the Gods favor us we will get there tomorrow—"Belle Fourche"—& then where, let the future decide. Grant killed a large rattle snake.[40] Several antelope were killed to day [by] Maj French, Lt Chance, comdg art, & Mr. Illingworth, special artist. Mr. I has had the good fortune not only to make numerous Photos but also to kill some 30 odd antelope—is a good shot as well as a good "Photograpist."[41] Musquitoes are quite plentiful so I will close for the night. I have killed so far 27 antelope & 13 deer.

18th [July]

After being bothered last night by mosquitoes for the 1st half of the night, the wind got so high that it was impossible to sleep & the wind blew all of the sand from its flat in [to] our tent.[42] The Black Hills look beautiful in the distance, but I fin[d] that distance lends enchantment to the view. Prof Winchell of Minneapolis seems to think that the soil generally is good, very good—but the want of rain will in my opinion prevent the country from ever being of any very great benefit to man, or civilized man. The noble Red Man of the West may waunder over & gain [a] subsistence by hunting but certainly never by cultivation unless he can ditch either from the Sheyenne River or Mo. With regard to fossils, Prof Grinnell has been rather disappointed. It is true some few bones been found but nothing of any great interest. Of one thing we are glad—the sun moon & stars take their natural course here as elsewhere, and even the comet gladdens us by making its nightly appearance.[43] We are in mountains at last. Mr. [William R.] Wood— Col Ludlows asst.—says that we reach[ed] this much talked of teritory yesterday. After crossing the bad lands we came in to a beautiful valley just beyond which we were glad to see timber—[the] first since leaving the Mo River. We are at present resting under the shade of large pines, and in fact almost under the shadow of the Black Hills—*most there*. I found a barrell on the bank of the creek just out side. Some one has been here before.[44] The remains show the goodness of the white man from the rising sun to his red bro of the West. We encamped to night on the North fork of the Cheyenne River at the foot of BH—nothing of interest having transpired during the day. Mchd only 17½ miles, part good & part bad. Just before reaching the river we came to a beautiful valley. Our camp is also situated in a very picturesque place surrounded by hills. The valley of the Cheyenne looks as if a white man might live here contented. So far we have seen few elk & deer—one of each killed to day by Scouts. We passed yesterday [an] Indian grave made not over 3 days ago. His spirit is wandering over the Black Hills—the Happy hunting ground of the Sioux.

19th [July]
We remain in camp to day. Much to our surprise & pleasure on awaking from our slumber this A.M. we found it raining—the 1st time since leaving Lincoln. There are times when rains are very refreshing, but they are too much so in camp. The soldier can well do without them, but then we could not stay in camp but for the rain. So like men elsewhere we must submit to the bad with the good. The rain to day was too much of a good thing, lasting from early morning until quite late. Chance came down to dinner.[45] Our conversation turned upon Indiana. He is acquainted with the Miss Howells. Hod[g]son came in about 5 pretty full of Smith's best. I have spent the day in reading *Jack Hinton, The Guardsman* by Liver.[46] Night—the camp fires remind me of the happy days gone by—when below Richmond we dreamed of a Confederacy & an independent government—& the men singing recalls the past—"Last Rose of Summer" & Home Sweet Home. I got wet going down to water my horse this A.M. and had to remain in wet clothes all day, which was certainly not very agreeable. Dreams of Home (Greenwood) make up a good part of my Camp Life. Lizzie['s][47] name is written on every page of my memory—and would I done over be written on every page of this book, but there are too many chances to loose it. While I think of it I will write the names of the Officers. Genl Custer

Col Ludlow	Genl Forsythe
" Grant	Col Hart
Lt Calhoun	" Benteen
Capt Yates	Lt Varnum
" Hale	" Hodgson
" McDougall	" Gibson
" Custer	" Watson
" Moilans	" Wallace
Col Wheaton	Lt. Chance
Cap —	Dr Williams
Lt. Gates	Profs Winchell, Donaldson & Grinnell.

There goes "Taps," so with the hope of many a good nights rest to Custer & his Command, I will take up "Jack Hinton" for [a]while.

Camp, 20th July, Blk Hills

Well we are encamped in the Black Hills at last. Nothing of interest having transpired in & around Hd Qts. We marched considerable distance in a round about way—19 miles they say.[48] Good camp, though water not quite as plenty as might be. Our friend Illingworth took a Photo of the camp & surroundings.

21st [July]

Sunrise found us on the march & a rough march it proved to be before the day was over. We marched up the Hill to march back again & after traveling 14 miles found our selves in about 5 miles of our starting point. During the day one of Lt Hodgsons men shot himself through the leg while mounting.[49] The shot did not do any very great damage. The country while quite pretty to look at would be of very little use. We find lots of iron ore, gypsium, magnesia, carbonized lime. We crossed a branch of the Red Water to day—the stream takes its name from the surrounding hills, which are red stones & rock. Capt McDougall found a tin cup marked [blank space], which shows that we are not yet in a country new to the white man.[50]

22 [July]

The usual hour found us on the march. One of Capt Benteens men died last night—has been sick several days [with] diarhea.[51] And one of Capt French['s] Co "M," 7 Cav., shot a private also in his company— some dispute about a horse.[52] The prisoner claims that he shot him in self defence. [The victim] is still living but the chances are that he will die before night. Our march so far has been one of the dryest yet— only crossed water once in about 12 miles—consequence men & horses [both] thirsty. Our march continued to be through a very dry country until just before getting to camp. We there found a spring sufficiently large to water the entire comd [command], viz. taken one or two at the time. As many as ten men though did manage to fill their canteens. Cool & fresh. I waited until after the command passed & then drank rather more than I should. The poor fellow who was shot this A.M. died this P.M. just as we were coming in camp. A great many of Col Wheatons[53] men gave out to day on acct of warm weather & no water. I remained

Scholars have speculated that this photograph was taken south of the Belle Fourche River in Wyoming. It may be one of the views Power mentions in his diary entry of 20 July. State Archives Collection, South Dakota State Historical Society

back with the wagons—found it rather dusty & think in future that I will try it with Hd Qts. Dont know that any thing of interest occurred. I came near getting too much Whiskey aboard last night & had quite a conversation with Hale[54]—Capt McDougall say that night, Power—I like to hear you talk so. My trip so far has been quite pleasant. I mess with Lt Chance, comdg art., & Lt Hodgson, Co B 7 Cav, both of who I

Just before entering the Black Hills proper, the expedition camped at the base of Inyan Kara, a landmark that served both Indians and explorers. The foreground shadow belongs to photographer William Illingworth. State Archives Collection, South Dakota State Historical Society

think like me. They are always playing some trick on me. So far we have not found the wonderful gold producing country. As to where it is, one would find it hard to say. The country to day has been rather more hilly on our flanks, but our road better than yesterday. We are camped on "Red Water" again to day. Lt Gibson is a fine fellow.[55] In fact I like all of the Officers of the Command and am glad to say that they like me or pretend to do so. I have just been over to see Dr Williams cut open the man who was shot, trying to find the ball. It entered his arm & pass[ed] through the stomach in to the spine.[56] The funeral was very impressive, as much so as I ever saw. The moon was shinning brightly when the poor fellows, not like Sir Jno Moore without shroud, but were put in their blankets and carried to their last resting place. Almost under the shadow of "Inyancair"[57] they sleep. The command was called out at 8 & marched down—the men first & then the Officers. The service was read by a Catholic belonging to French's Company, after which a salute was fired over their graves. Then "Taps," the most impressive I ever heard. The bugler sounded to the last for them.[58]

23rd [July]

Camp all day. On the Red Water still [at] Hungyakara. Our march yesterday was a little over 22 miles. We have marched 340 miles up to last night. We remained over in camp all day in the shade of Hungya-kara resting our weary bones & horses. I [am] reading *Jack Hinton the Guardsman* by Liver. Genl Custer accompanied by 2 companies went over to Hungyakara, the highest or one of the highest points in the Black Hills. They had a hard time & did not accomplish any thing worthy of note. The country for miles around can be seen, giving a very good idea of what might be expected on next days march. Our camp was on another branch of the Red Water with nothing very remarkable around it except the mountain already named. I neglected to say we saw where some several hundred Indians had been in there just before us. Their trail induced us to believe that they had gone down towards Laramie or the indian agency in that neighborhood.[59]

24th [July]

We only marched about 10¼ miles today through a very rough coun-try—in fact so rough that I thought it almost impossible for the Genl to get through but go he would. The 1st mile was very good, but then [came] a ravine so deep that the wagons had to be let down by ropes, which took considerable time. In the valley we found splendid soil, and the hills on either side had some what the appearance of [the] gran-diose. Imagine our surprise at finding straw berries in abundance. I found Cols Grant [and] Tilford[60] and Lt Gibson seat[ed] on the re-mains of a large tree enjoying straw berries, the 1st of the season. We find berries of all kinds in abundance & could we only get cream would be as well satisfied to remain here as else where. We have seen few Elk, some with antlers over six feet across. Several of the party—Genl Custer, Capts McDougall, French & others—will decorate their par-

After experiencing difficult travel into the Black Hills, expedition members reveled in the sights and smells of mountain meadows like those of Floral Valley, pictured here. State Archives Collection, South Dakota State Historical Society

lors at Lincoln with them, they being the fortunate ones to secure the prize. Our friend Illingworth has been at his old game shooting—shot a panther to day, wounding it—Unfortunate his rifle was not sufficiently large to kill it.[61] After getting out of this beautiful valley we cross a high hill to find our selves following the Genl into a valley more beautiful than our first, with more straw berries &c, with a stream as cool as ice running through it & disappearing in the ground.[62] The tale connected with the stream as told by Prof Donaldson is as follows (the Prof got his information from the Sioux Scouts of course)—its source is in a beautiful cave said to contain all of the luxuries of life, natural & artificial—fruits of all kind, wines, cakes, creams, mint juleps &c generally—with [illegible] beautiful to behold to serve—the wall of pure gold & floors of pearl. The cave has not yet been seen, but the Genl intends starting for it in a few days. The stream is swallowed by a snake of immense size, and he remains under ground in another cave.[63] Without the power of visiting this both I and Prof Donaldson insist on calling this camp "Echo." Lt Hodgson found a tent pole supposed to have been left here by Genl Warren in 1859.[64] Camp Echo is only the comm[enc]ement to a beautiful valley with the clearest of mountain streams flowing through it. The stream is filled with trout beautiful to behold but being so grassy prevents our gladening our eyes only at time. As yet we have not found time to catch them.[65]

25th [July]

We camped on the same stream, named by us "lost Water" from its disappearing several times under ground.[66] Our march to day was only 11 miles. The train had to cross the stream several times—on an average of twice in every mile. Game was as plentiful as we could expect, having a party of Sioux just ahead of us. The country is very hilly and approaches what might be called picturesque & grand—though not to that extent one might have expected.

26th [July]

We continued up the same valley to day until we crossed the ridge and came down a valley more beautiful. After passing to the east side we found an old encampment.[67] We marched on, coming some 16 miles. As [we were] coming into our present camp some one said that there was smoke ahead. Bloody Knife & several others started out to ascertain the cause. On the hill just in front of us there was a fire still burning where they [Sioux Indians] had camped in the morning. We—that is Genl Custer & staff and those with Hd Qts—made ourselves comfortable as circumstances would permit, lounging around in the old camp under trees &c. The Genl order[ed] Bloody Knife, Man the Bear Killed, Left Hand, Cold Hand, & Buffalo to go on down the valley. Bloody Knife sent one of the Scouts back to inform the Genl that he had found them. Capt McDougalls & Col Harts companies were with Hd Qts, also Lt Wallace with the Scouts.[68] The Genl had them saddled up in a few minutes and started for the front. Anticipating some fun, the Reporters Curtis, Bar-

Crossing a mountain divide, the expedition wound its way between the spectacular limestone cliffs of the Castle Creek Valley. As in Floral Valley, the lodgepoles of traveling Indians left a well-worn trail.
State Archives Collection, South Dakota State Historical Society

rows, Knappen & your humble serv[ant] accompanied them, and on getting around about two miles below camp our hearts beat faster than usual. Just ahead of us could be seen five Lodges. How many more we could not guess, as the end was hidden by a hill projecting out. Genl Custer led the way up on a hill commanding the camp. Much to our sorrow we found that the encampment only consisted of those five Lodges. The Ree Indians, our Scouts, were very anxious to go ahead & scalp the whole party but were prevented by Lt. Wallace.[69] The Genl went ahead, or rather at the head, with a white towel as a flag of truce and we all marched into their camp. We only found one man, Slow Bull. The rest were out hunting. They were all very much frightened, the Squaws & young ones thinking, I dare say, that their time had come. We found Red Clouds daughter, three [third] wife of Slow Bull, and some fifteen or twenty Squaws & children with 27 Bucks—about 50 in the outfit. The men came in from hunting, Long Bear & The Man Who Stabs, the latter the Chief of the band.[70] Genl Custer had some considerable conversation with them. They said they were about four suns from Red Cloud Ag[enc]y & about the same distance from Bear But[t]e, that they were a hunting party and had been in the Hills some four or five months. Knew nothing of our being in the Hills until we were up on them. The Genl offer[ed] them rations if they would come & stay with us a few days— to which they would not at first consent. Said that they must hurry up & get back to the agency but finally consented to remain there & to let us have a guide across the worst part of the way back. And also agreed to visit us in the afternoon to get some rations. The Genl & party, with the exception of a few of us, remained in their camp for a while conversing with the Squaws, making trades &c. They were coming up to bring their things a[nd] get some supplies. After being in camp an hour or so The Man Who Stabs, Slow Bull, Long Bear & another fellow came up on a visit. We conversed with them for some time & then sent them for rations, but [they] seemed rather uneasy the whole time. After getting their rations Long Bear & The Man Who Stabs concluded that they would go, the other two having already taken their departure. They started and had gotten about two hundred yards when the Genl called one or two of our Scouts & told them to go down & tell them to come back, that they should have some of our best men—"Sioux Scouts"—to go down & stay with them all night to prevent the Ree Indians from troubling them.[71] The Genl told the Scout to bring them back. So this fellow, after telling them & finding their unwillingness to come, caught

This camp was located at the foot of Limestone Peak in the Castle Creek Valley.
State Archives Collection, South Dakota State Historical Society

Long Bears horse by the bridle & started to bring him any how. Long Bear—not fancying such treatment—caught the Scout['s] gun & attempted to take it, but the fellow being quite active retained his hold and fell of[f] his horse. Thus securing his gun, Long Bear put spurs to his pony & disappear[ed]—not however until the Scout had taken a shot at him, wounding his horse.[72] With that the Scouts who were in camp leaped on their horses & started. Bloody Knife could not even wait to bridle his horse. On reaching their camp they found every thing gone. The Old Man was not so fortunate. He was captured & brought back. The Genl will keep him until after we are out of the Hills.[73] The

Scout[s] remained out until after 10 P.M. but could not over take the retreating Sioux. One of them returned saying they had the who[le] party down there but could not take them. The Genl sent L Co Col Custer[74] comdg to find out the facts & to protect the indians. On reaching there Col C found that it was all a big Lie [and] that they could not find them. So all returned to camp feeling some thing like sleep after the day['s] excitement. Genl Custer was very uneasy until they did return, fearing that our Scouts might over take & kill the whole party. After they returned he made Eagard[75] tell The Man Who Stabs that his party had all escaped & that no one should go after them, which news seemed to relieve the old fellow very much. Camp with the exception of the guards was soon reposing in the arms of Morpeus.[76]

27th [July)
Monday broke clear & brig[ht] and having had orders to remain over, the most of us did not arise quite as early as usual but rather refreshed our selves with a long nap. The men have been washing & cleaning up generally. I tried to wash for the 1st time & only managed tolerably well. Two companies went out to day with Col Ludlow.[77] We are at present in the heart of the unexplored country. The Col will give the world a map of it in a few weeks after getting in, giving the principal Butes Streams &c—& our friend Illingworth will furnish the finest of views that the country can afford. Lt Gates[78] while hunting discovered a trale 2 miles left of train. I & Yates both got pretty full of Smiths best & had a gay old time of it, so much so that I at one time thought it would end in rather an unpleasant way. Maj Sanger & Yates[79] dined with us this P.M. so the thing ended. We remain in camp all day. The party who went out this A.M.[80]

28th [July]
"The Man who Stabs," Genl Custer['s] prisoner, led the party this A.M. north of our former line of march across the hill. Our eyes were made glad by beholding a rolling prarie with a prospect of a good days march before us. On reaching the top or highest point, we found a pile of Elk horns, the work of Indians.[81] Our friend Illingworth was on hand as usual when there is any thing worthy of note—in other words with him—of being p[h]otographed or shot at. Last night we had frost. The night air is very very cold and the days pleasant, some times rather warmer than we care for some times. While photographing the Elk

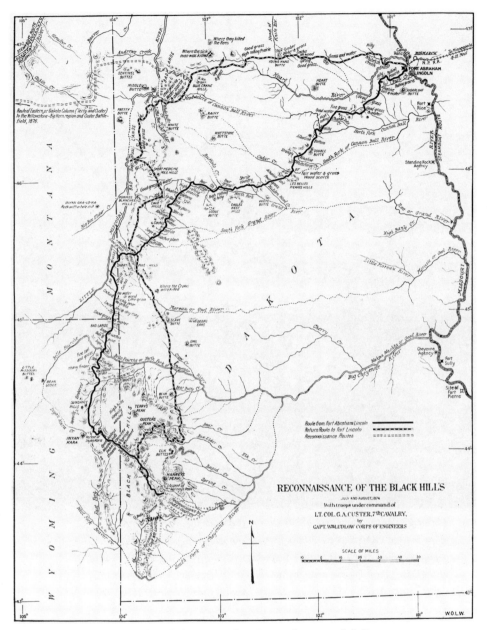

Captain William Ludlow led a corps of engineers that recorded distances and natural features along the entire expedition route. This map, redrawn by W. O. L. Westgard from Ludlow's original, appeared in the July 1927 issue of Motor Travel *magazine. South Dakota State Library, Pierre*

The origin of the pile of elk horns that expedition members found on what is now known as Reynolds Prairie remains a mystery, although correspondent Aris B. Donaldson speculated in the 15 August 1874 issue of the Saint Paul Daily Pioneer *that they were "a votive offering to some deity." State Archives Collection, South Dakota State Historical Society*

horns, Bloody Knife saw a pony over on the hill about a mile distant. The Scouts were sent out to ascertain who owned it.

29 & 30 [July]—15.10
The pony turned out to be a black tail deer & Mr. Reynolds[82] the fortunate man to own it. We remained on this hill some two or three hours

awaiting the return of the Scouts who were sent out to find the best route down, & not being able to find any that even Genl Custer could pass, we returned & camp[ed] at the old camping ground occupied by the Sioux on the evening of the 26, with water, wood & grass in abundance and only about three miles from our old camp of the night before.[83] The river—if I may so call a stream some 10 ft wide—supplied us with fresh fish [and] the surrounding woods with deer, so there was no lack of good eating. Straw berries were also plentiful. Our table besides being supplied with the nec[e]ssaries of life had some of its luxuries— a beautiful boquet adorned it, a gift of the valley, which abound[s] in flowers of all kinds. But like all things [illegible], our encampment came to an end & we took departure on the 29th not at all willingly— though I must confess with some curiosity as we were to follow the Indian trail, that being the only way to get out and that even taking [us] over a rough road. Genl & Hd Qts guard found at last a romantic spot over the hills & far away from our old camp, supplied with all the necessaries of life (Indian life): deer, Straw be[rrie]s, Water, Wood & grass, & determined there to pitch our tents, providence permitting, but it did not, & we slept beneath the blue skies with only our saddle blankets to protect us from the dews of heaven, the wagon train not making its appearance until the morning of the 30th.[84] Our road for the most part was over a beautiful country, hills & dales, with wood & water enough to establish a first class watering place suitable to visit during the summer months. The grand old hills that flanked us on either side looked on & [illegible] & seemed to wonder why it was that the white man should come to dist[urb] their rest. Rifle shot could be heard on all side[s], which told the death tale of some passing deer. Lt Chance brought his guns, a Gatlin, to bear on one, a fine buck, who seem to be admiring the passing troops & with one bound fell dead a few steps from the spot it had been stand[ing] a few moments before.[85] Sergt. Clair[86] of the Hd Qts detachment, not satisfied with killing two fine deer, shot one of the men through the arm (ball gla[n]cing). Lt C[hance] came in contact with the hind feet of Capt F[rench's] horse, which gave him a ride in the ambulance. Only for a short while, it is to be hoped, as the Lt is two good an artil[l]ery officer & understand[s] his guns too well to be spared. His wound is just below the knee & while it is quite painful is still not dangerous, being only a flesh wound. The Lt was also unfortunate enough to dismount one of his guns & render it unfit for action—one wheel being broking in coming down a hill. But that will be all OK just so soon as we go in camp to remain a day or so.

30th [July]

After spending a night in the open air & having our appetites sharpened by a fast of 24 hours, we were well prepared to enjoy a good breakfast. So after arranging our toilette we made our way to the mess tent, but alas for our stomach & hope. We were scarcely seated when Genl was sounded & then Boots & Saddle,[87] the aforesaid calls scarcely giving us time to drink a cup of coffee. About ten minutes before Capt McDougall might have been seen coming in to camp, having spent the night on the road with the wagons. Col Wheaton & Maj Sanger of the Infty also were on the go all night. Our march to day has not been a very long one—in fact the last three days they have only been about 12 miles. We pass[ed] Harney Peak early this A.M. & encamped about two miles below.[88] Harney Peak is in a line of Hills composed of rock. For miles & miles one can see them pointing their rocky crest toward heaven and although rugged & rough—yet they present a beautiful appearance. Tho I am some what of the impression that "distance lends enchantment to the view," Prof Winchell spends his time in finding out their hidden wealth. Some one suggest[ed] that it would not do to let him remain here very long, as the stones would not be large enough to supply building material.[89]

31st [July]

Our march happily was a short one and ended by encamping in the Blk Hills Park—a beautiful valley surrounded by grand hills whose heads had with stood the storms of many a winter & watered by [s]treams whose waters have flowed since the flood. Illingworth has with his camera assisted us the reporters in the Expd to give these things to the world as they are. We are certainly in one of the most beautiful valleys in the West—I had almost said in the world—the surrounds, grand & picturesque Hills rising on every hand of every shape & form imaginable, valleys on every hand abounding with flowers & streams of the coolest waters. A perfect fairy land in summer.[90] Gold has been found in quantities, also silver.[91] Every thing indicates beauty, grandeur & wealth.

*Travel became ever more difficult as Custer and his men moved through
the center of the Black Hills. This rugged terrain leads toward the
summit of Harney Peak, the highest point east of the Rocky Mountains.
State Archives Collection, South Dakota State Historical Society*

[1 August]
The 1st was spent herein.[92] Genl Custer & party started to Harney Peak
& did not return until after mid night.[93] Considerable uneasiness was
felt for fear that they would get in that night. The day was spent in
camp pretty much as all such days are spent, each one following his
own inclination as far as circumstances would permit. Most of my own

personal time was spent writing, getting my letters ready for the *Press* and thinking of home—Sister Bess, Carrie, Mary & Lizzie. Oh darling, I wonder how you are, what doing, and how often you think of me. I wonder am I forgotten by those I love so well. About sun set I went up to Hd Qts to learn the news, thinking Custer had ret[urne]d. I found Lt [James] Calhoun, Capt Morland, Yates comdg right wing, Fred Calhoun, Thos Custer & Boss.[94] We laughed, joked &c &c until I got tired. Visited Illingworth who was busy finishing some of the finest views that I had ever seen. Champagne supper in the Black Hills given by Capt Hale, Col Tilford, Benteen & Lt Hodgson. Capt McDougall, Col Grant, Lt Gibson & others distinguished themselves by making very appropriate addresses. Benteen had a quartette from his Co come up & sing for the amusement of the party. Champagne flowed plentiful, and also whiskey was not slighted. The whole party were pretty well hobbled. Hodgson found some difficulty in crossing the creek—but finally made it all "O.K." On reaching camp I found him dreaming sweetly. Capt Yates, comdg the right wing, got up an opposition party by him self— was monarch of all he surveyed. Hodgson & McDougall insisted that the right wing was not worth a damm. Mc[Dougall], not satisfied to bring him self & all the champagne that he could well carry, brought over Benteens quatello Club to serenade Power—"Power of Va," as he calls me—& insisted on my visiting his tent to partake of spiritual refreshments which I did, but not enough to feel its happy influences. The Glee Club sang several very fine pieces for us. "If I had but Thousand a year" &c. Stop[ped] to listen to the Band play the best Gallop in the world. Wish I had a pretty girl & good floor, but I have not. Barrows of the *N.Y. Tribune* went out & delivered a very appropriate little address after the[y] finished. Mc asked them to take another drink, [and] being soldiers they did not refuse.

[2 August]
The morning of the 2nd Mc & H paid their respects to Jno S[mith] quite early, thinking that by Sun up we would move, but the Genl not getting in until late did not feel very much like trying so early so remained in his little bed until after 7. McD, H, Barrows & myself discussed womans right over ½ gal of Smith[′s] best. I took one drink, they several. Genl was finally sounded, then Boots & S & the command started—N.E. march down the valley about five miles & camped.[95] The

Illingworth may have captured this view of an officers' table laden with champagne bottles and cigar boxes while Custer was away climbing Harney Peak. State Archives Collection, South Dakota State Historical Society

Genl informed us that the mail would leave some time with in the next 36 hours [and] to have our letters in readiness. From that time until after "Taps" I had my hands full writing two long letters to the *Press*, one home and a still longer one to my darling & a T[elegraphic] D[is-patch] to the *Press*, which was not finish[ed].[96] Every body spent their time pretty much as I did, writing.

*On 1 August, the expedition made "permanent camp" on French Creek,
not far from the present-day town of Custer, South Dakota. From here,
reconnaissance parties explored the country to the south and east.
State Archives Collection, South Dakota State Historical Society*

3d [August]

We mailed our letters, that is, took them to Hd Qts for Reynolds, who
was going to start to Laramie, some 200 miles [away]. Genl Custer went
with him one days march with five Co of the 7, taking three day rations.
I remained in Camp all day. Col Benteen went out with two (2) Co & Lt
Godfrey with one to Harney Peak[97] We remained quietly in camp, Fishing, prospecting & amusing ourselves generally, as best we could. Ross
got some good specimens of gold & McKay, silver qua[r]tz.[98]

4th [August]

Every thing continued in the same old way, Col Tilford being in comd
of camp. There was not much hunting—or infact outside sport of any
kind. I went over early to Knaps tent thinking to while away an hour
or so. McKay said something about hunting, so after an early dinner
McKay, Knappen, B[arrows of the] *Tribune* and I went out. Saw two
deer & one bear. My horse as usual went off. McKay got two shots into it

[the bear]. I wanted to charge him with pistol & rifle but McK & K were very much afraid that I would get hurt. My horse got "big fool" as he generally does when any thing of interest occurs. We followed the "Bar" about 2½ miles on foot through the tickist [thickest] of under growth but could not over take the gentleman. We retd to camp fully intending to go out next day & over take the old fellow if possible. On reaching camp found every thing in status co [quo], nothing having transpired since our departure.

[5 August]
Our dreams were pleasant. The morning of the 5th came too early. McK, Knappen, Ross & I went out with a detail to secure the bear if possible. We had a ride of some five miles before coming to the trail. We left our horses & prosceeded on foot some three miles up the valley. Could very easily follow the trail until he got in the rock at the foot of the hills and then had [to] give it up. We reached camp about ½ past 2, hungry and tired, not having had any thing to eat before going out. While [we were] out, Lt Godfrey retd with his two companies, having ridden some 88 miles. They saw nothing of interest.[99] Genl Custer & Escort also retd, they having traveled over 100 miles. They accompanied Reynolds to the South fork of the Scheyenne River, some 40 odd miles south of our camp at "Custer Valley." Col Grant "Fred" has just promised me a few notes taken with Custer from 3d to 5th inclusive. Beautiful country— Met Rock, [illegible], Car[bonized] Lime. Traveled 50 to 55. R[eynolds] left them at 12 Mid night and start[ed] on his lonely trip to Laramie with our letters & T.Ds. Found marble in small quantities. The country in parts beautiful. In one valley particularly they found fruit—goose berries, rasp berries, cherries &c &c. 3d day Sergt Clair saw Elk but unfortunately could not secure one.[100] The Comd recd camp 11 A.M. [on the] 5th. Horses considerably worn out. Capt French had 12 men dismounted the next day. They also had a hail storm, which we were fortunate enough to escape in camp. One horse was left or rather went of[f]. I spent a good deal of my spare time in camp thinking of home, Lizzie & the other dear ones. I wonder when I will be in old Va & what things look like there. Oh well, I hope to see home some time next mo.

6 & 7th Aug.
We followed our old trail back to the "Indian Camp," making that about 10 A.M. [in] the morning. From there our march was N.E. a little.

The sweeping valley pictured in this view became known as Illingworth Valley.
State Archives Collection, South Dakota State Historical Society

During the nine-hundred-mile expedition, more than one thousand big-game animals fell prey to members' guns, including this grizzly bear bagged by a party hunting with Custer near Reynolds Prairie. From left to right are Bloody Knife, Custer, Private John Noonan, and Captain William Ludlow. State Archives Collection, South Dakota State Historical Society

Crossed "Elk Horn" prairie and camped in a very fine valley filled [with] deer & a few bear. Genl Custer & Col Ludlow were fortunate enough to make way with one, a large old fellow, "Grisley," weighing it is suppose[d] some 1000 lb. to 1200. The Genl & Col had a photo taken by Illingworth. Camp known as Fruiting Brooke. The supplies of rasp berries was certainly equal to any I ever saw. "Red bird," a Santee Scout, killed the female bear—mate to the one killed by Genl. It took 13 balls to put them through the bear killed by Genl. [The bear] backed up to a large tree & stood on its hind feet and took the shots manfully.[101] The Scouts killed some 15 or 20 deer. Our marches [were] 23⅓ & 16¼ [miles].

8th [August]

We broke camp [at the] usual hour. Marched over hills—rock composed of mica, Schist & quartz, volcanic formation "Met Rock." McKay found gold just after leaving our camp. The march was a hard one, the country having been burnt over sometime since.[102] We encamped in a beautiful valley also filled with deer & beaver. Train did not get in until 12 & I dined at mid night—Hodgson came in—was too sleepy to eat much—was soon in the arms of Morpheus with my boots on. Had a pleasant dream of L., though[t] that we were married. Bloody knife reported Bears Butte about 5 miles N.E. of our camp.[103]

9th [August], Sunday

Sunrise found us [as] usual on the go. On reaching the top of a hill some 3 or 4 miles from camp, Bears Butte could not be seen and remains [unseen] yet. Our march continued from the top of the Potsdam Sand Stone Butte to the top of another Butte rather higher. Bears Butte is at present about 20 or 25 miles N.W. by W.[104] Cant be seen from our camp, which is in a valley about 12 miles from our camp last night. Plenty of wood & water & grass. We have had an abundance of all the above. A great many deer killed now by men of the comd, killing or participating in killing one [hundred] or more.[105] Got in camp early, about 12 or ½ past 12. Hodgson & I went to sleep and slept until dinner, nearly sunset. The prairie is in full view from the top of the Bluffs.

[10 August]

The 10th we continued our march down the valley & camped in the lower end of the ravine. Two companies were sent ahead to find a rode.

We found fish in great abundance & enjoyed the sport very much. Just after getting our camping ground selected it comin [commenced] to rain. I being about ½ mile in advance of the train went fishing and enjoyed the rain all by my self, which was not at all agreeable.

[11 August]

The 11th we laid over in our camp. Lt Godfrey & Escort went over to Bear Butte and retd that P.M. The two companies went fowd [forward] to make the road.[106] Took with them the co wagons and camped out.

[12 August]

Our march on 12 [August] was through a beautiful valley flanked on each side by high bluffs that presented a beautiful appearance, and watered by quite a large stream. Now I will remark that although we have seen quantities of fish they have been of the poorer kind.

13th [August]

Our march was a short one, just over the Hills about 5 miles.[107]

14th [August]

We struck the plains. March[ed] about 30 miles & camped at the foot of Bear Butte, from which place we sent in a mail. The Black Hills present a fine picture from the Butte & looming up in the distance may be seen Dogs Ears Buttes, Slave Butte and others.[108] Since starting home ward the men have been quite anxious to get in—the excitement over & little chance of meeting Indians. We crossed to day an encampment occupied by the Indians not long since but no Indians. No[r] did we find them at the Butte as informed that we would. In my humble opinion they are all West of the Mo hunting & getting in their winter supply of meat and dont care to trouble their white Bros. We made camp about Sun Set & were soon ready to Sleep.

15th [August]

We camped last night at the foot of Bear Butte & spent to day in getting off our letters to go to night by the Indian Scout.[109] I got one for the paper & one for my little darling—I wonder if she spends as much time in thinking of me as I do of her. My letter to day was but a poor one, but under the circumstances the best I could do. Oh well, if I could express the thoughts in words I am sure that she would be satisfied. My

On 13 August, shortly before the expedition left the Black Hills, thirty-eight officers and members of the scientific corps assembled in front of the headquarters tent for this group photograph. State Archives Collection, South Dakota State Historical Society

time to day has been fully occupied after breakfast. I went down & had a good wash. Watered & fed "Coon" my horse. Retd, wrote to Lizzie & then managed ½ col[umn] for the *P[r]ess.* Ate dinner rather earlier than usual. Fed & water[ed] horse at 12, finished letter [and] took it over. Saw Brass about picture.[110] Mailed letters, a TD, fed, watered & curried my horse & spent some time afterwards in dreaming of a certain little girl in Va. So goes the world, so good night.

16th [August]
Marched to day 29¾ miles. Crossed the Belle Fourche and camped not far from Slave Butte on a branch of the B.F. I made a Bet with Curtis [of the] *Inter Ocean* that we would march 35 miles, so I lost the whiskey for 5. When in sight of the B Fourche several (4) Indians were seen. Genl Custer fow'd 3 of our Scouts—Bloody Knife, Left Hand &

The expedition's arrival at Bear Butte, the remains of an ancient molten-rock uplift on the northern edge of the Black Hills, marked the beginning of the long march over the plains back to Fort Abraham Lincoln. State Archives Collection, South Dakota State Historical Society

another—to interview them. They said that we would find in the neighborhood of our old camp on the Mo some thing over 1000 Indians—Sioux's—awaiting us. And also that there was buffalo on this side of [illegible]. Genl C, thinking that they were awaiting us, would give them a chance, so left the B Fourche & struck out in a bee line for our camp of the 17 Ulto, but contented himself with camping east of "Slave Butte," making about 31 miles.[111] Our camp had water but very poor grass and horses very much jaded.

17 [August]

Early found old Custer on the war path. Passed Slave Butte & camped on the Owl (Moreau) River. Mch 27 miles. Nothing of interest except passing an Indian trail at Slave Butte. Dog Ears Butte are in full sight of camp. Same thing—wood & water—but very poor grass. Several horses gave out, but not catching any more Indians. We did not hear any thing of the Sioux.[112]

18th [August]

We crossed the Moreau River or rather south branch of it & marched N.W., making some 30 miles. Camped about 4 miles west of our old camp—"Prospect [Valley] Camp"—wood, water & better grass than for the past few days.

19th [August]

Started from camp in a N.Wly direction & marched all day over a rough broken country. No timber & very little water. Deer & antelope in abundance. Several of the former & a great many of the latter killed. Marched 37½ miles & camped on Grand River some where near the cave.[113] A great many horses & mules played out & were shot, the want of water being in my opinion the cause. We camped in good grass. Water impregnated with alkali but was partaken of very freely by everyone. Did not get in Camp until late, nearly 9.

20 [August]

We were awakened this A.M. to find it raining. Genl Custer determined not to move quite so early, so much to our gratification we remained there until after 8 A.M. & started across the prairie. Traveled West & camped on the Little Mo about 30 miles from our old camp. The prairie we found burnt over. No grass for the horses until getting to camp & not very good even then.[114] The Little Mo we found to be impregnated with alkali, which is not very palateable but had to be endured.

21st [August]

The command remained in camp for rest. The horses required rest & grass. About 12 or soon after I went to Jno Smiths and got drunk—remarkably so. That was the last that I remember, Col Benteen [name is crossed out], Lt Hodgson, Lt Gates & several other officers being the cause to some extent. Of one thing I am confident, that is that I made myself a precious fool—as all drunken men do—so much so, that I am disgusted with whiskey & will I am confident go without for some time to come.

22d [August]

We marched 28¼ miles & camped just in the edge of the bad lands.[115] They certainly present a novel sight, and to one who has never had the pleasure of traveling in them quite a pretty picture. They are hills of all conceivable form & from very small to large. The genl appearance is white & red. One can see Cities, Fortifications, Castles, Hay stacks, and any thing that they would or could wish for. "Distance certainly lends enchantment to the view."

23 [August]

Our march was a continuation of yesterday, that is, just on the edge of the bad lands, and towards mid day we crossed Stanley['s] old trail [from] 1872, & followed it until we reached camp.[116] The camp is well supplied with water & grass, neither of very good quality. I am glad that my time now with the Expedition is nearly out, or in other words, that we have only a very few days to remain out and then St. Paul will catch me very soon. I am building my hopes on going east but as to whether I will or not I cant say—that remains to be seen—sorter of an after act. Nothing of interest occurred in camp, or in fact in the command worthy of note. We have been blessed with the sight of several black tail deer, & a few antelope have paid the penalty of their curosity. Several were killed.

24th August 1874

We broke camp this A.M. rather earlier than usual & continued our march on Stanley 1872 trail until after 11. There is nothing to divert our attention from the march. The prairie is burnt over—seeing *nothing* & no game of any consequence.[117] Prof Donaldson says that it is very monotenous. I did get a shot at a wolf, but too far to hit it. The old Prof [was] with me and I think enjoyed the sport of seeing me shoot equally as much as I enjoyed it myself. And the old gent remarked to me, Well, Power, I would not be in that fellows place for all that A. T. Stewart is worth.[118] We marched 24¾ miles to day & camped on the "H[e]art"

A constant search for water and grass characterized the last leg of the journey, during which the expedition traveled nearly thirty miles each day. Here, men and horses rest during a noonday break.
State Archives Collection, South Dakota State Historical Society

[River]. I was saying something about being drunk a few days since. Col Hart came in to day equally as full as I was & insisted in my going down in the woods with him to get out of sight. He fell off of his horse while dismounting & I left him alone in his glory. "Antelope Benj," "Pride of Prairie," "Jack Harts" and Chance have been trying their best to plague me but not succeeding very well [have] quit. Strange to say "Antelope" has been on his good behavior for the past three days and has been perfectly sober since getting tight with me [on the] 21st. I made a perfect dammed ass of myself—so much so that I dont think that [I will] try it again. Camp not very good. Wood enough but water & grass very poor. Nothing of special interest occurred to day. My thoughts run on something else. I have been dreaming of Va—Lizzie & home—and in fact have spent a great deal of my time in thinking of her since coming out. Well—I could not occupy my time better—that is, on an expedition where there is so much vulgarity & profanity—even, I am sorry to say, among the office[rs]. One could not expect much more from the privates, but officers, men who represent the "U. S.," should to some extent be moral. Well I am almost as bad as the worst of them—but I shall try to mend my way after getting back in the states.

25 [August]
"B" Co. went ahead. Consequently I had to get my breakfast sooner than usual and be ready for the march. Barrows, [of the] *N.Y.T*, & I started off towards sunrise by our selves & B got in the mud—steady found it hard work to extricate him self, but finally got out and we went on our way rejoicing. Struck Stanley & Whistlers old Trail which the Genl will follow in, it is supposed.[119] Nothing of interest occurred during the days march. The Genl went in camp earlier than usual—did not march over 17¾ miles. The country is rolling prairie, we having left the "Bad Lands" behind. Antelope were few & far between—no other game what ever. I got a shot at one but too far to do any good. Our camp is a good one—wood, water & grass in abundance. We were blessed with a little rain to day, but none worth speaking of. I am getting home sick—want to get back to old Va. I am heartily tired of the West, that is, the "Far West." Chicago and St Louis will do, but this Western Country generally is a poor place. If I had a good situation & was married, why then I could stand it for awhile & be contented, but as I am, I think that I prefer the East. This P.M. every thing looks gloomy. The sky is over cast with clouds. The prairie is burnt off and things wear a dull look generally.

26th [August]

Our march to day continued over the burnt prairie with very little to interrupt the monotony of our ride. We past the grave of "Dan Malloy" [the] teamster killed last year.[120] It was in a state of good preservation to all appearances, not having been molested by Indians or beasts. The dullness of the march was broken in upon on several occasions by shots fired at antelope and other game. My gun had the honor of ending the career of one. The day was hot and hard on the stock—several old horses departed this life. A Sergt in Custers Co died last night & was burried this P.M.[121] The usual honors were paid—4 men since leaving "Lincoln" [have had] "Taps" sounded for their last sleep. Poor fellows. May their sleep be sweet until call[ed] to render their account at the last "grand roll call," and may they then be reported as good "Soldiers" & rec[eive] a Soldiers & Christians reward. We marched 32 miles & camped on the head waters [of] Knife River. Got in camp quite early. Wood & water—but no grass. "Coon" got his picket pin up & wandered off. Could not find him until this morning. Our trail will be another added to the great thorough fare to the Black Hills. We are now following the line of the N[orthern] P[acific] RR survey.

27 [August]

It rained some little last night and gave every indication of giving us a benefit this A.M. The fog was very thick but finally clear[ed] off very prettily. Our march was very short, only [17] miles. Camped in a beautiful valley. Good grass & water [but] no wood. I rode with Hodgson & Col Forsythe during the greater portion of the day. A few words about Genl Forsythe—he comd the right wing of our Expd, is A[ide] D[e] C[amp] to Genl Sheridan, is an accomplished gentleman & officer, affable & agreeable, a man of good conversational powers and pleasant manner. I was introduced to him a few days before starting from the post. A few days since [the] 23d inst I was riding with him. The day after my "drunk" at lunch he insisted on my joining him, remarking that it would not hurt me to eat even so much infact that to the contrary it would do me good after being on "a tare" to eat. So I joined [him]. The Genl has traveled considerably south & converses well with references to the lost opportunities of men there. [He] observes every thing & consequently knows considerable to talk about. I was surprised to find that he knew so much about farming &c &c.[122] Fruit raising also seems to have attracted his attention. The fact is the Genl['s] idea seems to be, do well what you under take, but he cant keep the men of his companies. Sometimes makes a mistake in his Roster but that is caused by keeping it in his head. Long may he wave. Benj H Hodgson, my friend & tent mate—What shall I say about the "Old Boy." 1st of all that to plague me seems to be his greatest delight. In camp & tent has named me F[red] Coffee—say[s] my greatest ambition is to return to the states, stop at some good Hotel, sign myself F. Coffee Power, part my hair in the middle & spit through my front teeth. With it all, H is a good fellow.

28th [August]
We marched only 15¾ miles to day & camped on the Muddy, which was certainly in keeping with its name, though our camp was a good one—wood, water & grass. Nothing of interest except that we are again march[ing] on good unburnt prairie again which is consoling. The horses seem to enjoy it to the fullest extent of the law. I spent most of my time with Capt Yates, 7th. Our conversation was about things & matters in general.

29th [August]
A short & good march to day—only 20 miles. Camped on a branch of the H[e]art, Sweet briar Creek. Wood, W. & g. I killed an antelope [and] gave the head to [Lieutenant] Gates, 20 Infy, who took lunch with me. Lt [Edward G.] Mathey[123] also joined us & dined on hawk and light bread, which was very good. Two Scouts came in from [Fort] Rice to inform Col Hart that one of his children was at the point of death.[124] The Col will leave us tomorrow night. Our time is drawing to a close & most of us are looking forwd with pleasure to getting in [to] Lincoln, getting letters &c &c from home & other places. After two months absence from civilization it makes one Oh d____t I am going to sleep & put off writing until tomorrow. . . .

AFTERWORD
Power's account of his Black Hills adventure ends abruptly with the notation, "Prof Donaldson with his Mule made their appearance on top of a Bluff in full view of Lincoln." Power may have found the incident significant enough to record because Custer had posted forward pickets as the expedition neared Fort Abraham Lincoln to prevent any of his men from slipping into the fort ahead of himself. At any rate, the command marched into Fort Abraham Lincoln on 30 August to the cheers

One of Illingworth's last expedition photographs was probably this view down the Heart River toward its confluence with the Missouri. On the afternoon of 30 August 1874, Custer and his men marched into Fort Abraham Lincoln, located just south of where the two rivers joined. State Archives Collection, South Dakota State Historical Society

of those in both the garrison and Custer's camp.[125] Custer's reconnaissance had been eminently successful, accomplishing more than anyone expected. The expedition had recorded the topography of hitherto unexplored areas of the Dakota, Montana, and Wyoming territories. Its engineers had mapped the courses of major rivers and streams. Its scientists had gained new information on the botany, geology, and zoology of the Black Hills region. Finally, the expedition's miners had verified long-standing rumors of gold. Although the expedition press corps had blared news of the gold discovery to the world, Power made only passing references to gold in his diary, and his newspaper dispatches lacked the other correspondents' sensationalism. In his dispatch of 2 August, he casually informed readers, "Oh! I forgot to say gold has been discovered."[126]

Soon after the expedition returned to Fort Abraham Lincoln, Power "shook his picket rope," in the words of the *Bismarck Tribune* editor, "and went home with the remainder of the boys."[127] His stint with the *Saint Paul Daily Press* over, Power gradually worked his way back to Chicago, always on the lookout for suitable employment. During the Panic of 1874, however, he did not have much luck. On the last day of October, he confided to his diary, "I am out of money and friends," adding, "a bad state of affairs but a true one."[128] Several weeks later, though, he was working again, writing an installment travelogue about Joliet, Morris, Lasalle, and other towns along the Illinois River. At this point his 1874 diary ends.

By 1877, Power had returned to Virginia, ready to settle down. Continuing in his earlier vocation, he began a lifelong career with the Northwestern Mutual Life Insurance Company. After his return, Lizzie Quarles dropped completely from the picture. In January 1878, he married Medora Beckwith Woodfin from Buckingham County, about sixty miles west of Richmond. She was seventeen; Power was thirty-one. Power became a traveling auditor for Northwestern Mutual, and the family moved to various locations across the South. Their first child, Frederick William, evidently died in infancy or early childhood. A daughter, Mary Randolph, was born in 1887 while the Powers were in Virginia. The last child, Marjorie Beckwith, was born in 1889, when the family resided at Covington, Georgia. According to a later family story, they also lived for a period in Meridan, Mississippi. By 1900, the Powers were in Washington, D.C., where they lived in a rented residence at 1006 B Street NW.[129]

Fred Power died on 28 April 1901 at his home on B Street. His cause of death was recorded as cardiac neuralgia, probably a form of heart disease. He was buried three days later in the Congressional Cemetery in a plot he had purchased before his death. Today, Power rests in an unmarked grave in range 141 of Washington's most historic cemetery.[130] Although he died at age fifty-three, he lived longer than either of his parents and, according to known information, survived his other siblings.

But what of the adventurous men and powerful landscape Power had left behind him twenty-six years earlier? The lure of gold opened the

Fred Power and his wife, Medora Beckwith Woodfin Power, were photographed around the time of their marriage in 1878. Faye and Clyde Bryant, Red Lion, Pa.

floodgates to the Black Hills, and prospectors poured into the region. By 1876, the Great Sioux War erupted on the Northern Great Plains, sparked in part by these violations of the Fort Laramie Treaty of 1868. A scant two years after the 1874 Black Hills Expedition ended, "Antelope Benj" Hodgson, Captain Yates, Bloody Knife, Sergeant Clear, and other comrades with whom Power had ridden through the Hills rode into legend by dying with Custer at the Battle of the Little Bighorn, another instance in which, to paraphrase the words of Power, distance lent enchantment to the view.

NOTES

1. Standard sources on the 1874 Black Hills Expedition include John M. Carroll and Lawrence A. Frost, eds., *Private Theodore Ewert's Diary of the Black Hills Expedition of 1874* (Piscataway, N.J.: CRI Books, 1976); Lawrence A. Frost, ed., *With Custer in '74: James Calhoun's Diary of the Black Hills Expedition* (Provo, Utah: Brigham Young University Press, 1979); Max E. Gerber, "The Custer Expedition of

1874: A New Look," *North Dakota History* 40 (Winter 1973): 4–23; Donald Jackson, *Custer's Gold: The United States Cavalry Expedition of 1874* (New Haven, Conn.: Yale University Press, 1966); Herbert Krause and Gary D. Olson, *Prelude to Glory: A Newspaper Accounting of Custer's 1874 Expedition to the Black Hills* (Sioux Falls, S.Dak.: Brevet Press, 1974); James D. McLaird and Lesta V. Turchen, "Exploring the Black Hills, 1855–1875: Reports of the Government Expeditions— Colonel William Ludlow and the Custer Expedition, 1874," *South Dakota History* 4 (Summer 1974): 282–319; Cleophas C. O'Harra, "Custer's Black Hills Expedition of 1874," *Black Hills Engineer* 17 (Nov. 1929): 221–86; Donald R. Progulske, *Yellow Ore, Yellow Hair, Yellow Pine: A Photographic Study of a Century of Forest Ecology*, Agricultural Experiment Station, Bulletin no. 616 (Brookings: South Dakota State University, 1974); Donald R. Progulske with Frank J. Shideler, *Following Custer*, Agricultural Experiment Station, Bulletin no. 674 (Brookings: South Dakota State University, n.d.); Philip H. Sheridan, *Record of Engagements with Hostile Indians within the Military Division of the Missouri from 1868 to 1882* (1882; reprint ed., Bellevue, Nebr.: Old Army Press, 1969).

2. For more on the explorations of Warren and Raynolds, *see* James D. McLaird and Lesta V. Turchen, "Exploring the Black Hills, 1855–1875: Reports of the Government Expeditions—The Dacota Explorations of Lieutenant Gouverneur Kemble Warren, 1855–1856–1857," *South Dakota History* 3 (Fall 1973): 360–89, and "Exploring the Black Hills, 1855–1875: Reports of the Government Expeditions—The Explorations of Captain William Franklin Raynolds, 1859–1860," *South Dakota History* 4 (Winter 1973): 19–62.

3. *Army and Navy Journal*, 4 July 1874.

4. Jackson, *Custer's Gold*, pp. 14, 23–24. The quotation is from article 2 of the Fort Laramie Treaty of 1868, which is reprinted ibid., pp. 127–36.

5. *Army and Navy Journal*, 4 July 1874.

6. Jackson, *Custer's Gold*, pp. 18–19, 34.

7. Ibid., pp. 52–60, 64–65, 81–82; Krause and Olson, *Prelude to Glory*, p. 40.

8. Krause and Olson, *Prelude to Glory*, pp. 40, 98, 188.

9. *Bismarck Tribune*, 8 July 1874, reprinted in Krause and Olson, *Prelude to Glory*, p. 15. *Prelude to Glory* is an excellent compilation of the correspondents' published articles and the official expedition reports. Subsequent references to correspondents' articles will include the newspaper name, date, and the page number(s) from *Prelude to Glory* on which the article appears.

10. Power was born 15 March 1847. Power Family Bible, in possession of Faye and Clyde Bryant, Red Lion, Pa.

11. Unless otherwise noted, all information about the Power family comes from a compilation of family records held by the Bryants.

12. George W. Randolph to Superintendent, 12 May 1863, Alumni Biographical Files, Virginia Military Institute (VMI) Archives, Lexington, Va.

13. Frederick W. Power, Sr., to Superintendent, 15 May 1863, ibid.

14. Frederick W. Power, Jr., Records, ibid. Essentially, a state cadet was one who received a scholarship in return for promising to teach for two years to repay the cost of his education. In 1863, tuition at VMI was $375 per year. Fifty of the institution's three hundred students were state cadets.

15. Ibid.

16. Tracy Chernault and Jeffrey C. Weaver, *18th and 20th Battalions of Heavy Artillery* (Lynchburg, Va.: H. E. Howard, 1995), pp. 26–44. Although published sources give varying information about which unit Power served with, records of the Point Lookout prison camp examined by the Bryants at the National Archives firmly established his service with Company C of the Twentieth Battalion.

17. Douglas S. Freeman, *Lee's Lieutenants*, Vol. 3: *Gettysburg to Appomattox* (New York: Charles Scribner's Sons, 1942–1944), p. 711; Register of Prisoners, 1863–1865, Point Lookout, Md., Records of Individual Prisons or Stations, Selected Records of the War Department Relating to Confederate Prisoners of War, 1861–1865, War Department Collection of Confederate Records, Record Group 109, National Archives Microfilm Publication M598, roll 119, p. 25.

18. The former Power lands today make up a large portion of Colonial National Historical Park at Yorktown. The house is in private ownership.

19. Power, Diary, 12, 20, 24 June, 20 Oct. 1874, in possession of Kirk Budd, Rushville, Nebr. In *Prelude to Glory*, Krause and Olson speculated that the *Saint Paul Daily Press* correspondent, who signed his dispatches simply "Power," was James B. Power, a prominent Saint Paul businessman (p. 80). A notation accompanying the diary at the time it was purchased indicates that Olson acknowledged the error in a 7 April 1982 letter to Dale Anderson.

20. Krause and Olson, *Prelude to Glory*, p. 80.

21. Power, Diary, 24 June 1874.

22. Frost, *With Custer in '74*, p. 9.

23. *Saint Paul Daily Press*, 16 Aug. 1874, p. 90.

24. Kenneth Hammer, *Men with Custer: Biographies of the 7th Cavalry* (Hardin, Mont.: Custer Battlefield Historical Museum Assoc., 1995), p. 158.

25. *Saint Paul Daily Press*, 15 Aug. 1874, p. 83.

26. Power, Diary, 15 July, 2, 15 Aug. 1874.

27. *New York Tribune*, 29 Aug. 1874, p. 223.

28. Marguerite Merington, ed., *The Custer Story: The Life and Intimate Letters of General George A. Custer and His Wife Elizabeth* (New York: Devin-Adair Co., 1950), p. 273.

29. Custer took his entire entourage into training camp to prepare both men and animals for the long march to the Black Hills. Jackson, *Custer's Gold*, p. 22.

30. Captain George B. Dandy, who had been a brigadier general in the Civil War, was the quartermaster officer in charge of building Fort Abraham Lincoln.

31. This dispute may have arisen because of an unflattering woodcut portrait of Custer that ran with the article on 24 June. Custer soon relented and allowed Knappen to come along.

32. Custer had learned of this cave from an Arikara scout, Goose, who told him that Lakotas had left the items inside to guarantee success in the hunt. In his 15 July dispatch, Power described the cave as twenty feet high and twelve to fourteen feet wide. It extended into the rock for 230 feet, "or rather that was as far as we could go" (*Saint Paul Daily Press*, 28 July 1874, p. 81). Custer officially named this geographical feature "Ludlow's Cave" after the expedition's chief engineer. It is located in the Cave Hills of Harding County, South Dakota, west of the present-day town of Ludlow. McLaird and Turchen, "Exploring the Black Hills—Colonel William Ludlow and the Custer Expedition," pp. 290–91.

33. The "General" was the cavalry bugle call to strike tents and prepare to move.

34. Custer wrote to his wife on 15 July that the column stopped at the place he named "Prospect Valley," Dakota Territory, to rest the animals, repair wagons, and "give the men a chance to wash their clothes" (Merington, *The Custer Story*, p. 272).

35. Bloody Knife was a Hunkpapa-Arikara scout who had served the army since 1868. He would die with Reno's battalion in the valley fight at the Little Bighorn. Hammer, *Men with Custer*, p. 27. A scouting detail followed the smoke and spotted a small group of twenty Indians. Power told his newspaper readers, "Should the Indians make their appearance at anytime during the day I shall get under the ammunition wagon and there remain" (*Saint Paul Daily Press*, 28 July 1874, p. 82).

36. Second Lieutenant Fred D. Grant, son of President Ulysses S. Grant, graduated from West Point in 1871 and became an aide de camp and lieutenant colonel in 1873. Custer had requested that he accompany the expedition, although it appears he was only along for the ride. Jackson, *Custer's Gold*, p. 20.

37. *New York Tribune* correspondent Samuel Barrows reported the command marched until 9:00 P.M. with dinner served at 10:30. *New York Tribune*, 21 Aug. 1874, p. 203.

38. In his next dispatch, Power informed his readers that Knappen had fallen asleep in the shade of a "sage bush" along the trail. *Saint Paul Daily Press*, 15 Aug. 1874, p. 84.

39. Although Donaldson was critical, Lieutenant James Calhoun wrote that some portions of the valley contained "an abundance of everything capable of sustaining a dense population" (Frost, *With Custer in '74*, p. 37).

40. Power told his readers, "Col. Grant came in contact with an old fellow who surrendered after some considerable resistance, but the colonel, having something of his father's disposition, determined to fight it out on that line if it took the whole summer" (*Saint Paul Daily Press*, 15 Aug. 1874, p. 85).

41. Captain Thomas H. French, Company M, Seventh Cavalry, served in the Civil War and joined the regiment in 1871. A member of the Reno battalion at the Little Bighorn, he would survive the battle. First Lieutenant Josiah Chance, Seventeenth Infantry, commanded the expedition's artillery detachment. William H. Illingworth, a professional photographer from Saint Paul, had been hired by Ludlow, who supplied his camera and equipment. Hammer, *Men with Custer*, pp. 115–16; Frost, ed., *With Custer in '74*, p. 5; Krause and Olson, *Prelude to Glory*, pp. 33–35. Power wrote that Illingworth brought in more game than any other man "and keeps our mess all the time supplied" (*Saint Paul Daily Press*, 28 July 1874, p. 55). For more information, *see* Ernest Grafe and Paul Horsted, "In Illingworth's Footsteps: Rediscovering the First Photographs of the Black Hills," *South Dakota History* 31 (Fall/Winter 2001): 289–316.

42. The storm during the night of 17–18 July impressed expedition members. Power told his readers, "Tents might be seen a half mile from camp," and "hats were plentiful" (*Saint Paul Daily Press*, 15 Aug. 1874, p. 85).

43. These two items of scientific interest stand out from the first segment of the expedition's journey. Custer reported that the large leg bone found on 14 July "evidently belonged to an animal larger than an elephant" (Frost, *With Custer in '74*, p. 35). Correspondent William Curtis called the bright comet that attracted expedition members' attention each night "a treasure of scientific satisfaction if seen as plainly in 'the States'" (*Chicago Inter-Ocean*, 15 Aug. 1874, p. 115).

44. The expedition was camped near the trail of Captain William F. Raynolds, who had skirted the northern Hills in 1859. Upon reaching the timber after days of travel with only horses for shade, correspondent Samuel Barrows wrote with delight of "the prospect of having a real, live tree—a tree that would not tread on you just as you had dropped to sleep" (*New York Tribune*, 24 Aug. 1874, p. 204).

45. Power reported that while on the march "being very fashionable we only eat two meals a day, breakfast and dinner, at 3 a.m. and 6 p.m." (*Saint Paul Daily Press*, 28 July 1874, p. 82). This layover relaxed the rules and gave everyone a welcome break.

46. Power assured readers that his leisure activities did not include partaking of the whiskey sold by John W. Smith, the expedition's trader, even though it was "some of the best, . . . [but] not being a drinkist I can only say so from heresay" (ibid., p. 84). Charles J. Liver wrote the popular English adventure novel that Power was enjoying.

47. Lizzie Prentis Quarles of Virginia is frequently mentioned in Power's diary.

48. Custer reported on this date that the expedition was "feeling" its way carefully along the outlying ranges, "seeking a weak point through which we might make our way to the interior" (quoted in O'Harra, "Custer's Black Hills Expedition," p. 272).

49. Private Hoener, Company B, Seventh Cavalry, was the man who accidentally shot himself. His commander, Second Lieutenant Benjamin H. Hodgson, was an 1870 graduate of West Point. At the Little Bighorn, he would serve as acting adjutant of Reno's battalion and die during the retreat to the bluffs. Frost, *With Custer in '74*, p. 41; Hammer, *Men with Custer*, p. 158.

50. The officer who found the cup was First Lieutenant Thomas M. McDougall, Company E, Seventh Cavalry, who had joined the regiment in 1870. At the Little Bighorn, he would guard the pack train and take part in the hilltop fight. Correspondent Barrows reported that the cup was marked "William Robertson," a name John Smith recognized as belonging to a mixed-blood man. Hammer, *Men with Custer*, p. 227; *New York Tribune*, 24 Aug. 1874, p. 207.

51. Private John Cunningham died of acute pleurisy. The men of his company were bitterly critical of the lack of care he received from the expedition medical staff. *See* Frost, *With Custer in '74*, p. 42, and Carroll and Frost, *Private Theodore Ewert's Diary*, pp. 34–36. Cunningham's commanding officer, Captain Frederick W. Benteen, Company H, had served with the Seventh Cavalry since 1866. He commanded a battalion in the hilltop fight at the Little Bighorn and, after retiring in 1888, was brevetted a brigadier general for his actions there. Hammer, *Men with Custer*, pp. 21–22.

52. Private William Roller shot Private George Turner, the man with whom he had enlisted four years earlier. Turner was quarrelsome, abusive, and, according to Lieutenant James Calhoun, "received no sympathy from the other men" (Frost, ed., *With Custer in '74*, p.49).

53. Power refers to Captain Lloyd Wheaton, Company I, Twentieth Infantry, by his brevet rank, which he attained as a commander of volunteers during the Civil War. Wheaton would rise to the rank of major general before retiring in 1902. Francis B. Heitman, comp., *Historical Register and Dictionary of the United States Army*, 2 vols. (Washington, D.C.: Government Printing Office, 1903), 1:1023.

54. Captain Owen Hale, Company K, joined the Seventh in 1866. He would not be present at the Little Bighorn but would die in the Snake Creek fight with the Nez Perce in 1877. Ibid., 1:487.

55. First Lieutenant Francis M. Gibson, Company H, joined the Seventh Cavalry in 1867. He would fight with the Reno battalion in the valley and hilltop fights at the Little Bighorn and survive to retire in 1891. Ibid., 1:453.

56. Dr. John W. Williams, assistant surgeon, was the chief medical officer on both the Black Hills Expedition and Terry's staff during the Little Bighorn campaign. Hammer, *Men with Custer*, p. 125; Heitman, *Historical Register*, 1:1041.

57. Inyan Kara mountain, a familiar landmark on the northwestern edge of the Black Hills, was described by Winchell as an inverted saucer with still another inverted saucer lying on top. Power also called it "Hungyakara," a variation of a Sioux term meaning "rocky mountain goat." Gerber, "Custer Expedition," p. 11; *New York Tribune*, 24 Aug. 1874, p. 207.

58. Sergeant Michael Walsh of Company H, Seventh Cavalry, read the service, and Private Theodore Ewert, also of Company H, played taps. Afterward, a fire was lit to obliterate any trace of the graves. Jackson, *Custer's Gold*, p. 72; Carroll and Frost, *Private Theodore Ewert's Diary*, p. 39. The marked graves are located about thirteen miles south of present-day Sundance, Wyoming, on State Highway 585.

59. Other expedition members also noted trail signs, including Lieutenant Calhoun, who wrote, "Indian trails visible in all directions" (Frost, *With Custer in '74*, p. 49).

60. Major Joseph G. Tilford, Seventh Cavalry, commanded one of the expedition's two battalions. According to Frost, he was not particularly fond of Custer and resented leaving his post at Fort Rice for the hardships of an expedition. Ibid., p. 85.

61. Expedition members also picked up shed elk antlers. Donaldson wrote that Custer intended to send several pairs to the Smithsonian Institution. The animals that Power and Donaldson called panthers were correctly identified by Grinnell as mountain lions. *Saint Paul Daily Press*, 15 Aug. 1874, p. 60; Jackson, *Custer's Gold*, p. 55.

62. Custer designated this area "Floral Valley" because of the profusion of wild flowers. Donaldson reported, "Some [officers] said they would give a hundred dollars just to have their wives see the floral richness for even one hour" (*Saint Paul Daily Pioneer*, 15 Aug. 1874, p. 60). Custer noted, "It is no unusual sight to see hundreds of soldiers gathering wild berries" (quoted in *New York World*, 16 Aug. 1874, p. 175).

63. Power elaborated on the tale for his *Saint Paul Daily Press* readers: "Those who are fortunate enough to enter this paradise are so enchanted that they desire to spend the rest of their lives there, and after life take it for their heaven. The disappearing is accounted for in pretty much the same way; that is, it flows into a cave just opposite of the above. One, the happy hunting ground, the home of the departed brave; the other, the last resting place of the unfortunate and the coward" (15 Aug. 1874, pp. 87–88). Another correspondent labeled the tale a product of the professor's fertile imagination. *Chicago Inter-Ocean*, 18 Aug. 1874, p. 120.

64. The discovery of the tent pole and other debris conjured up similar speculation among other expedition members. However, neither Warren nor Raynolds penetrated the Hills near this point.

65. Power explained to his readers that because they were late in making camp, they "did not enjoy a supper of the finny tribe" (*Saint Paul Daily Press*, 15 Aug. 1874, p. 88).

66. This campsite was located in what is now known as Cold Springs Valley.

67. The command had passed over the divide into the Castle Creek Valley, which Custer named for the rugged, castellated hills bordering it. At this point, expedition members believed they were following the main trail from Red Cloud Agency to the hunting grounds. Gerber, "Custer Expedition," p. 12.

68. Captain Verling K. Hart, Company C, a three-year veteran of the Seventh Cavalry, would be promoted to the Fifth Cavalry late in 1875. Second Lieutenant George D. Wallace joined the Seventh fresh from West Point in 1872 and commanded the scouts on the Black Hills Expedition. He would fight with the Reno battalion at the Little Bighorn and be killed at Wounded Knee on 29 December 1890. Heitman, *Historical Register*, 1:506; Hammer, *Men with Custer*, p. 362.

69. Shortly before the expedition had left Fort Lincoln, Lakota Sioux warriors attacked an Arikara village, killing several relatives of the scouts, including Bloody Knife's son. The Arikara, or Ree, were eager for revenge. *Chicago Inter-Ocean*, 18 Aug. 1874, p. 121.

70. The daughter of Red Cloud was apparently Plenty Horses, later known as Libbie Slow Bear. The Man Who Stabs was also known as One Stab or Stabber; he claimed association with both the Red Cloud and Spotted Tail agencies in northwest Nebraska. Custer reported that the entire party numbered twenty-seven. Interview with Lula Red Cloud, Hermosa, S.Dak., 12 Apr. 1997; *Army and Navy Journal*, 22 Aug. 1874; *New York World*, 16 Aug. 1874, p.174.

71. Custer had Lieutenant Wallace send fifteen Santee scouts to watch over the camp. *Saint Paul Daily Pioneer*, 15 Aug. 1874, p. 62.

72. The next day, expedition members found provisions and a saddle blanket covered with blood but no trace of Long Bear. Grant's Report, reprinted in Krause and Olson, *Prelude to Glory*, p. 250.

73. The village inhabitants reported at the agencies that Custer's men had killed The Man Who Stabs, but in fact, Custer would release him on the night of 4 August to the consternation of the Arikara scouts who had destroyed what remained of the vacated Sioux camp and wanted to kill the prisoner. *Army and Navy Journal*, 8 Aug. 1874; *Saint Paul Daily Pioneer*, 15, 25 Aug. 1874, pp. 62, 69.

74. Captain Thomas W. Custer had received the brevet rank of colonel for his service in the Civil War. The younger brother of George A. Custer, he would later

die with the Custer battalion at the Little Bighorn. Hammer, *Men with Custer*, p. 80.

75. Louis Agard, a Frenchman who had married into the Sioux tribe, accompanied the expedition as a guide and interpreter. Jackson, *Custer's Gold*, p. 20; *Bismarck Tribune*, 24 June 1874, p. 12.

76. In Greek mythology, Morpheus is the god of sleep or dreams.

77. Companies F and H, Seventh Cavalry, were divided into platoons and sent out with the engineers and scientific party. Major Forsyth reported that the accompanying miners found indications of silver in quartz deposits along the creek bottoms. *Chicago Tribune*, 27 Aug. 1874, p. 256.

78. Second Lieutenant Julius G. Gates, Company I, served with the Twentieth Infantry from October 1873 until his dismissal in June 1880. Heitman, *Historical Register*, 1:449.

79. Captain George W. Yates, Company F, was assigned to the Seventh Cavalry in 1866 and would die with the Custer battalion at the Little Bighorn. Captain Louis H. Sanger, Company G, Seventeenth Infantry, commanded the infantry detachment for the expedition. Hammer, *Men with Custer*, p. 384; Frost, *With Custer in '74*, p. 15.

80. Power must have been interrupted, for the last half of the diary page is blank.

81. Donaldson wrote that the stack of horns had probably been twelve or fifteen feet high but had settled to five or six feet. *Saint Paul Daily Pioneer*, 15 Aug. 1874, p. 61. Today the spot is known as Reynolds Prairie and is located just north of Deerfield Lake.

82. Charles ("Lonesome Charlie") Reynolds was a well-known scout and hunter who accompanied the expedition as a guide. He would perish in the valley fight at the Little Bighorn. Hammer, *Men with Custer*, p. 292.

83. Today, the locations of the Indian campsite and Custer's camp of 28 July lie beneath Deerfield Lake.

84. The camp of 29 July was about seven miles north and west of present-day Custer, South Dakota.

85. No other correspondent or diarist mentions this incident involving a Gatling gun.

86. Elihu F. Clear (also known as Clair and Claire) enlisted in the Seventh Cavalry in 1867. He would die at the Little Bighorn during Reno's retreat to the bluffs. Hammer, *Men with Custer*, p.60.

87. "Boots and Saddles" was the cavalry bugle call to mount up and move out.

88. The marches, as Ludlow recorded them, were 10.0 miles on 28 July, 15.0 miles on 29 July, and 10.2 miles on 30 July. Frost, *With Custer in '74*, p. 48. On

30–31 July, the expedition camped near French Creek seven miles south and west of Harney Peak. The western portion of the present-day town of Custer now occupies the site.

89. Rather than Winchell, Power is probably referring to Donaldson, who wrote at some length about building stone in his dispatch of 15 July. *Saint Paul Daily Pioneer*, 15 Aug. 1874, p.62.

90. Donaldson agreed with Power, writing, "In my attempt at describing it, there is no danger of exaggeration. . . . No one ever saw anything to equal it" (ibid., p. 63). Ludlow named the area "Custer's Park."

91. While other expedition members also reported that gold had been found, Lieutenant Colonel Grant expressed skepticism in his official report, writing that the expedition's miners "showed the same pieces every day." He concluded, "I don't believe that any gold was found at all" (Grant's Report, p. 252).

92. The events Power records in this entry actually occurred on 31 July.

93. Custer, Forsyth, Ludlow, and three others reached the summit of Harney Peak at 4:30 in the afternoon. Once at the top, they were treated to what Forsyth called "by all means the grandest [sight] I had ever seen" (quoted in *Chicago Tribune*, 27 Aug. 1874, p. 256).

94. First Lieutenant James Calhoun, of Company C, had been appointed to the Seventh Cavalry in 1871. In 1872, he married Margaret Emma Custer, sister of George, Thomas, and Boston. Captain Miles Moylan, Company A, had been commissioned into the Seventh Cavalry in 1866. He would survive the valley fight at the Little Bighorn to retire as a Tenth Cavalry major in 1893. Frederic S. Calhoun, the younger brother of James Calhoun, evidently accompanied the expedition as a civilian employee. "Boss" was Boston Custer, the frail, youngest Custer brother, who worked on the expedition as a forage master. Both he and James Calhoun would die with the Custer battalion at the Little Bighorn. Hammer, *Men with Custer*, pp. 50, 78, 251; Thomas R. Buecker, "Frederic S. Calhoun: A Little-Known Member of the Custer Clique," *Greasy Grass* 10 (May 1994): 16–25.

95. This camp was actually made on 1 August at a point 3.5 miles down French Creek where grazing conditions were better. The expedition remained here in "Permanent Camp" from 1–5 August. Frost, *With Custer in '74*, p. 60.

96. Power's letters to the newspaper concluded with the statement, "This is written by fire light and in a hurry" (*Saint Paul Daily Press*, 16 Aug. 1874, p. 92). His telegraphic dispatch, sent from Fort Laramie on 8 August, was published the next day. *Saint Paul Daily Press*, 9 Aug, 1874, p. 93.

97. Custer and his men struck south, exploring the country to the South Fork of the Cheyenne River. The two companies Power mentions as being led by Benteen were actually led by Captain Hart and included a mapping party under First Lieu-

tenant Edward S. Godfrey, all of whom were to explore French Creek southeast to the Cheyenne River. Godfrey, Company K, Seventh Cavalry, was an 1867 graduate of West Point. He would be with the Benteen battalion at the Little Bighorn and have a distinguished military career, retiring as a brigadier general. He died in 1932, one of the last surviving officers of the battle. Frost, *With Custer in '74*, p. 67; Jackson, *Custer's Gold*, pp. 86–87; Hammer, *Men with Custer*, p. 129.

98. George Custer had invited Horatio N. Ross, an experienced miner from Bismarck, and William McKay, an early settler of Fort Randall and one-time member of the Dakota Territorial Legislature, to accompany the expedition in an unofficial capacity. Confusion exists over when and where gold was first discovered in the Black Hills, but most accounts agree that Ross made the discovery. Frost, *With Custer in '74*, pp. 60–61; Jackson, *Custer's Gold*, p. 82.

99. Because of rugged terrain, the detachment could not reach the Cheyenne River. Jackson, *Custer's Gold*, p. 87.

100. Sergeant Clear told Donaldson he saw a herd of "not less than one hundred Elk" (*Saint Paul Daily Pioneer*, 25 Aug. 1874, p. 69).

101. Lieutenant Calhoun reported that Custer, Ludlow, Bloody Knife, and Private John Noonan of Company L, Seventh Cavalry, all shot at the male bear, which he judged to weigh six hundred pounds. Forsyth estimated the bear's weight at eight hundred pounds. Frost, *With Custer in '74*, pp. 70–71; *Chicago Tribune*, 27 Aug. 1874, p. 258.

102. Donaldson estimated that the forest had been destroyed some twenty to thirty years earlier. According to Forsyth, the remaining stumps and downed logs made the day's march one of the expedition's hardest. *Saint Paul Daily Pioneer*, 26 Aug. 1874, p. 71; *Chicago Tribune*, 27 Aug. 1874, p. 258.

103. Bear Butte, the eroded remains of molten rock that pushed its way to the earth's surface, rises twelve hundred feet above the prairie on the northern edge of the Black Hills, where it serves as an excellent reference point.

104. Due to rough terrain, the command had been unable to move northeast toward Bear Butte and was forced to turn south to find adequate passage out of the Hills. *Chicago Tribune*, 27 Aug. 1874, p. 258.

105. Expedition members killed an estimated one thousand deer while in the Hills, one hundred of them on 9 August alone. Interestingly enough, they did not see a single buffalo on the entire journey. O'Harra, "Custer's Black Hills Expedition," p. 252; *Chicago Inter-Ocean*, 17 Aug. 1874, p. 118.

106. The expedition had been traveling down Box Elder Creek and began to experience difficulty as it attempted to leave the narrow canyon. Companies were detailed to cut down trees, dig out hillsides, and bridge streams to prepare the way for the ponderous wagon train. *Chicago Tribune*, 27 Aug. 1874, p. 258.

107. Strangely, Power did not record the death of Private James King of Company H, Seventh Cavalry, who died of chronic diarrhea on the night of the thirteenth. As in the case of Private John Cunningham, the men of Company H were "exceedingly displeased" at the medical attention he received. Frost, *With Custer in '74*, p. 74.

108. Power refers to Deers Ears and Slave (now Castle Rock) buttes, two prominent landmarks thirty-five miles northeast and north, respectively, of present-day Newell.

109. The command also used the day to reload and refit for the long march back to Fort Abraham Lincoln. Forsyth, Ludlow, and others climbed to the top of Bear Butte. Frost, *With Custer in '74*, p. 76.

110. Power may be referring to a group photograph of officers and staff that Illingworth took on 13 August. Power sent his fourth and last article for the *Saint Paul Daily Press* from Bear Butte. *Saint Paul Daily Press*, 26 Aug. 1874, pp. 93–95.

111. After the scouts talked with the four Lakotas from the Cheyenne River Agency, rumors spread through camp that Sitting Bull and six bands of Indians were waiting to intercept the expedition in the Short Pine Hills. Even so, Custer adhered to his original plan to explore new country and head north and then east in returning to Fort Abraham Lincoln. Frost, *With Custer in '74*, pp. 80–81; O'Harra, "Custer's Black Hills Expedition," p. 285.

112. Lieutenant Colonel Grant recorded on 17 August, "All expect a fight with Indians tomorrow if not this evening" (Grant's Report, p. 251). The anticipated confrontation never occurred, the story having been either a fabrication by the four Lakotas or a product of camp rumor.

113. The expedition camped near the northwest base of the Cave Hills, approximately six miles northwest of their camp of 11 July.

114. Captain Ludlow reported that Indians had burned the prairie from the Grand River north to above the Heart River, but the expedition was able to find areas with enough grass to provide passable campsites. *New York Tribune*, 14 Sept. 1874, p. 261.

115. This site was approximately twenty miles west of present-day Amidon, North Dakota.

116. At this point, the expedition followed the trail of Colonel David S. Stanley, who had escorted Northern Pacific Railroad surveyors west into the Yellowstone country in 1872 and 1873.

117. Despite the lack of grass and wildlife, correspondent Barrows reported that the burnt prairie "made an excellent road; the cactus had been consumed with the grass, and not a spine was left to torture man or horse" (*New York Tribune*, 14 Sept. 1874, p. 226).

118. Alexander T. Stewart was a wealthy Irish-American merchant of the time.

119. Major Joseph G. Whistler had led the first railroad survey expedition from Fort Rice toward the Yellowstone in the fall of 1871. While Barrows refrained from telling his readers of his adventure in the mud, he wrote with relief that finding Whistler's trail "was like striking an old familiar turnpike, though devoid of toll-gates and keepers" (*New York Tribune*, 14 Sept. 1874, p. 226).

120. Dan Malloy (or John Mullory) was a teamster with the 1873 Yellowstone Expedition who died after being run over by his wagon. Frost, *With Custer in '74*, p. 85.

121. Sergeant Charles Stempker of Company L, Seventh Cavalry, died of chronic diarrhea, "his mind wandering the last twelve hours" (Carroll and Frost, *Private Theodore Ewert's Diary*, p. 80). Correspondent Donaldson read the burial service in "an impressive manner" (Frost, *With Custer in '74*, p. 86).

122. In his report to General Sheridan, Forsyth was as enthusiastic about the agricultural possibilities of the Black Hills as he was about the discovery of gold. "The interior of the Black Hills," he wrote, "offers splendid inducements to farmers and stock-raisers of all descriptions" (*Chicago Tribune*, 27 Aug. 1874, p. 253).

123. First Lieutenant Edward G. Mathey, Company M, had been appointed to the Seventh Cavalry in 1867. He would command the pack train at the Little Big-horn and retire as a major in 1896. Hammer, *Men with Custer*, p. 220.

124. An examination of the *Bismarck Tribune* in the weeks immediately after the expedition returned revealed no information concerning a death in the Hart family.

125. Carroll and Frost, eds., *Private Theodore Ewert's Diary*, pp. 80–81.

126. *Saint Paul Daily Press*, 16 Aug. 1874, p. 92.

127. *Bismarck Tribune*, 2 Sept. 1874.

128. Power Diary, 31 Oct. 1874.

129. Family Records, Faye and Clyde Bryant, Red Lion, Pa.

130. Record of Interments, Congressional Cemetery, Washington, D.C.

Leander P. Richardson

"I KNOW . . . BECAUSE I WAS THERE"

REPORTS OF THE BLACK HILLS GOLD RUSH

James D. McLaird

When in 1894 a Mr. Adler claimed in an article for the *Denver Republican* that he had witnessed the murder of James Butler ("Wild Bill") Hickok in 1876, newspaperman Leander P. Richardson called him a liar. In his article, Adler claimed Hickok to be an expert gambler and a partner of Jack McCall, who, after a disagreement, murdered Wild Bill while he played cards. According to Adler, Hickok fell face first into the poker chips when shot. In contradiction, Richardson contended that there were no poker chips at the table when Hickok was killed, nor had Hickok and McCall ever been companions. In fact, Hickok was not even a good card player. "I know," said Richardson, in a letter to the *New York Sun*, "because I was there."[1] Richardson was indeed in Deadwood that day and had made Hickok's personal acquaintance. Although he did not witness the shooting, he arrived at the murder scene soon afterwards and wrote about the event at various times in later years.

Numerous historians of the Black Hills gold rush and biographers of Wild Bill Hickok have used Richardson's testimony about events in Deadwood in 1876, but the man himself and his credentials are rarely discussed.[2] His publications about the Black Hills included contemporary dispatches, magazine articles, reminiscences, and

This essay originally appeared in *South Dakota History* 31 (Fall/Winter 2001): 239–68.

even dime novels. While these accounts published over a twenty-year period display some discrepancies, they are relatively consistent, perhaps because he based his writing on notes kept during his visit. His best-known narrative, "A Trip to the Black Hills," appeared in *Scribner's Monthly* in 1877 and led to extensive publicity for the author.[3] Richardson based his Black Hills writings on a five-day visit to Deadwood that began on 30 July 1876. Although his time in the Hills was brief, he immersed himself in gold-rush life, camping with Hickok and C. H. ("Colorado Charley") Utter. In addition, Richardson met and later described Martha ("Calamity Jane") Canary, Richard ("Bloody Dick") Seymour, Kitty Arnold, Jack Langrishe, and other Deadwood celebrities. The writer's firsthand accounts reveal his interest in colorful characters, the common people, and the theater, as well as his penchant for irony, humor, and exaggeration. Although at times Richardson, like Adler, stretched the truth, his descriptions help to document life during Deadwood's colorful "days of '76."

Leander Pease Richardson was born in Cincinnati, Ohio, on 28 February 1856, the son of Albert D. and Mary Louise Richardson. Little is known about his early life, although he evidently attended school in Cincinnati. His father, a well-known journalist, served as an important role model. Albert Richardson was born in Massachusetts but traveled to the West to begin his journalistic career. He served as correspondent for the *Cincinnati Gazette* in Kansas during the bitter conflict there between proslavery and abolitionist forces. In 1859, while visiting Denver, he met Horace Greeley, beginning a lifelong association with the famous editor of the *New York Tribune*. During the Civil War, he served as the *Tribune* correspondent with General Ulysses S. Grant and was captured during the siege of Vicksburg. His wife died during his imprisonment, leaving their three children virtually orphaned. Albert Richardson later described his war adventures and escape from a Confederate prison camp in *The Secret Service, the Field, the Dungeon, and the Escape*. After the Civil War, his literary reputation grew with the appearance of his major work, *Beyond the Mississippi*, narrating his travels through the American West, and of his *Personal History of Ulysses S. Grant*. Richardson was murdered in the offices of the *New York Tribune* in 1869 as the result of a relationship with another man's ex-wife.[4] The impact of his father's death on Leander, only thirteen, and of the sordid revelations at the murderer's trial, is not known, but it must have been considerable. Nevertheless, like his father, Leander Richardson pursued a journalistic career, even imitating his father's travels to the West.

By age sixteen, young Richardson was a correspondent for the *Chicago Inter-Ocean*. Four years later, he made his famous visit to Deadwood. The Black Hills gold rush, wrote Richardson, "has probably been the subject of more newspaper discussion than any discovery in America" since the 1849 California gold rush. So little was known with certainty, however, that he deemed an investigation of conditions there worthwhile. A small Massachusetts press, the *Springfield Republican*, funded his trip, and therefore his means were modest. The journalist's intent was to send regular dispatches describing his western tour to attract readers, boost newspaper sales, and, of course, give the author desired publicity.[5] Both Richardson's contemporary dispatches and his article published a year later in *Scribner's Monthly* commanded national attention. In them, he provided a narrative of his trip, descriptions of Deadwood's unique society, and an assessment of the resources of the Black Hills.

Richardson probably traveled by rail to Cheyenne, Wyoming, where he hired a driver to take him to the Black Hills. While in Cheyenne, he heard fantastic stories about the large quantities of gold in the Black Hills and immediately decided they were "false impressions" circulated to increase migration. Richardson worried about the influence of such exaggerated reports, not only because they might entice people to give up their jobs in a foolish pursuit for easy wealth, but also because he believed that young men who began to "chase after fortune" might continue "a life of perpetual endeavor to accumulate money without giving its equivalent in labor." Thus, one of Richardson's goals was to blunt "reports of the vast resources and abounding beauty of the country," with their "exaggerated hopes of the brilliancy of its future," much to the chagrin of Black Hills boosters.[6]

Richardson began his narrative with his departure from Fort Laramie on 22 July 1876. His party, he said, was comprised of eight men, a lumber wagon, and a wagon called a "jerky," each of the latter drawn by four horses. Inclined to highlight the least enjoyable aspects of his experiences for humor, Richardson reported that the "jerky" lived up to its name and proceeded to detail unpleasant travel conditions. In the Platte River region, the party struggled through "deep and heavy sand" under an unmerciful sun. The group was also "surrounded and harassed by innumerable sand-gnats, which darted into our eyes, crawled into our nostrils, buzzed in our ears, and wriggled down our necks in a most annoying fashion."[7] These problems, encountered during the first fifteen miles, were but a prelude to what was to come.

The travelers' first stop after leaving Fort Laramie was a ranch called Government Farm, where small parties joined together for safety.[8] There, Richardson's group prepared its first meal. "I don't think the dinner was a very decided success," he concluded. "Everything became covered with bacon-grease; I burned my fingers in a most unprofessional manner, and there was more dust in the food than I was accustomed to eating." After their repast, the men hurried to join a larger wagon train at Rawhide Buttes, which they reached that evening despite finding the road through the bluffs and gulches difficult to traverse. There they took the party's "jaded teams . . . down the steep hillside to an almost imperceptible creek for water and grass." After caring for the animals, again came that "horrible mockery" called supper, followed by an effort to sleep in the wagon.[9]

The second day's travel from Fort Laramie, according to Richardson, was even worse:

July 23d. Cold and damp. The horizon completely hemmed in by clouds, and a drizzling rain setting in. The party has eight colds, all told. Breakfast—a swindle. We started at four o'clock in the morning, traveling along the side of the Buttes until about ten, when Running Water was reached. Here we went through the one-act farce of dinner, and fed our horses; never animals needed it more! Two men who had up to the present time been following beside the coach, having overtaken us at Government Farm, turned back at this point, being afraid to go through with so small a party. We sha'n't miss them much, however, except at dinner-time, when it has been their habit to borrow our frying-pans and coffee-pots.

The landscape was bleak and "unpleasant to the eye, producing little besides sage-brush and cactus." To add to their misery, the men were drenched in a rainstorm as they approached Hat Creek.[10]

On the trail, the group met several travelers heading back to Cheyenne, including some gamblers returning for more equipment. Richardson found them "reticent" when asked about mineral prospects, confirming his suspicions about the prodigious reports of gold. At Hat Creek station, Richardson's party found a small contingent of soldiers and a hotel, saloon, and store known as Johnny Bowman's

Ranch. There, the men were informed that the danger of Indian attack increased dramatically as they neared the Black Hills, and the party camped nearby for the night.[11] This time, Richardson tried sleeping in the jerky rather than the lumber wagon, only to be deluged when another storm struck. "After daylight I fell into a doze," he reported, "under the impression that by twisting and doubling myself into serpentine form, I had managed to evade the pools of water which had gathered at various places upon the blankets." Waking up an hour later, he discovered that the puddles "had all united so as to form a kind of lake, in which I was an island." Completely miserable, the small party left for the Hills, deciding to risk the danger from Indians.[12]

Mud, not hostile Indians, became their problem. All day they traveled in a steady drizzle with a chilling wind and found the going on wet ground difficult. "The revolving wheels quickly became solid masses of heavy mire," Richardson wrote, "the spaces between the spokes and between the wheel and wagon-box being completely filled, so that every hundred yards or so it became necessary to dismount and pry it with a crow-bar." To relieve the tired horses, most of the passengers got out to walk, but "after a half a dozen steps their boots would pick up great slabs of the earth, and they too were forced to resort to the crow-bar."[13]

They made only fourteen miles that day, spending the night at a deserted cabin along Indian Creek, where they ate a "melancholy meal of raw ham and hard tack." During Richardson's turn at watch, a loud splashing was heard, "as though all the Indians between New York and the Pacific Coast were crossing the creek." Fearful, the party remained alert all night, only to discover that the noise had come from a portion of the bluff collapsing and falling into the water. Then, as they cooked breakfast, the group heard "a series of . . . infernal yells" and readied their weapons, only to learn the noise came from coyotes, whose cry, described Richardson, is "a fearful and blood-curdling sound."[14]

While Richardson worried about an Indian attack, his death at their hands was reported in Cheyenne. Word of his demise reached the front page of the *New York Times* on 27 July 1876. According to the newspaper, a scalped body riddled by at least twenty bullets was found a hundred miles north of Fort Laramie. John Marsh of Deadwood said he had buried the body, on which he found Richardson's memorandum book with directions to send it to A. C. Snyder, the Associated Press agent in Cheyenne. It was Snyder who had warned Richardson of the dangers of Black Hills travel and asked him to carry written instructions to notify him in case something happened. In fact, the story was merely a prank, for John Marsh was with Richardson when the party arrived in Deadwood.[15] Afterwards, the *Cheyenne Leader* referred to the journalist as "Puttyhead Richardson" for reporting his own death.[16]

Meanwhile, Richardson continued on to the Black Hills. As the rain subsided, travel conditions improved, although the country became "wilder than ever." Within sight of Buffalo Gap, the group passed the trail ("path" in Richardson's account) leading to Red Cloud Agency. There the travelers descended into the valley of the Cheyenne River, which, they were told by passing drivers, was so dry they had had to dig to get water for their animals. "When we arrived, the river was fifty yards wide and from four to nine feet deep," exclaimed Richardson, and though warned not to cross, their driver made the attempt. Soon the wagon was mired in quicksand and mud, and fully two hours were consumed in the struggle to bring it back to dry land. "This was the second drenching for us, and we were not very amiable, — in fact we almost came to blows two or three times within an hour."[17]

Across the Cheyenne River was a road ranch, where Richardson purchased dry clothes and a venison dinner. There the party remained a couple of days before traveling to the mouth of Red Canyon, where they passed a soldiers' camp. After their evening meal, they traveled through the canyon, well aware that the Charles Metz party had been killed there by Indians earlier that spring.[18] Once again, however, it was not hostile Indians that caused difficulty for Richardson's party. As the men traveled in the dark, their driver fell asleep and, at about two o'clock in the morning, overturned the wagon. "I have a dim recollection of executing a semicircular transit through the air," wrote Richardson, "followed by a kind of ricocheting movement along the surface of the ground." He soon found himself "sitting upon a rock, surrounded by boxes, bundles, and such dancing lights as one is apt to see in times of skating accidents." After repairs, they continued their trip in daylight, finally arriving at Custer City in the southern Black Hills. Although he estimated the houses at about a thousand, Richardson believed that only about one hundred and fifty people remained there, the others having been drawn to Deadwood by reports of gold in the northern Hills. In fact, decided Richardson, there never had been enough gold in the Custer vicinity to warrant a mining rush. "Not more than $20 per day has ever been taken out on French Creek, along the banks of which lies the town," he asserted. Nevertheless, he speculated the town might

Richardson found Custer and Hill City depopulated, the inhabitants lured away by reports of greater riches in Deadwood. This engraving of Hill City illustrated his Scribner's Monthly *article.* Scribner's Monthly, *April 1877*

become "the leading post for supplies, and there seems no reason why it should not be as important a center to that district as Denver is to the Colorado mines."[19]

Richardson's party tarried only briefly at Custer; nevertheless, the journalist treated himself to a hotel room and dinner before leaving that afternoon. After crossing Spring Creek innumerable times and making only twelve miles, the group camped. The next morning they passed Hill City, which, like Custer, was practically deserted. As they neared the Rapid Creek district, they discovered more mining activity. Now in a hurry, the party pressed on for twenty-seven hours straight to reach Deadwood, wearing out their animals. When they arrived at the steep hill leading down to Deadwood Gulch, Richardson observed dead timber on the hills, which, he assumed, gave the town its name.[20]

Richardson estimated Deadwood Gulch to be about ten winding miles in length, with a "long line of shanties and tents, forming, in all, four towns": Montana City, Elizabethtown, Deadwood City, and Gayville. As they entered Deadwood, the party was "immediately surrounded by a crowd of miners, gamblers and other citizens, all anxious to hear from the outer world." Because it was Sunday afternoon, everyone was spending the day in town. "Taken as a whole, I never in my life saw so many hardened and brutal-looking men together, although of course there were a few better faces among them," Richardson wrote. "Every alternate house was a gambling saloon, and each of them was carrying on a brisk business. In the middle of the street a little knot of men had gathered, and were holding a prayer-meeting, which showed in sharp contrast to the bustling activity of wickedness surrounding it."[21] There were, Richardson estimated, about fourteen thousand people in Deadwood that August, of which "about 10,000 would have started out large beads of cold, apprehensive sweat upon the stone walls of any penitentiary in the world."[22]

Before reaching the Black Hills, Richardson had met Steve Utter, who gave him a letter of introduction to his brother, C. H. ("Colorado Charley") Utter, who had arrived in Deadwood a few weeks earlier.[23] When located, Colorado Charley at once invited the reporter to share his camp and introduced him to Wild Bill Hickok, his partner.[24] "Of course I had heard of him, the greatest scout in the West," Richardson wrote, "but I was not prepared to find such a man as he proved to be." In the writer's opinion, most famous frontiersmen were "frauds." Consequently, Hickok came as a surprise. "In 'Wild Bill,' I found a man who talked little and had done a great deal," said Richardson.[25]

Hickok's appearance, as well as his demeanor, impressed the young reporter. "He was about six feet two inches in height, and very powerfully built; his face was intelligent, his hair blonde, and falling in long ringlets upon his broad shoulders; his eyes, blue and pleasant, looked me straight in the face when he talked; and his lips, thin and compressed, were only partly hidden by a straw-colored mustache." Hickok's voice was "low and musical" but contained "a ring of self-reliance and con-

Richardson clearly admired James Butler ("Wild Bill") Hickok, and the engraving that accompanied his article portrayed a man notable for his "rapidity of motion, courage, and certainty of aim." Scribner's Monthly, *April 1877*

sciousness of strength." He wore "a curiously blended union of the habiliments of the borderman and the drapery of the fashionable dandy." Included in his costume were "two silver-mounted revolvers."[26] During his visit, Richardson asked Hickok to display his skill with the guns:

> At his request I tossed a tomato-can about 15 feet into the air, both his pistols being in his belt when it left my hand. He drew one of them, and fired two bullets through the tin can before it struck the ground. Then he followed it along, firing as he went, until both weapons were empty. You have heard the expression "quick as lightning?" Well, that will describe "Wild Bill." He was noted all over the country for rapidity of motion, courage, and certainty of aim. Wherever he went he controlled the people around him, and many a quarrel has been ended by his simple announcement, "This has gone far enough."[27]

Richardson also described Utter when he reminisced about his experiences in the Hickok-Utter camp eighteen years later. Colorado Charley, he said, was "a natty, handsome, courageous little man" with long blonde hair and a moustache. Regarded as "the dandy of the country," he wore "beaded moccasins, fringed leggings and coat, handsome trousers, fine linen, revolvers mounted in gold, silver, and pearl, and a belt with a big silver buckle." In addition, he had a "rather startling" habit of taking a bath each morning, a process that spectators came out to view with "interest . . . not wholly unmixed with wonder." Utter also slept "between fine California blankets, and he had a real mirror, and real combs, brushes, razors and wisp brooms." The attractive frontiersman, according to Richardson, drew the attention of Calamity Jane, "who bossed a dancehouse" and appeared to aspire to the twin goals of winning Colorado Charley's heart and "the consumption of all the red liquor in the gulch."[28]

Richardson found Wild Bill less fastidious than his partner. Hickok was willing to sleep in an army blanket in the wagon. Each morning, just before breakfast, the frontiersman would "crawl out, clad in his shirt, trousers, and boots, tie his hair in a knot at the back of his head, shove his big revolver down inside the waistband of his trousers, and run like a sprinter down the gulch to the nearest saloon." His morning cleanup occurred only after he had had a few drinks.[29]

What impressed Richardson most about the relationship between Hickok and Utter was the control Colorado Charley exercised over Wild Bill. "I never heard anybody take 'roastings' with as little concern as that with which Bill used to take the fierce tongue lashings of his dudesque little partner," he noted. "I suppose, perhaps, they fully understood each other, and knew perfectly well that behind all the words there was an impenetrable wall of manly affection." One tongue-lashing occurred after Hickok violated Utter's rule ("a shooting point with him") that no one was to enter his tent. Having stayed out all night and arrived drunk at the deserted camp in the morning, Hickok went to sleep in Utter's tent. When Richardson and Utter happened by about an hour later, a furious Colorado Charley grabbed the nearly unconscious Hickok by the feet and dragged him out. Hanging his blankets in the trees to air out, Utter continued "straining his vocabulary for fresh epithets to hurl at the offender." Hickok, meanwhile, "stared at him with lazy lethargy, and then, with a parting grunt, climbed into his wagon and went peacefully to sleep again."[30]

Hickok's only other activities during Richardson's two days with him were relaxing in camp and playing cards. According to the reporter, Utter gave Hickok money for gambling, and "if he ever won, nobody knew it." Near sundown, the trio would have supper, eating bear steak or beef, elk milk, fried potatoes, flapjacks, and coffee. Because Utter was a good cook and hospitable host, they had numerous visitors. "After

According to Richardson's account, Wild Bill Hickok did his part to augment the mountain of bottles found behind Deadwood saloons in 1876. State Archives Collection, South Dakota State Historical Society

supper the pipes were lighted and Bill would tell stories of New York, and Boston, and Philadelphia, and other cities where his companions had never been," Richardson wrote. "Whenever any of them ventured to express a doubt as to his veracity, he would turn to me and ask me if he hadn't adhered strictly to the facts. I always said that he had understated rather than embroidered the situation. I love truth, but I do not yearn to obtrude my preferences so far away from home."[31]

Occasionally the men walked around town to look things over, observing "shooting scrapes, stabbing affairs, a lynching, fisticuffs, and various kinds of shindigs of high and low degree." One afternoon, they saw two men, neither of whom was a particularly good shot, dueling with six-shooters. According to Richardson, "Bill stood near the belligerents, passing derisive remarks on their lack of ability to hit anything and apparently as unconcernedly amused as if the fighters had been merely throwing soft boiled potatoes at each other." They also observed a saloon fight; when shots were fired, the crowd exited so fast that the entire building front fell outwards. "Bill said he thought it was a breach of hospitality for a man's guests to carry away the bulk of his house like that," Richardson recalled. Another fight occurred while the party relaxed in a different saloon. When the proprietor "produced a sawed-off shotgun" and ordered everyone out, Hickok told Richardson not to move. "'Young man, never run away from a gun,' he said. 'Bullets can travel faster than you can. Besides, if you're going to be hit, you had better get it in front than in the back. It looks better.'" Afterwards, Richardson asked Hickok how he kept his nerve, and Wild Bill responded, "'When a man really believes the bullet isn't moulded that is going to kill him, what in hell has he got to be afraid of?'"[32]

Richardson, who loved the theater, managed to make a couple of visits with his new companions to the Deadwood productions of Jack Langrishe. The actor and his company of eight played numerous roles. Langrishe, according to Richardson, "went considerably beyond the others, in that he added to his labors as an actor the combined task of selling tickets at the box office, painting much of the scenery, stage managing and productions, and getting out the advertisements." The primitive theater "was constructed mainly of unplaned boards" and had a canvas roof. Wooden benches served as seats. The stage rose about six feet above the dirt floor and had a drop curtain "with a picture labelled Lake Como, probably to obviate the quite simple misapprehension that it might represent a large green tomato," described the young critic.

One young man with a "cottage melodeon" served as the orchestra. "In the pathetic scenes in which he was not engaged on the stage this young man would pullout the tremolo stop in his melodeon and contribute untold agony to the situation." Richardson found Langrishe's Deadwood theater inadequate, to say the least.[33]

One Deadwood theatrical performance, *The Streets of New York*, was made especially famous by Richardson, who attended with Hickok, Moses ("California Joe") Milner, and a Mr. Myers.[34] The audience, though primarily male, included a few "mining camp damsels," the most noteworthy being Kitty Arnold, whom Richardson identified as "Kitty Austin." She paraded down the center aisle of Langrishe's theater "clothed in splendor and smoking a brunette cigar with a band around it which bespoke the fact that it had cost 75 cents." Her dress was yellow silk with green trim, a long train, and a low-cut neck "revealing a plentitude of charms that would evoke comment almost anywhere outside of the Metropolitan opera house in New York." When the "dancehouse" proprietress took a seat next to Myers and gave him a cigar, the "ever gallant" Myers returned the favor, giving her a chew of his tobacco.

While in Richardson's opinion the actual play was "horribly performed," the crowd loved it. Langrishe's wife, a woman in her fifties and "imposing in point of adipose tissue," played the leading lady. To Richardson's amusement, she had to lift her overly long skirt each time she moved, an action that always seemed to occur at particularly dramatic moments. Near the end of the play, the two female characters decide to commit suicide but are saved when the hero bursts into their apartment. As the curtain fell, there was a brief moment of silence. Then, wrote Richardson:

> there is the sound of expectoration and a voice is heard that penetrates to every part of the building—the voice of Kitty Austin, the belle of Deadwood City. It says, in the accents of one whose finer sensibilities have been trifled with:
> "Oh, h—l! That was a put-up job."
> For a part of an instant the big, bare auditorium with its canvas roof is as still as death. Then there is an outburst of yells, cheers and wild laughter, such as one does not often hear. In the course of this hilarious turmoil, which dies away and then rises again and again, Miss Austin hastily withdraws from the theater, and at least a third

of the audience goes with her, putting in a considerable portion of the night carousing in her establishment.[35]

In 1881, Richardson told a different version of this story, identifying the tobacco spitter as Calamity Jane rather than Kitty Arnold. Apparently, he found it acceptable to modify his own stories of early Deadwood, even while challenging erroneous accounts by other writers.[36]

According to Richardson, "Miss Austin was the prettiest, and possibly at that period the most elegant girl in camp." Her rival in the "young and boiling metropolis" was Calamity Jane, who also "kept a dance house." In contrast to Kitty Arnold, who was "admitted to hold the palm in the matter of looks and wardrobe," Richardson observed that Calamity Jane had arrived in Deadwood without any clothes except the man's suit she was wearing. She, however, could "outride, outdrink, and outshoot Miss Austin," he reported. "These claims of superiority she was wont to demonstrate, once in a while, by first consuming a sufficient quantity of the liquor sold in her own establishment to awaken her ambition, and then mounting a horse man fashion and riding up and down the street howling like an Indian. As a fitting wind-up for these harmless little bursts of innocent enthusiasm . . . Jane would usually shoot in all the windows of Miss Austin's vaunted temple of Terpsichore."[37] Except for her carousing and chasing after Colorado Charley, Calamity Jane is unmentioned in Richardson's articles.

Richardson also reported on a hanging that happened, he said, the morning after Kitty Arnold displayed her spitting skills at the theater. News arrived that a murderer had been captured at Fort Laramie by a man named Cuny, who brought his captive to Deadwood to claim the reward. Richardson described the prisoner as "a long, lean, angular Missourian, with a yellow skin, a black moustache, and thin, straggling chin whiskers reaching nearly half way to his waist." The man also sported a "little glass eye" that never moved in tandem with the real one. His crime, said Richardson, was the stabbing death of his companion for the gold dust he was carrying. The assembled crowd had to be convinced that there should be a trial before the hanging, and Richardson found it "strange that the man on trial that morning did not receive more sympathy among those fellows—he was so much like the majority of them." Upon conviction, the prisoner was sentenced to be hanged within the hour. Richardson described the execution in vivid detail: "The noose was adjusted, the horse was led out from under the mur-

COPYRIGHT 1895, BY H.R.LOCKE

Martha ("Calamity Jane") Canary was also a part of the Deadwood scene in 1876. State Archives Collection, South Dakota State Historical Society

derer's form, and at the same moment the men holding the opposite end of the rope ran up the hill with it for a few paces. The body of the tall Missourian, writhing horribly in agony, flew upward. A dozen shots from pistols and rifles rang sharply out. . . . The body, twisting with the strain upon the rope, swayed to and fro in the freshening breeze." Afterwards, the crowd, "sobered and reflective, turned slowly away and dispersed," said Richardson, and the "first tragedy of Deadwood Gulch was avenged."[38]

Unfortunately for Richardson's credibility, this hanging never occurred. The incident he described began with the murder of John Hinch on 9 July. Although reports about the killing differ, two men, Jerry McCarty (or McCarthy) and J. R. Carty, were involved. McCarty evidently stabbed Hinch while Hinch was struggling with Carty during a saloon quarrel. Afterwards, the two men fled, McCarty going to Cheyenne and Carty joining a logging outfit operated by E. Coffey & Cuny that was leaving Fort Laramie. When he learned of the murder, Deputy United States Marshal J. C. Davis pursued and captured Carty and with "Mr. Cuny accompanying him" brought his prisoner to the Black Hills on 31 July, the day after Richardson's arrival in Deadwood. On 1 August, a meeting of Deadwood miners was held to try Carty for murder. Described in the *Black Hills Pioneer* as a large man with one eye, Carty testified that Hinch had started the saloon fight, that he had hit Hinch over the head with his revolver, and that McCarty had stabbed Hinch. The jury found Carty guilty only of assault and battery. "Thus ended the first murder trial in Lawrence County," reported the newspaper, which called it "fair and honest." Carty was not executed.[39]

Richardson was more accurate when he described Wild Bill Hickok's murder at the hands of Jack McCall. The *Black Hills Pioneer* reported that when word of the killing circulated about 3:00 P.M. on Wednesday, 2 August, the *Pioneer* editor hurried to the building of Nuttall and Mann, where he "found the remains of Wild Bill lying on the floor." The assassin, Jack McCall, "was captured after a lively chase by many of our citizens, and taken to a building at the lower end of the city." Upon investigation, the newspaper continued, it was learned that Hickok had been playing cards when McCall entered the saloon. Walking to within three feet of Hickok, he "raised his revolver, and exclaiming 'Damn you, take that,'" he fired. Death was instantaneous. A meeting of citizens was held at the theater to plan McCall's trial. A jury was selected the next day, and at two o'clock that afternoon the trial commenced, with

Judge W. L. Kuykendall presiding. Court lasted until six o'clock, with the defense asserting that "at some place in Kansas" Hickok had "killed the prisoner's brother," causing him to seek revenge. The jury found McCall not guilty. Meanwhile, Wild Bill was "being laid in the cold, cold ground" in the valley of Whitewood Creek "by kind hands that were ever ready to administer to his sufferings while living, and ready to perform the painful duty of laying him in his last resting place."[40]

Richardson was not with Hickok at the time of his murder and, like the Deadwood editor, hurried to the scene as soon as word of the killing reached camp. Wild Bill, he wrote, "had been sitting at a table playing cards, when a dastardly assassin came up behind, put a revolver to his head and fired, killing his victim instantly." While his description of the murder is similar to that of the newspaper, Richardson reported the time of McCall's trial incorrectly, claiming that the assassin was brought before a miners' court the evening of the murder. In Richardson's version, once McCall made a statement, he "was discharged, put on a fleet horse, supplied with arms, and guarded out of town."[41] The reporter probably gained this information through hearsay, for he evidently remained with Hickok's friends that night and the next day attended the funeral rather than the trial. To his secondhand description of the trial, Richardson appended an explanation of McCall's intent in a September 1876 dispatch published in Denver: "There were a dozen or so men in Deadwood who wanted to kill Wild Bill because he would not 'stand-in' with them on any 'dead-beat' games, but not one man among them all dared to pick a quarrel with him. They were all waiting to get a chance to shoot him in the back." It was this "clique" that put McCall up to the killing, according to Richardson, and ensured that he was not convicted afterwards.[42] Later, when Richardson learned that McCall again had been arrested, tried for murder, and sentenced to death in Yankton, Dakota Territory, he amplified his comments: "At the trial it was proved that the murderer was hired to do his work by gamblers who feared the time when better citizens should appoint Bill the champion of law and order, — a post which he formerly sustained in Kansas border life, with credit to his manhood and his courage."[43] This premise was not proven at the trial, however, and most likely reflects the feelings of Hickok's friends. McCall's actual motives probably involved alcohol and a petty gambling quarrel the night before the murder.[44]

Unlike his observations on McCall's trial, Richardson's description of Hickok's burial seems to be firsthand. Colorado Charley "took charge of the remains of the great scout," he said, "and announced that the funeral would occur at his camp." Richardson described the final rites:

> The body was clothed in a full suit of broad-cloth, the hair brushed back from the broad forehead, and the blood washed from the pallid cheek. Beside the dead hero lay his rifle, which was buried with him. The funeral ceremony was brief and touching, hundreds of rough miners standing around the bier with bowed heads and tear-dimmed eyes,—for with the better class "Wild Bill" had been a great favorite. At the close of the ceremony the coffin was lowered into a new-made grave on the hillside,—the first in Deadwood. And so ended the life of "Wild Bill,"—a man whose supreme physical courage had endeared him to nearly all with whom he came in contact, and made his name a terror to every Indian west of the Missouri.[45]

Newspaperman Richard B. Hughes disagreed with Richardson about Hickok's reputation and later wrote that "mourning over his fate . . . was confined chiefly to those of his own kind." Similarly, Joseph ("White-Eye") Anderson, one of Hickok's companions, remarked that many dance-hall girls, including Calamity Jane, were present at the funeral.[46] Oddly, Richardson did not comment on Hickok's recent marriage to Agnes Lake, who should have been notified of his death. He also omitted mention of the disturbance that occurred during the preparation of Hickok's body when a man identified as a Mexican rode into town carrying the head of an American Indian to claim the reward offered for the grisly "trophy."[47]

Although Richardson left the Black Hills shortly after the funeral, he remained in the West for some time. One of his letters, published in the *Denver News* on 1 November 1876, described another meeting with Charley Utter, who at that time was "running a freight line to Deadwood." Utter reportedly gave his former guest a lock of Hickok's hair "more than a foot long, . . . fine and glossy as a woman's locks." Concerning Deadwood, Utter informed Richardson that everything became "very quiet" when winter made its appearance with a snowstorm on 3 October. "The theatre and dance houses have been closed, and business of all kinds is in a rather precarious condition," the town's residents having left for Custer and other points.[48]

With the closure of Deadwood's 1876 mining season, Richardson's personal descriptions of the Black Hills ended. He had experienced much during his five-day visit to Deadwood, but his observations were

Charles H. ("Colorado Charlie") Utter sits by the grave of Wild Bill Hickok.
State Archives Collection, South Dakota State Historical Society

limited to particular aspects of its society and focused on saloons, dance halls, the theater, and notorious characters. Missing, for example, were discussions of mining companies, commerce, Deadwood's leading businessmen, and the development of government institutions. Concerning the town's future, Richardson decided it was bleak. Placer mining, he observed, produced just enough for "grub." Only in rare instances were miners earning a real living wage. "Seven out of every ten men in the whole region have no money and no means of getting any," he concluded, because the ground in Deadwood "is all taken up, and men do not dare to go out prospecting away from the main body, on account of the Indians."[49]

The only remaining opportunity was to extract gold from quartz ore, a process requiring machinery and heavy investment. Richardson saw little future for this enterprise, believing that "men of wealth will hesitate about sending capital into a country so far from railroad communication, and about which so little is definitely known." Further, the region had few other resources that could be easily tapped. "Farming there is out of the question," he observed, because of a short growing season. "Snow-storms did not cease last spring until the eleventh day of June," he noted, and "heavy frosts begin in September." Therefore, the region would always have to import the "necessaries of life . . . at immense cost." As a result, Richardson predicted, "the Black Hills will eventually prove a failure. The trip there would be a severe trial for most men, even if the danger of being murdered were removed. At present the journey is exceedingly dangerous, and if by good fortune the gold-hunter succeeds in surviving its hardships and getting through alive, his chances for success are few and his expenses necessarily will be large."[50] It is hardly surprising that some Black Hills boosters angrily claimed Richardson had never reached Deadwood.[51]

Despite his negative views concerning gold prospects, Richardson's articles popularized the region. To his serious publications describing the Black Hills, he added at least three dime novels. The first, *I'm No Slouch: A Romance of Pike's Peak; A Story of Wild Bill* (1881), featured Colorado Charley Utter and Wild Bill Hickok. Although Richardson claimed in the foreword that many of the incidents were based on fact, historian Agnes Wright Spring observed, "It is difficult to find a word of truth or fact in the entire yarn." The plot was evidently based on the 1879 Meeker Massacre in Colorado, which occurred three years after Hickok's death.[52] Richardson's descriptions of Hickok and Utter, however, were probably based on personal observations.

In 1889, *The Road Agents: A Tale of Black Hills Life* appeared, and while the plot and characters were invented, Richardson clearly based his physical descriptions of the region on his trip to Deadwood. In his story, a party travels toward the Black Hills in the spring of 1876, stopping en route at Fort Laramie, Rawhide Buttes, and Hat Creek (where soldiers are stationed) and struggling through mud, just as Richardson's party had. In standard dime-novel form, the heroes, Oregon Bill and Silas Clark, have as their companion a tame mountain lion, Deathgrip. They battle villainous road agents headed by Jack Watkins and his partner, Cherokee Bob, who terrorize travelers. Both Oregon Bill and Jack Watkins fall in love with Rose Bailey, a married woman also traveling to the Hills. Recruiting some Indians, the road agents attack her party, killing her husband. Eventually, the heroes defeat the villains, and Oregon Bill marries the widowed woman. Filled with romance, adventure, racist characterizations, humor, and unlikely events, *The Road Agents* typified dime-novel literature.[53]

Captain Kate: The Heroine of Deadwood Gulch (1896) features a woman who wears buckskins and is a good shot but is not patterned on Calamity Jane or Kitty Arnold. Richardson took great pains to describe why Kate chose her unique apparel. Having made a harrowing trip to get help after her party was stranded in a blizzard, she deemed a buckskin outfit best suited for frontier conditions. Kate was strictly feminine in all other respects. The other heroic figure is California Joe, who spins fantastic yarns; whether this characterization is realistic is uncertain. The novel's villain, Tom Hemingway, kills the captain of a wagon train, steals their livestock, and leaves the party stranded in a blizzard. Kate, sister-in-law of the dead captain, is elected leader and leaves with California Joe to secure aid. After he kills a deer, Kate sends him back with the desperately needed meat. Alone, she falls and breaks her leg but manages to shoot a mountain lion as it leaps toward her from a tree. Soldiers from Standing Rock Agency led by a Colonel Archer hear the shot, rescue Kate, and hurry to save the starving party. Meanwhile, California Joe discovers gold, and Deadwood is born. Before the happily-ever-after ending, Colonel Archer is almost lynched and villain Tom Hemingway is killed. Archer and Kate, of course, marry, and California Joe, worth more than a half-million dollars from his gold claims, lives nearby, telling tall tales to willing listeners.[54]

Richardson's numerous articles and stories about the Black Hills accounted for only a small portion of his literary career. A few years after he returned from his western travels, Richardson journeyed to England and wrote about his experiences there.[55] His complaints in *The Dark City; or, Customs of the Cockneys* (1886) mirror those about the Black Hills. From "the smoky city of Liverpool," he traveled to the "equally

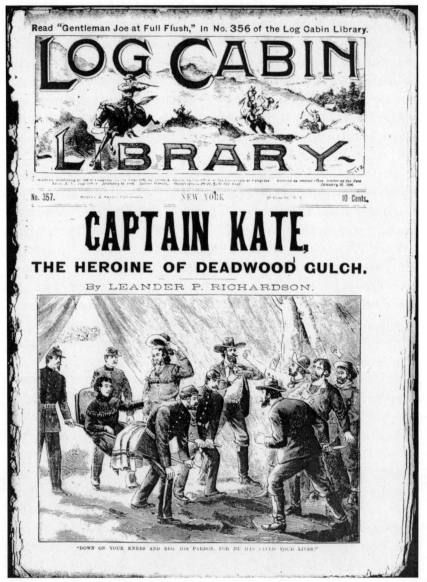

Captain Kate *was Richardson's third dime novel set in the*
Black Hills. James D. McLaird, Mitchell, S.Dak.

smoky city of London." The streets were muddy even in dry weather because sprinkling wagons were used to keep down the dust. This mud, he found, "was of the consistency of glue, and twice as nasty."[56] As a drama critic, Richardson also visited London's theatrical performances and found them no more to his liking than Langrishe's Black Hills dramas. He warned his readers to "fill your pockets with insect powder before you visit Her Majesty's Theatre," but not to expect it to stop the vermin. "They like it. I think it makes them fat," he concluded.[57] Richardson's description of the English people also recalled his assessment of Deadwood's 1876 population: "We think in this country that we have a good many roughs in our population, but when we have been introduced to the British workman, on his native heath, we are apt to believe our ruffian is the most polite, genteel, and refined personage on the face of the earth."[58]

Just as his Black Hills experiences became the basis for dime novels, Richardson fictionalized his experiences with the English in a novel, *Lord Dunmersy* (1889), which satirizes American deference to English nobility and shows his love of irony.[59] Rather than travel commentaries and fiction, however, it was journalism and the theater that dominated Richardson's literary passions. He became a foremost drama critic, translated and adapted French plays for the American stage, and wrote and produced several plays of his own. His dramatic works include *The Millionaire* (1891) and *Under the City Lamps* (1893). From 1889 to 1896, he served as editor of the *New York Dramatic News*. He also remained active as a newspaperman, reporting for the *New York Times*, serving on the staff of the *New York Morning Telegraph* between 1896 and 1900, and then becoming editor of the *New York Inquirer*. In later years, he became manager and publicity director for the Playhouse in New York and worked with the World Film Corporation.[60]

Upon Richardson's death from pneumonia at age sixty-one on 2 February 1918, the *New York Times* reviewed his significant career. In its description of his extensive work as reporter, drama critic, and editor, the newspaper failed to mention the trip to the Black Hills that helped launch his career and provided him with material for the remainder of his life.[61] Richardson's eloquent descriptions of Deadwood's colorful characters and turbulent society help to document that important dimension of early Black Hills life. Though based on a brief visit and filled with personal opinion, hearsay, and exaggeration, these observations by the youthful reporter deserve a significant place among accounts of Deadwood during the gold rush of 1876.

NOTES

1. Richardson, "Last Days of a Plainsman," *True West* 13 (Nov.–Dec. 1965): 22. "Last Days of a Plainsman" is actually a reprint of Richardson's lengthy letter to the *New York Sun*, taken from the 15 February 1894 issue of the *Weekly Press*, a New Zealand newspaper. The issue of the *New York Sun* in which Richardson's letter originally appeared has not been located. *See also* Agnes Wright Spring, *Colorado Charley, Wild Bill's Pard* (Boulder, Colo.: Pruett Press, 1968), pp. 98–101, which includes a portion of Richardson's letter as it appeared in several installments of the *Georgetown* (Colo.) *Courier* in 1937.

2. Lloyd McFarling, who edited one of Richardson's articles, found no information about him other than details "incidentally revealed by the article" (McFarling, "A Trip to the Black Hills in 1876," *Annals of Wyoming* 27 [Apr. 1955]: 35). Another researcher discovered only that Richardson was "from someplace 'back East'" (Earl Scott, "The Killing of Wild Bill Hickok," *Denver Westerners' Monthly Roundup* 21 [May 1965]: 6–16).

3. Richardson, "A Trip to the Black Hills," *Scribner's Monthly* 13 (Apr. 1877): 748–56.

4. William Coyle, *Ohio Authors and Their Books* (Cleveland, Ohio: World Publishing Co., 1962), p. 528; *New York Times*, 3 Dec. 1869, 5 Apr.–11 May 1870; Don C. Sietz, *Horace Greeley, Founder of the* New York Tribune (Indianapolis, Ind.: Babbs-Merrill Co., 1926), pp. 27, 99, 109, 310–15.

5. Richardson, "Trip to the Black Hills," p. 748.

6. Ibid.

7. Ibid., pp. 748–49.

8. Located fourteen miles from Fort Laramie, Government Farm at one time accommodated soldiers who experimented in raising grain and vegetables for the military post. By 1876, it was a private station and the original log structures were gone. Agnes Wright Spring, *The Cheyenne and Black Hills Stage and Express Routes* (Glendale, Calif.: Arthur H. Clark Co., 1949), p. 118.

9. Richardson, "Trip to the Black Hills," pp. 749–50.

10. Ibid., p. 750.

11. Ibid. Hat Creek station, actually on Sage Creek, was established in 1876 by John ("Jack") Bowman at a site located earlier by the military. More than forty soldiers were normally garrisoned there, but only six remained when Richardson arrived, the others having joined a scouting expedition under General Wesley Merritt that would follow General George Crook into northern Wyoming in pursuit of

the Sioux. Spring, *Cheyenne and Black Hills Stage*, pp. 122–23; Don Russell, *The Lives and Legends of Buffalo Bill* (Norman: University of Oklahoma Press, 1960), pp. 220–39.

12. Richardson, "Trip to the Black Hills," p. 752.

13. Ibid.

14. Ibid., pp. 752–53.

15. *New York Times*, 27 July 1876, p. 1. According to the *Cheyenne Daily Leader* for 17 August 1876, C. H. Cameron, Richardson's driver, returned to Cheyenne on 8 August, reporting that Marsh, Richardson, and Wild Bill Hickok were drinking together when he left them in Deadwood. William B. Secrest, ed., *I Buried Hickok: The Memoirs of White Eye Anderson* (College Station, Tex.: Creative Publishing Co., 1980), p. 114n31.

16. Spring, *Colorado Charley*, pp. 108–9.

17. Richardson, "Trip to the Black Hills," p. 753.

18. Ibid., p. 754. Cheyenne River Ranch was built early in 1876 by J. W. Dear. Camp Collier and Red Canyon Station were located near the canyon entrance. Although Red Canyon offered the most practicable route into the Black Hills, its steep walls and narrow gorge caused travelers to fear hidden attackers. In April, a small party comprised of a baker from Custer named Charles Metz, his wife, and their cook, had been killed at their camp near the canyon mouth. Spring, *Cheyenne and Black Hills Stage*, pp. 124–25, 135–37.

19. Richardson, "Trip to the Black Hills," p. 754.

20. Ibid.

21. Ibid., pp. 754–55.

22. Richardson, "Last Days of a Plainsman," p. 23.

23. Ibid. Steve Utter entered the Black Hills with Colorado Charley Utter and Wild Bill Hickok in June 1876. Secrest, *I Buried Hickok*, pp. 92–115. Confirming that Steve Utter had left the Black Hills is a brief notice in the 9 September 1876 *Black Hills Pioneer* that Colorado Charley had left Deadwood for Georgetown, Colorado, upon receiving word that his brother "had got into a scrape there and was badly wounded."

24. Colorado Charley and Wild Bill Hickok organized a wagon train into the Black Hills from Cheyenne in early 1876. No record tells the date of their departure, but John Hunton mentions them stopping at his road ranch on 30 June 1876. L. G. ("Pat") Flannery, ed., *John Hunton's Diary, 1876–77* (Lingle, Wyo.: By the Editor, 1958), pp. 115–16. *See also* Secrest, *I Buried Hickok*, pp. 92–115.

25. Richardson, "Trip to the Black Hills," p. 755. The authoritative works on Hickok are Joseph G. Rosa, *They Called Him Wild Bill: The Life and Adventures of James Butler Hickok*, 2d ed. (Norman: University of Oklahoma Press, 1974),

and Rosa, *Wild Bill Hickok: The Man and His Myth* (Lawrence: University Press of Kansas, 1996).

26. Richardson, "Trip to the Black Hills," p. 755. Rosa comments, "It is a matter of conjecture how much of the truth is to be found in Richardson's accounts." While certain that Richardson was there, Rosa concludes, "his remarks leave much to be desired," especially because "he only knew Hickok for two days, whereas his reports suggest it was a relationship of several weeks" (*They Called Him Wild Bill*, p. 295).

27. Richardson, "Trip to the Black Hills," p. 755.

28. Richardson, "Last Days of a Plainsman," p. 22. The best account of Charley Utter is found in Spring, *Colorado Charley*. Oddly, Richardson does not mention the "pony express of Seymour & Utter" that carried mail to Laramie and Cheyenne, as noted in Deadwood's *Black Hills Pioneer* for 22 July 1876. The 14 October 1876 edition of the same newspaper announced the opening of a Deadwood bathhouse more than two months after Richardson's visit, but others may have preceded it.

29. Richardson, "Last Days of a Plainsman," p. 22.

30. Ibid., p. 23.

31. Ibid. pp. 22–23.

32. Ibid., p. 23.

33. Richardson's description, entitled "Tragedies in '76: They Were Performed on the Stage in Deadwood," was reprinted in the *Saint Paul Pioneer Press* for 12 March 1894. It originally appeared in an unidentified issue of the *New York Sun*. The Langrishe theater is discussed in numerous publications about the Black Hills. *See*, for example, John S. McClintock, *Pioneer Days in the Black Hills: Accurate History and Facts Related by One of the Early Day Pioneers*, ed. Edward L. Senn (Deadwood, S.Dak.: By the Author, 1939), pp. 73–74, and George W. Stokes, *Deadwood Gold: A Story of the Black Hills* (Yonkers-on-Hudson, N.Y.: World Book Co., 1926), pp. 89–91. In contrast to Richardson, the *Black Hills Pioneer* editor waxed enthusiastic about the theater. "The inhabitants of Deadwood City and vicinity have now a place of entertainment they can visit, and enjoy as pleasant an evening as can be spent in any Eastern city," he wrote on 29 July 1876.

34. *Saint Paul Pioneer Press*, 12 Mar. 1894. California Joe was a friend of Hickok's and is described fully in Joseph E. Milner and Earle R. Forrest, *California Joe* (Caldwell, Idaho: Caxton Printers, 1935). "Mr. Myers" may refer to C. W. Meyer, the reporter for the *Cheyenne Daily Sun* whose arrival in Deadwood was announced in the *Black Hills Pioneer* on 29 July 1876.

35. *Saint Paul Pioneer Press*, 12 Mar. 1894.

36. The tobacco spitter is identified as Calamity Jane in the *Black Hills Daily Times* for 24 February 1881. In 1920, actor Charles Chapin, who performed in

Deadwood in 1881, claimed that the incident occurred while he was there and identified Calamity Jane as the culprit. Chapin most likely incorporated the story, which appeared in the newspaper while he was there, into his own account. *See* Charles E. Chapin, *Charles E. Chapin's Story, Written in Sing Sing Prison* (New York: G. P. Putnam's Sons, 1920), pp. 30–32.

37. *Saint Paul Pioneer Press*, 12 Mar. 1894. Kitty Arnold arrived in Deadwood with the Hickok-Utter party, as did Calamity Jane, according to McClintock, *Pioneer Days in the Black Hills*, pp. 105, 117. Arnold visited Deadwood again in 1892 as a married woman, and the newspaper reminisced about her 1876 appearance, when she "wore the regular buckskin suit, trowsers and all" and took her turn as a guard as her party trekked to the Hills. Like Calamity Jane, she was "generally found in dance halls," yet "commanded universal respect" because of her acts of charity. *Black Hills Daily Times*, 7 May 1892. Arnold may be "Kitty the Schemer," discussed by H. N. Maguire, who said in 1876 that she and Calamity Jane were two of Deadwood's notable "soiled doves." According to Maguire, "Kitty the Schemer" had made several fortunes, having owned "two splendid establishments" in Hong Kong and Yokohama. She reportedly spoke fluent Japanese and tolerable Chinese and, in her resorts, entertained such notable figures as Prince Albert and Grand Duke Alexis. Maguire speculated that she was next planning to try South Africa, as the "Black Hills were getting too civilized for her." Maguire, *The Coming Empire: A Complete and Reliable Treatise on the Black Hills, Yellowstone and Big Horn Regions* (Sioux City, Iowa: Watkins & Smead, 1878), pp. 63–64.

38. *Saint Paul Pioneer Press*, 12 Mar. 1894.

39. *Black Hills Pioneer*, 5 Aug. 1876. *See also* McClintock, *Pioneer Days*, pp. 96–97, and Jesse Brown and A. M. Willard, *The Black Hills Trails: A History of the Struggles of the Pioneers in the Winning of the Black Hills*, ed. John T. Milek (Rapid City, S.Dak.: *Rapid City Journal* Co., 1924), pp. 344–47.

40. *Black Hills Pioneer*, 5 Aug. 1876. The best account of McCall is Joseph G. Rosa, *Jack McCall, Assassin: An Updated Account of His Yankton Trial, Plea for Clemency, and Execution* (n.p.: English Westerners' Society, 1999).

41. Richardson, "Trip to the Black Hills," p. 755.

42. *Saint Paul Press and Tribune*, 8 Sept. 1876, quoted in Rosa, *Wild Bill Hickok*, p. 197. Rosa observes that Richardson "later wrote several contradictory accounts of the event" (p. 196).

43. Richardson, "Trip to the Black Hills," p. 755.

44. The newspaper reported that McCall was arrested in Laramie and taken to Cheyenne for a hearing, where a witness would testify that "when McCall stopped at Horse Creek, on his way to this city, he stated that Wild Bill never killed a brother of his, but that he killed Wild Bill merely because Bill snatched a card from

his hand during the progress of a game between them" (*Black Hills Pioneer*, 9 Sept. 1876). *See* Rosa, *Jack McCall, Assassin*, pp. 8–11, for trial testimony.

45. Richardson, "Trip to the Black Hills," pp. 755–56.

46. Hughes, *Pioneer Years in the Black Hills*, ed. Agnes Wright Spring (Glendale, Calif.: Arthur H. Clark Co., 1957), pp. 162–63. For a description of the funeral, *see* Secrest, *I Buried Hickok*, p. 121.

47. All the events Richardson described did indeed occur on 2 August 1876. "An exciting day in Dead Wood," recorded Jerry Bryan in his diary, listing the arrival of the murderer (who soon was released), Hickok's death, and the arrival of a man carrying an Indian's head. Clyde C. Walton, ed., *An Illinois Gold Hunter in the Black Hills: The Diary of Jerry Bryan, March 13 to August 20, 1876* (Springfield: Illinois State Historical Society, 1960), p. 35. *See also* Secrest, *I Buried Hickok*, p. 120.

48. Richardson to Editor, *Denver News*, 1 Nov. 1876, quoted in Spring, *Colorado Charley*, p. 107. According to Rosa, Richardson gave the lock of Hickok's hair to Wild Bill's widow, Agnes Lake Hickok. Rosa, *They Called Him Wild Bill*, p. 301.

49. Richardson, "Trip to the Black Hills," p. 756.

50. Ibid. Lloyd McFarling defended Richardson, asserting that in August 1876 "there was considerable justification for pessimism in Deadwood Gulch" because only one rich placer deposit had been located. McFarling, "Trip to the Black Hills in 1876," p. 41.

51. *See*, for example, *Black Hills Daily Times*, 29 Apr. 1878.

52. Spring, *Colorado Charley*, pp. 121–22.

53. Richardson, *The Road Agents: A Tale of Black Hills Life* (New York: Street & Smith, 1889). The copy I consulted is from the "Log Cabin Library," Vol. 1, No. 33. There actually was a purported road agent named Jack Watkins in the Black Hills, suggesting that Richardson continued reading newspaper accounts from the region after his departure. Spring, *Cheyenne and Black Hills Stage*, p. 252.

54. Richardson, *Captain Kate, The Heroine of Deadwood Gulch* (New York: Street & Smith, 1896). The copy I examined is from the "Log Cabin Library," No. 357.

55. Some of Richardson's publications were pedestrian when compared to his works on the Black Hills. In 1878, for example, his article "The New York Post-Office," appeared in *Appletons' Journal* 5 (Sept. 1878): pp. 193–203. Little is known of his other travels in the West, but in various publications he mentions having spent time in Colorado, Montana, and Arkansas.

56. Richardson, *The Dark City; or, Customs of the Cockneys* (Boston, Mass.: Doyle & Whittle, 1886), pp. 1–35. His trip probably occurred in 1882.

57. Ibid., pp. 62–63.

58. Ibid., p. 164.

59. Richardson, *Lord Dunmersey: His Recollections and Moral Reflections, By Himself* (New York: John Delay, 1889).

60. *Who Was Who in the Theatre, 1912–1976* (Detroit: Gale Research, Inc., 1976), 4:2024; *New York Times*, 3 Feb. 1918.

61. *New York Times*, 3 Feb. 1918.

3

Lucretia Marchbanks

A BLACK WOMAN IN THE
BLACK HILLS

Todd Guenther

Early in the summer of 1876, a determined former Tennessee slave woman in her mid-forties took her place in
the predominantly young, white, and male throng that
crowded the streets of the booming new town of Deadwood in the Black Hills of Dakota. In addition to her
race, gender, and age, Lucretia Marchbanks differed further from many of her contemporaries in that she was a
veteran of other mining booms. As a teenager, she had
been taken in bondage across the continent to California during the greatest of all American gold rushes. She
and several siblings spent the decade after the Civil War
in Colorado mining camps. Moving on to Deadwood, she
parlayed her worldly experiences into success and fame.
Independent and unmarried, she supported herself as a
cook, boardinghouse manager, and, later, hotel owner.
Ten years after her arrival in the Black Hills, she "retired"
to a homestead across the border in Wyoming, on the
western edge of the Hills, and took up ranching.

From the time of her arrival until her death in 1911,
Marchbanks was one of the best-known figures in the
Hills, recognized far and wide as "Aunt Lou." When her
reputation filtered back to the East Coast, a perplexed
New York newspaper editor queried, "Who is Aunt Lou?,"

This essay
originally
appeared in
*South Dakota
History* 31
(Spring 2001):
1–25.

to which the *Black Hills Daily Times* responded, "We'll Tell You Who She Is":

> Aunt Lou is an old and highly respected colored lady who has had charge of the superintendent's establishment of the DeSmet mine as housekeeper, cook and the superintendent of all the superintendents who have ever been employed on the mine. Her accomplishments as a culinary artist are beyond all praise. She rules the ranch where she presides with autocratic power by divine right, brooking no cavil or presumptuous interference. The superintendent may be a big man in the mine or mill, but the moment he sets foot within her realm he is but a meek and ordinary mortal. Aunt Lou is believed to be the first lady of color who set foot in the Hills. Her check is good at the banks for all she may sign for, and no one stands higher in the community than the sable lady of the DeSmet.[1]

That 1881 response amounts to little more than a teaser and offers little substantive information to identify who she was, how she came to be a prominent figure in Black Hills history, and what kind of life she, as a female of a racial minority, experienced in the community she helped to shape.

Other evidence reveals that Marchbanks identified so completely with the dominant white, European-American culture that, late in life, she claimed to have been the first white woman in the Black Hills,[2] even though the color of her skin was "black as the ace of spades."[3] She was considering the "big picture" when she made her claim, and such a statement was not unique. George Bonga, who was "so black that his skin glistened," described himself as one of the first two white men in the fur country of Minnesota. Though frontier race relations were complex and African Americans were unarguably second-class citizens in comparison to whites, Marchbanks, Bonga, and their contemporaries, whether black or white, ultimately recognized only two kinds of people: Indians and "us."[4] Marchbanks and other African-American pioneers were part of, not distinct from, the European-American cultural front engaged in conquering the landscape and native inhabitants of the West. American Indians regarded the racial situation in much the same way, making little or no distinction between African Americans, whom they sometimes called "black white men," and white settlers. They saw people dressed similarly, using identical tools and weapons, living in comparable houses, and threatening their ages-old way of life.[5]

In some ways, Marchbanks's gender made her stand out as much as her race did. Although female gold-rushers were less numerous than their male counterparts, western opportunities had attracted "gentle tamers," too. Women, African Americans among them, sought their fortunes in the mountains and prairies of the western territories.[6] Life on the frontier may have seemed risky, especially for an unattached woman without a husband to protect her, but from the moment of her birth, Lou Marchbanks had nowhere to go but up.

She was born a slave near Turkey Creek, east of Algood in Putnam County, Tennessee, about seventy-five miles due east of Nashville, on 25 March 1832 or 1833. Her owners, a white family named Marchbanks, had roots in South Carolina. Her father was the product of one of the horrors of slavery: the son of a slave woman and her white master. He was thus the illegitimate half-brother of the master's legitimate white son, Martin Marchbanks, who inherited their father's property, an inventory that included his own siblings and their offspring. Prior to the Civil War, Lucretia Marchbanks's father somehow managed to buy his freedom by paying his half-brother the unimaginable figure of seven hundred dollars.[7]

Lucretia was the oldest of eleven children. Her name was of Latin origin, suggesting that she may have been christened by her owners rather than her uneducated parents. She had four sisters, Margaret, Martha Ann ("Mattie"), Charlotte, and Mirah ("Myra"), and six brothers, Walter, Chester, Charlie, Finella, Finley, and Crocket. She grew up on her uncle/master's plantation, where she was trained as a housekeeper and kitchen slave. She never attended school and never learned to read or write. When Lucretia was in her late teens, Martin Marchbanks gave her to his youngest daughter, and she became the property of her cousin. Her new owner took her to California in 1849 or the early 1850s during the gold rush there. Although she eventually returned to her childhood home in Tennessee with her owner, the young black woman had seen the possibilities inherent in the developing West. Like others of her race, she viewed it as a place of economic opportunity and potential refuge from racial restrictions.[8]

Freed during the turmoil of the Civil War, Marchbanks returned to the land of opportunity. Several of her siblings also succumbed to the westering urge that shaped the nation and settled in Colorado.[9] By

1870, the Marchbankses were among 284,000 African Americans who lived in the western states and territories, where they comprised about 12 percent of the regional population. In Wyoming and Dakota, they represented a smaller proportion of the overall population, no more than 1 or 2 percent. As a region, the West was not a utopia, and several territories limited black freedom with prohibitions against voting, jury service, and interracial marriage. School segregation was a recurrent issue. Even so, the West was a place comparatively full of possibilities, where new rules might be written for new communities. Between 1867 and 1869, several measures were enacted that enfranchised black men throughout the nation, and while these and other federal measures were sometimes protested by territorial citizens, the West still offered greater economic and political freedoms in comparison, for example, to Marchbanks's native Tennessee.[10]

Lucretia Marchbanks's relocation to the Black Hills was a direct result of publicity surrounding Custer's 1874 discovery of gold in the area. In 1876, lured by the stories of wealth, she traveled to Deadwood, a boomtown in Dakota Territory, via Cheyenne. A later, probably embroidered account relates that the party she traveled with had their horses stolen near Piedmont at the eastern edge of the Hills. The travelers recovered their stock with the help of a man identified as Wild Bill Hickok, whom Marchbanks otherwise had little use for and remembered as a rounder and broken-down gambler who ate in her restaurant, or so the story goes. Whether it happened to Marchbanks or not, the tale underscores the risks travelers took. A less-fortunate black woman named Rachel Briggs also traveled the Cheyenne-Deadwood Trail that summer, but she was not rescued from her attackers and paid with her life. Such experiences were not unique that dangerous year; many people were robbed or killed by white criminals or American Indians, including Lieutenant Colonel George Armstrong Custer and his command not too far away at the Little Bighorn River.[11]

When Marchbanks first stepped down into the dirty streets of Deadwood on 1 June 1876, she found a crowd that differed little from those she had seen in California and Colorado. "Like all previous mining frontiers," explained mining historian Rodman Paul, "the Black Hills attracted a mixture of the restless, the ambitious, the curious, and the outlaws."[12] On any given Sunday, when prospectors and miners came to town to get mail and supplies, you could find representatives from "every prominent mining district" in the West and newcomers

Bustling with fortune-seekers in 1876, Deadwood offered Marchbanks and others the chance to make money providing essential services to miners. State Archives Collection, South Dakota State Historical Society

from all over. Here the buckskin-wearing hunter "jostled the dandi-fied gambler and the pilgrim from New England." Everywhere were signs and sounds of new construction. On either side of the street, one could hear "the impassioned call of an itinerant minister of the Gos-pel" or "a loud-voiced gambler crying his game."[13] The majority of these fortune-seekers were United States citizens still reeling from an eco-nomic downturn that struck the nation in 1873. News of gold in the

Black Hills attracted thousands of men and a few women looking for ways to support their families or, as in Marchbanks's case, themselves. They were determined to better their lots in spite of all obstacles.[14] "I will lose my life or find out what there is in the Black Hills or die, you bet," one man wrote of his quest.[15]

Marchbanks was after gold, too, but had no intention of becoming a miner herself. That was man's work. While a few women tried their hands at prospecting, most worked in support or service industries, supplying the wants and needs of miners in exchange for some of their gold. Providing meals for the prospectors whose time was devoted almost exclusively to toiling through rock and mud in search of an elusive bonanza was one important source of income. Marchbanks promptly secured employment as a cook in Carl Wagner's Grand Central Hotel, a two-story frame building with offices, saloon, dining room, and kitchen on the first floor and a parlor and sleeping rooms upstairs. Cooking was a job that allowed Marchbanks to support herself and still maintain her feminine respectability. Generally speaking, women during the Victorian era were expected to remain home tending the family unless circumstances required them to enter the realm of gainful employment. Occupations such as cooking and cleaning were seen as extensions of the home and therefore acceptable for women.[16]

Maintaining feminine decorum was sometimes a challenge during the first violent summer. A little over two months after her arrival, a situation arose that would have terrified a less intrepid individual than Marchbanks. In August 1876, a Mexican man cut off the head of an Indian who had been killed by a third man and paraded the gruesome trophy around town. His riotous debauch eventually took him to the Grand Central, where he "boasted that he had killed an Indian and perhaps let it be known that he wasn't above adding another notch to his gun." As the nervous customers sipped their coffee and kept a watchful eye on the strutting killer, "Aunt Lou decided he wasn't exactly an attraction to the establishment and confronted him with a gleaming knife in hand and fire in her eye." Noting her keen blade, the man "decided he had urgent business elsewhere."[17] In an era when women were expected to be quiet, submissive, and retiring, Lucretia Marchbanks gained a reputation for being unintimidated by male bravado or death.

On the lighter side, the Grand Central hosted Deadwood's first ball, a crude affair, on 4 July 1876, to celebrate the United States centennial. The floor and walls constructed of recently milled lumber wept "great amber tears" through decorations of barrel hoops twined with pine boughs. The celebrants' heads were protected from dripping sap by yards of unbleached fabric tacked across the ceiling. Candle shavings facilitated the dancers who glided across the sticky, unplaned floor. Only nine women were present, but that was enough for two quadrille sets as the one-fiddle "orchestra" serenaded partygoers. Whether Marchbanks was counted among the nine or excluded because of race or occupation is unknown.[18]

Marchbanks, nicknamed "Mahogany" that first summer, was in charge of the Grand Central's kitchen. It quickly became evident that she was no ordinary boomtown hash slinger. Though the hotel's guest rooms were crude, the board on her table was justly famous. The cost for room and board at hotels varied from twelve to twenty dollars a week. At about eight to ten dollars, boarding houses were cheaper, but people were willing to pay higher prices at the Grand Central to enjoy the results of Marchbanks's efforts over the stove. Her sunny temperament, outstanding biscuits, and wondrous plum puddings, among other delights, set the culinary standard for the whole town.[19] A competing hotel, the Overland, advertised that their kitchen was "presided over by a clean, neat, and intelligent white man."[20] The race-based advertising campaign apparently failed, and the Overland cook's name, unlike Marchbanks's, has been forgotten. In mid-September 1876, General George Crook and his staff, just arrived from the field, obtained quarters at the Grand Central, "the only first-class hotel in Deadwood City." Crook's adjutant, John G. Bourke, commented that, though the hotel was crude, the board was "decidedly better than one had a right to look for" in such a community.[21] Not surprisingly, Marchbanks was soon offered a better position in the well-known Golden Gate Hotel. During these years, she became renowned among the camps for her wizardry in the kitchen and for her noble character. An employer's dream, she reputedly observed "the principles of right living—industry, frugality, honesty, and love of mankind."[22]

While at the Golden Gate, the illiterate ex-slave's fame took a tremendous leap. In August of 1879, the community held a fundraiser to build a Congregational church. A diamond ring was to be raffled off and given to the most popular woman in the Hills. The contest created great excitement, and prominent among the competitors was Lou Marchbanks. Miners and mine officials alike rallied to the support of their "sable benefactress." Over thirteen hundred votes were cast at fifty cents

The mansard-roofed mansion at the DeSmet mine, where Marchbanks earned a reputation as the finest cook in the Black Hills, appears at lower right in this 1886 photograph. State Archives Collection, South Dakota State Historical Society

each for three contestants, and Marchbanks won handily with a total of 652. She was declared the most popular woman in the Black Hills and took home the diamond. The affair raised seven hundred dollars after expenses and was considered a great success. In a similar contest, she won a valuable silver service including a sugar bowl, a butter dish, a cream pitcher, and a spoon holder.[23]

As her renown grew, Marchbanks continued up the ladder of success. An offer of still better wages convinced her to manage the boardinghouse of the rich Father DeSmet Mine and cook for the executive table at its headquarters mansion near Central City. She worked there for four successive superintendents at the impressive salary of forty dollars a month. Marchbanks was by now considered the finest cook in the Black Hills, a compliment not to be regarded lightly. Won-

Marchbanks's culinary talents won her both accolades and the silk dress she wore for this 1881 portrait. Adams Museum, Deadwood, S.Dak.

derfully varied and delightfully high-quality dining could be found in many mining boomtowns. Lonely miners tended to eat out often, and those with enough gold in their pockets were willing to pay large sums for elaborate tables spread with well-prepared, even imported, foods. Competition among the various eateries was stiff, but Marchbanks was in a league of her own. She once baked such a marvelous mince pie for a man that he bought her a silk dress. The best-known photograph of Marchbanks, taken 8 November 1881, shows her wearing the dress.[24]

Her time at the prestigious DeSmet was not without turmoil. In May of 1880, the superintendent of the mine resigned. After the evidently unpopular foreman was promoted to the superintendency, the purchasing agent, the mill superintendent, the assistant superintendent, the superintendent of the ditch that supplied the mill with water, the mill engineer, and "Aunt Lou, the colored housekeeper, threw up the sponge" and resigned en masse.[25] The foreman did not last long, and after his departure, Marchbanks returned to the DeSmet. The following January, she accomplished a magnificent feat, feeding one hundred people in the "DeSmet mansion." The occasion was a testimonial dinner marking the departure of another superintendent and one of the finest gatherings to line a table in the Hills.[26] Within the course of a few years, she became so completely associated with the mine in the public's mind that she was known as "Aunt Lou DeSmet," "Mother DeSmet," and "the last survivor of the DeSmet outfit."[27]

Marchbanks's personal life is harder to discover, but a few episodes are recorded. On 25 July 1881, for instance, she attended a mountain picnic with mine superintendent Harry Gregg's wife, two children, and two other women. While gathering berries, they got lost and spent nearly the entire night in the forest, as "a host of friends were barking their shins as they waltzed over the hills looking for them."[28] Later that same month, Marchbanks received a telegram informing her that one of her brothers was dying in Leadville, Colorado. She caught the next stage to Sidney, Nebraska, where she continued her hurried journey by train. She finally arrived at Leadville, high in the Colorado Rockies, "just in time to close his eyes and feel his warm breath once more upon her cheeks before he breathed his last." She remained in Colorado, perhaps visiting other relatives, for nearly a month. She was welcomed back to Deadwood on 13 September.[29]

In 1883, having worked for others for most of her fifty years, she resigned permanently from the DeSmet payroll. The *Black Hills Daily Times* reported that "Aunt Lou, relict of Father DeSmet, . . . has severed her connection with [the mine] and opened a private boarding house in Sawpit Gulch [near Central City], [and] is doing well and looks twenty years younger." She christened her establishment the Rustic Hotel. Within days, the venture was "overrun with custom," a situation a newspaper reporter predicted was likely to continue "as long as she provides such dinners as we partook of."[30] In previous years, Marchbanks had worked hard for a salary. Now, she worked even harder for herself. She would not accept money from just anyone, however, and was not above turning away unsatisfactory customers. She was consid-

Marchbanks hosted boarders at her Rustic Hotel, one of the buildings
that lined the gulches leading down into Central City's main street.
State Archives Collection, South Dakota State Historical Society

ered a good judge of human character. A boarder related that she would study an applicant for shelter at the Rustic and, if she did not like him, would say, "My dear boy, you had better board somewhere else." She could be even harsher. She once took in a penniless fourteen year old, kept him for two months, and affectionately called him her boy. When he foolishly loaned ten dollars to a man who would not repay the debt, she kicked the lad out, saying she would spank him if he did not go.[31]

Lucretia Marchbanks was not the only African-American business-person in the Black Hills, though she was certainly among the most respectable. Edmond Colwell ran a saloon in Deadwood in 1880. In Sturgis, then known as Scooptown because of the money that could be scooped from the pockets of troops stationed there, a black man named Abe Hill owned a saloon that catered to black soldiers at nearby Fort Meade. Though the Hills populace was mobile and often visited between communities, it is doubtful that Marchbanks associated with either Colwell or Hill, given their less-than-savory professions. It is also unlikely that she had much to do with the black "soiled doves" who entertained the soldiers in Abe Hill's tawdry establishment. But there were others among whom she could seek friendship, for she was only one of a sizeable African-American community. Negro Gulch, one of the many valleys draining Negro Hill in the northwestern Black Hills, was named for a half-dozen black miners who took out seventeen hundred dollars in gold (about one hundred ounces) in a single day. Another group of black miners washed out fifteen hundred dollars in half a day. In 1880, the one hundred African Americans in the Hills were among the most easily distinguished minorities among the many races and nationalities to participate in the gold rush (the Chinese were another).[32] Marchbanks did not lack for opportunity for companionship with others of her race, but there is no evidence that she was romantically involved with anyone of any race.

Mirroring the general population, most blacks in the region were male and single. Though less cohesive than the Chinese community, African Americans met in large numbers on at least one occasion. On 1 August 1879, they held a large picnic celebration and ball to honor the anniversary of freedom for blacks on the Caribbean island of Santo Domingo. They were obviously concerned with issues related to racial equality around the globe. A white reporter described them as appearing to be "industrious, enterprising, [and] frugal citizens."[33] Even though the African-American community had a recognizable presence, its members did not control great wealth nor have sufficient numbers to influence the political process. Although blacks were generally regarded as intellectually and morally inferior to whites, white politicians nevertheless occasionally tried to court their vote.[34] "In 1880," recorded historian Watson Parker, "a certain 'Colonel John Lawrence' of Silver City, 'a town composed of one deserted log cabin somewhere at the head of a small gulch in the Bald Mountain District,' was busy trying to work up black support for his favorite political candidates, although neither he nor his candidates had 'ever been known to do a disinterested act for the good of our colored citizens.'"[35]

A significant black military presence also played a role in the settlement and development of the Black Hills. Their presence does not seem to have directly affected Lucretia Marchbanks, but it did catalyze race relations in the Hills for several years. In August of 1880, units of the black Twenty-fifth United States Infantry marched into Fort Meade, on the north end of the Hills, to join the white Seventh Cavalry in monitoring the Lakota Sioux Indians on reservations after the Custer debacle. During the early 1880s, the Twenty-fifth proved to be a consistently disciplined, meritorious outfit. In August 1884, however, a series of killings, rape charges, and lynchings of whites and blacks who frequented the red-light districts of Sturgis, including Abe Hill's establishment, came to a head. A black corporal who was accused of murdering a respected local doctor was dragged from the jail and lynched. His compatriots believed him innocent and responded by shooting up the town. Military investigators blamed the community for the problems. By 1888, peaceful relations had been restored, but the soldiers' services were necessary elsewhere, and the Twenty-fifth Infantrymen were transferred to posts in Montana.[36]

Throughout the years of gold-rush excitement, racial harmony, and racial tension in the Black Hills, Lucretia Marchbanks's personal reputation continued to grow. Her nickname, "Aunt Lou," is evidence of broad acceptance on two levels. Admirers singing her praises often associated Marchbanks with their own mothers. And, indeed, she was a surrogate mother to many. She reportedly "guarded the human flotsam and looked after the health, comfort and welfare of the miners as if she were their natural mother." One miner stated that, next to his own mother, Marchbanks was the finest woman he ever knew. An early woman resident claimed that "Aunt Lou" was like a mother to all the women in the Hills. She delivered their babies and nursed young and old when they were sick or hurt. Her services to the victims of mountain fever were especially appreciated. She assumed roles typically played by family members back home. This familial warmth and responsibility contributed to her nickname.[37] The sobriquet, however, was commonly applied to black women all over the West who "knew their place" in society. Being called "aunt" was a sign of white acceptance, a flag signifying that this black woman was not "uppity." African Americans who openly questioned race-based social stratification or related issues were often regarded as dangerous.[38] Marchbanks's social prominence, her positions of responsibility in hotels and boardinghouses, and her subsequent status as an independent businesswoman could have caused some consternation, but the force of her remarkable personality seems to have overcome many stigmas. Even so, some people could not accept that a woman of her caliber and success could be black. On one occasion, when asked if she had any white blood in her veins, she responded, "No child, . . . all I evah seen was red."[39]

With reddish hair and dressed conventionally in bustle, ruffles, stays, and a long chain around her neck, Marchbanks was an attractive woman. In a community with many men and few eligible females, she was much sought after in spite of the stumbling block of race. Although there is no evidence to suggest that she ever encouraged any suitor, her playfulness with gender and racial roles is on record. A "backward" young German immigrant who had never seen a black person before behaved awkwardly in her presence. "Asking him in a joking way if he would like to marry her, a query that completely cowed the young man," an early historian noted, "she pretended to be much discomfited because he did not accept her overture." The same source maintains that many "an ebony colored man, and probably not a few lonely prospectors of lighter hue, would have been proud to call her his wife. . . . If anyone is to believe the oldtime miners, Providence left her a virgin that the people of the Black Hills might call her Aunt Lou. Possessed of a deep religious nature, she was a sincere, devout Christian, a communicant of the Methodist church. The smut of early-day scandal never touched the life of this lowly colored woman. There was truth in her quaint remark, intended no doubt as a jest, that she was the first respectable woman in the Black Hills."[40]

When the boom ended and the crowds departed, leaving hotels and restaurants sparsely populated, Marchbanks chose to remain. She encouraged her family to come to the Hills that had been so good to her and find work themselves. Her younger sister, Martha Ann, called Mattie, finally took her advice. On 27 March 1885, she arrived on the stage after a long, cold trip from Sidney, Nebraska. The newspaper noted the event, listing "Miss Marchbanks" in the Arrivals and Departures column.[41] The younger Marchbanks became popular and did not remain single long, marrying Harry Marshall, an African-American barber at Lead City. Not too long afterwards, the couple moved to Pueblo, Colorado, where he served as a policeman and she raised a family.[42]

A few months after Mattie first arrived in the Hills, and only two years after opening her own Rustic Hotel, Marchbanks announced that following a half-century spent slaving in the kitchen, she was tired of cooking and cleaning for the hordes, even in her own establishment. By June, she had a ranch near Rocky Ford in the western Black Hills between Beulah and Sundance, Wyoming. The ex-slave woman and former hotelier was going into small-time ranching across the border where women, regardless of color, had been able to vote and participate fully in governing their affairs since 1869. That fall, she did some remodeling on the Rustic before selling it, and by 1886, she owned a small herd of forty-nine range cattle worth $784. In October of that year, she paid $500 to A. C. Settle to complete the purchase of her ranch and became a deeded landowner, attaining an equal footing with the grandfather who had owned her as a child.[43]

The transition was not without its rough spots. In June 1885, Marchbanks was returning to Central City, Dakota, still her primary place of residence, after a visit to the ranch when she was involved in a buggy accident. Thrown violently from the vehicle, she was fortunate that only her left arm was broken. Within a few weeks, the Deadwood paper reported that she and Mattie had visited both that city and Lead to do some shopping and that all her many friends were pleased to see her. "She has so far recovered as to be able to attend to business again, but she has but one arm she can use."[44]

As Marchbanks prepared to move to her ranch, she found that some aspects of Wyoming geography and demographics were not markedly different from those in Dakota. For one thing, she would still be in the Black Hills, which overlapped into eastern Wyoming. In both territories, the population was largely rural and worked in mining or agriculture. Most residents were white or Indian, with only a tiny fraction being African American. In 1890, only 541 blacks lived in all of South Dakota, while Marchbanks was soon to be one of 922 in Wyoming.

Hundreds of black troops stationed at Wyoming forts artificially inflated the latter figure. According to census data, by 1900, there were only two black farms or ranches in Wyoming and seventeen in South Dakota. In 1885, Marchbanks's new home was still part of the Wild West by eastern standards. It was sparsely populated by cowboys and American Indians, with lonely homesteads and mines scattered across miles of dangerous, virgin wilderness. Only twelve years before Marchbanks acquired her spread, Custer's first exploring expedition, accompanied by Sarah ("Aunt Sally") Campbell, a black cook who really was the first non-native woman in the Black Hills, had camped just a mile or two west of Marchbanks's ranch site. In 1885, the famed Johnson County War between cattle barons and homesteaders was years in the future, and periodic "Indian scares" still kept the "white" people of Wyoming and Dakota on edge.[45]

Marchbanks did not immediately take up residence on her ranch, choosing instead to board for a time with H. Cole in Sundance and keep her primary address in Central City. In 1887, she at last moved onto the ranch, which at that time consisted of a part-frame house on 160 deeded acres with access to portions of the open range. Her deeded real estate was valued at $750. Later, through purchase and by taking advantage of homestead laws, Marchbanks enlarged the size of her ranch, claiming an additional 80 acres to give her a total of 240 deeded acres.[46]

County tax records reveal interesting details about her life on the ranch. In 1887, she sold most of her cattle and began acquiring other types of goods and equipment necessary for country living. The county placed a total value of $1,019 on her property. She had two milch cows ($70), ten range cattle ($135), one "ordinary" horse ($75), two ponies ($50), a carriage or wagon ($20), and miscellaneous household and other goods. She registered her own brand, an "ML" burned onto her horses' left hips. In 1888, her land dropped in value to $650, but her total valuation was $1,115. She still had two milch cows but only two range cattle, one "American" horse and two ponies, a twenty-four-dollar wagon, and fifty dollars' worth of farming tools and household furniture. She had acquired two hundred dollars' worth of musical instruments. Clearly, Marchbanks was settling into her new home.[47]

During the following years, the value of her land and other property rose and fell, reflecting the national and regional economies and events such as the recession of the 1890s. The number and types of stock she raised also fluctuated annually. Changes were so drastic that one suspects she traded not simply for profit but because she enjoyed dickering and visiting with her neighbors. In 1889, for example, she had twelve cattle and five horses. In 1890, she owned only three cattle, two horses, and a pig. In 1895, she was taxed on twenty cattle, twelve horses, and two pigs. In 1902, at about seventy years of age, she was down to eight cattle and two horses, but four years later she had thirteen cattle, two horses, and five pigs. In 1908, her stock included fourteen cattle and four horses.[48]

Although Marchbanks had retired from the hotel and cooking business, one source erroneously claims that she operated a roadhouse at Rocky Ford. This contention is probably an outgrowth of her reputation as a cook and boardinghouse manager in the gold districts and the fact that her ranch was located about a mile east of the Beulah-Sundance trail near the two-story way station called the Rocky Ford Inn. Nevertheless, on infrequent occasions, she did again perspire over large commercial cookstoves during these years, either as favors to friends or to augment her income. She cooked off and on at a cafe in Beulah, Wyoming, and at Guidinger's hotel in the same town, where meals were fifty cents a plate.[49]

Well liked by many local families, Marchbanks played an intimate part in their lives during the next two decades. Most residents were new people, not the old-time bachelor prospectors who remembered her from boom times a quarter century earlier. They were families who came from diverse locations to settle on homesteads and build stable communities in which to raise their children. Except, perhaps, for the color of their skin, they were her kind of people. One clan far from their own relatives considered Marchbanks to be essentially one of their family matrons. Her neighbors often called upon "Aunt Lou" to act as a midwife, and she delivered babies for many families. At least one white child, Annie Lucretia Smith, was named for her. They all depended on Marchbanks, who always seemed to be on hand when someone was ill.[50]

As before, Marchbanks was not the only African American in her rural neighborhood. When she moved onto the ranch, she engaged Moses W. ("George") Bagley to undertake the heavy labor of stock-tending, plowing and planting, fencing, fuel hauling, and so on. Bagley, born in 1845, probably began life as a slave. He started working for Marchbanks during the mid-1880s but may not have taken up residence on the ranch until 1895. In that year, Marchbanks began paying

Pictured here in front of her ranch house sometime after 1905, Marchbanks spent her later years managing her holdings and helping her neighbors. Crook County Museum Archives, Sundance, Wyo.

poll taxes for two people. It is unknown if he lived in the main house or had his own bunkhouse on the ranch. Oddly, Marchbanks seems not to have paid him. Years later, after she died, Bagley submitted a claim against her estate, stating that he had worked for her without remuneration for twenty-five years. He received $450 from the estate and the proceeds from the 1912 crop. Why he would work so many years without compensation is unknown, but there is no evidence to suggest that theirs was anything more than a business relationship. Had they been "living in sin," Marchbanks's reputation for respectability most likely would not have survived her neighbors' Victorian-era judgments, nor would she have been described as the virgin mother to everyone in the Hills.[51]

In 1896, Marchbanks welcomed two more family members to the Hills. Her sister Margaret's son, Burr Officer, and his son Ted settled near Beulah and, on 8 March 1901, applied for a homestead almost immediately north of hers. Like Marchbanks, Burr Officer was born a

Tennessee slave. His son was born in Algood, Tennessee, on 10 October 1882. Burr's wife had died about 1891 and never lived in the West. Burr went to work cowboying. Ted spent the winters in school in Lead and devoted his summers to riding the range and becoming famous for his whistling. He apparently finished school, and by the time he was grown, he was better educated than many of his cowboy compadres. In 1905, the young Officer was Marchbanks's agent to the county assessor's office.[52] Ted Officer also became good friends with Kate Reynolds and her niece, another black family homesteading on Little Spearfish Creek about twenty-two miles south of Spearfish and only two and a half miles from the Wyoming border, roughly fifteen miles east of Marchbanks's ranch.[53]

Lou Marchbanks's holdings were relatively small, and she did not make a concerted effort to pursue wealth. According to one possibly apocryphal rendition of her life on the ranch, she "enjoyed her last days—she would sit on her porch and happily puff on her pipe. Occasionally she would go back to the Hills and visit her many friends in Central City and Lead. They would also visit her and sometimes their children would spend several days on the ranch. The area people also thought a lot of her and during round-ups she was well-supplied with choice quarters of beef."[54]

In the early 1900s, Lucretia Marchbanks's health began to fail. Sundance, Wyoming, physicians R. C. Knode and J. F. Clarenbach did what they could for her. The bill Clarenbach submitted to her estate suggests urinary-tract problems, as does a bill from a pharmacist for kidney pills. Beginning in February 1907, Clarenbach performed many tests including numerous urinalyses. Finally, on 19 November 1911, he made his last "call to the ranch," and the tired old woman passed away the next day at about seventy-eight or seventy-nine years of age. Sundance Undertaking Company charged the estate $99 for one bottle of preserving fluid, four bands of crepe, a lady's robe and cap, an octagon-end casket, black cloth and trimmings, and an "R. Box," plus two days' time for work and travel to the ranch and back. The Deadwood Granite and Marble Works charged $65 for her monument and placement. The half lot in the Beulah cemetery cost $6. The estate also paid a $19.50 bill for boarding several relatives and friends who came for the funeral.[55]

The funeral service, conducted by Reverend M. C. Roberts from the Methodist church in Sundance, was held in her ranch house. "When she died," Roberts later recorded, "I had the honor to go to Beulah and conduct services. A large crowd of friends and admirers were present to pay their last tribute of respect to one whom they loved, although her skin was black. I remember well the occasion. I preached from the text, 'She hath done what she could.' We returned her body to the earth, believing her soul had gone to the God who gave it."[56] Early historian Thomas Odell recorded, "Loving white hands laid to rest the good woman—Lucretia Marchbanks, the black queen of the Hills. . . . When the Recording Angel opens the great Judgment Book, the name of Lucretia Marchbanks . . . deserves to head the list of all the argonauts who followed the rainbow to the wild Black Hills in quest of the pot of gold." White hands alone did not lay her to rest, however. A number of African-American relatives and friends, including Marchbanks's only surviving sibling Mattie Marshall, also attended the funeral. All the regional newspapers printed lengthy eulogies and obituaries as the Hills mourned her passing.[57]

Her simple estate, the end result of a lifetime of labor begun in slavery but ended in freedom on the front porch of her own ranch, was offered for auction on 15 June 1912. The inventory, consisting of one old mare, two younger mares, three calves, two yearling colts, two dozen chickens, four geese, a half share in a breaking plow, a wagon, one yearling heifer, one yearling colt, three cows, a set of harness, two oil paintings, one grindstone, chairs, a trunk and contents, one gray mare, a mower, a harrow, a kitchen range and utensils, one commode, two beds, one clock, cupboards, dishes, chairs, stands, and a "whatnot," fetched a total of $504. Augmenting the meager list of belongings were her real estate holdings, which were valued for tax purposes at $1,840. She also had a life insurance policy valued at $2,400, a small savings account, and other lesser assets. Her physical estate did not reflect the wealth of affection she had received from the friends and loved ones whose lives she had enriched.[58]

By the time of Marchbanks's death, only a handful of African Americans still remained in the Black Hills. Deadwood had only thirty-eight black residents in 1900. During the following years, more people moved away and only a few new residents immigrated to the area. Her nephew, Burr Officer, remained in Beulah as late as 1915. Ted Officer cowboyed for George Berghoffer of Sundance and other area ranchers, eventually becoming a range and timber foreman. He passed away in 1946 and is buried in Beulah. George Bagley died 20 June 1922 and is buried beside Marchbanks in the Beulah cemetery.[59]

Lucretia Marchbanks, ex-slave and veteran of the California gold rush, came to the Black Hills in 1876 at the height of the boomtown excitement. In doing so, she fulfilled the 1855 prophecy of San Francisco minister Darius Stokes who, in addressing the first state convention of the Colored Citizens of California, declared, "The white man came, and we came with him; and by the blessing of God, we shall stay with him, side by side. . . . Should another Sutter discover another El Dorado . . . no sooner shall the white man's foot be firmly planted there, than looking over his shoulder he will see the black man, like his shadow, by his side."[60] Lucretia Marchbanks personally played a role in the process of settling and developing the American West. Moreover, the single, female, nonwhite cook, hotel owner, and rancher was not content to be a mere shadow. Instead, she worked diligently to live her own life on her own terms, to the greatest extent possible. The reputation she established and the property she acquired under difficult frontier circumstances were nothing short of remarkable for a woman who had started out her life as someone else's property. Altogether, she gained the respect and even love of those who knew her—black and white—and was able to live a modestly comfortable life in spite of the complex world of frontier race relations.

NOTES

1. *Black Hills Daily Times*, 12 Dec. 1881. A reference in a story about the DeSmet Mine published earlier in the *Times* had prompted the exchange. The words, "Aunt Lou, mother of Father DeSmet, still reigns supreme in the mansion" (14 Nov. 1881), piqued the curiosity of staff on the *New York Daily Stock Report*. *See also* Vernice White, "Lucretia Marchbanks, A Former Slave," in *Pioneers of Crook County, 1876–1920* (Sundance, Wyo.: Crook County Historical Society, 1981), pp. 310–11.

2. Interview with Karen Glover, Sundance, Wyo., 12 May 1994. Glover is an area historian and former Crook County treasurer whose family was well acquainted with their neighbor Lucretia Marchbanks.

3. George W. Stokes with Howard R. Driggs, *Deadwood Gold: A Story of the Black Hills*, Pioneer Life Series (Yonkers on Hudson, N.Y.: World Book Co., 1926), p. 75.

4. W. Sherman Savage, *Blacks in the West*, Contributions in Afro-American and African Studies, no. 23 (Westport, Conn.: Greenwood Press, 1976), p. 70.

5. Kenneth Wiggins Porter, *The Negro on the American Frontier* (New York: Arno Press, 1971), pp. 392–93; Barbara A. Neal Ledbetter, *Fort Belknap Frontier Saga: Indians, Negroes and Anglo-Americans on the Texas Frontier* (Burnet, Tex.:

Eakin Press, 1982), pp. 114–18, 135–37; John W. Ravage, *Black Pioneers: Images of the Black Experience on the North American Frontier* (Salt Lake City: University of Utah Press, 1997), p. 44. Patricia Nelson Limerick examines the complexities of frontier race relations in *The Legacy of Conquest: The Unbroken Past of the American West* (New York: W. W. Norton, 1987).

6. *See* Dee Brown, *The Gentle Tamers: Women of the Old Wild West* (New York: G. P. Putnam's Sons, 1958).

7. Thomas E. Odell, "She Was Mother to All Folks in Early Deadwood" (unidentified newspaper clipping, probably the *Sundance Times* or the *Queen City Mail* of Spearfish, S.Dak.), ca. 1946, Scrapbook, Crook County Public Library, Sundance, Wyo. Odell is identified as a "Spearfish writer and Black Hills historian." His article, based on old *Black Hills Daily Times* articles and interviews with gold-rush survivors, seems to be the source for much of the published information about Marchbanks.

8. Odell, "She Was Mother to All"; Aaron Paragon (nephew of Lucretia Marchbanks) to Clerk of District Court L. Mauch, 26 Dec. 1911, and Vincen Gardenshire to executor of the estate, 15 Mar. 1912, both in Probate Files, Crook County Courthouse, Sundance, Wyo.; Quintard Taylor, *In Search of the Racial Frontier: African Americans in the American West, 1528–1990* (New York: W. W. Norton, 1998), p. 81. Slavery was illegal in California but existed nevertheless. By 1852, thousands of slaves worked in the goldfields, as house servants, or in other capacities in urban areas. In 1860, there were over four thousand blacks in California, almost equal to the total white population of Dakota Territory. Taylor, *In Search of the Racial Frontier*, pp.76–78.

9. *Black Hills Daily Times*, 16 Aug., 13 Sept. 1881; Paragon to Mauch, 26 Dec. 1911. In Colorado, at least one brother lived in Leadville, another in Brother, and a sister in Pueblo. Her nephew, Walter Paragon, also moved west and resided in Estic, Nebraska.

10. Taylor, *In Search of the Racial Frontier*, pp. 104–5, 121. The most pertinent federal acts were the Territorial Suffrage Act (1867) and the Fifteenth Amendment (ratified in 1870), which gave black men the right to vote. White pioneers with southern origins or sympathies resisted on the floors of territorial legislatures and with street violence in Helena, Montana, and at South Pass City, Wyoming. Perhaps the most extreme response came from the first Wyoming legislature, which responded by granting women suffrage in its territorial constitution. The rationale, according to Senator William Bright, a South Pass City saloonkeeper and sponsor of the legislation, was that if black men could vote, then supposedly superior white women should also be able to cast ballots. Ibid., p. 125; Sidney Howell Fleming, "Solving the Jigsaw Puzzle: One Suffrage Story at a Time," *Annals of*

Wyoming 62 (Spring 1990): 27–28, 59–61; Michael A. Massie, "Reform Is Where You Find It: The Roots of Woman Suffrage in Wyoming," *Annals of Wyoming* 62 (Spring 1990): 8–10; Todd Guenther, "At Home on the Range: Black Settlement in Rural Wyoming, 1850–1950" (M.A. thesis, University of Wyoming, 1988), pp. 5–18.

11. Irma H. Klock, *Black Hills Ladies: The Frail and the Fair* (Deadwood, S.Dak.: By the Author, 1980), pp. 12–13; Jesse Brown and A. M. Willard, *The Black Hills Trails: A History of the Struggles of the Pioneers in the Winning of the Black Hills* (Rapid City, S.Dak.: *Rapid City Journal* Co., 1924), pp. 95–96; Watson Parker, *Gold in the Black Hills* (Pierre: South Dakota State Historical Society Press, 2003), pp. 133–36; Sydney B. Spiegel, "History of Laramie County, Wyoming, to 1890" (M.A. thesis, University of Wyoming, 1961), pp. 147–52; Agnes Wright Spring, *The Cheyenne and Black Hills Stage and Express Routes* (Glendale, Calif.: Arthur H. Clark Co., 1949), pp. 135–36. Briggs was a servant for the Charles Metz family, who were traveling from the gold fields to their home in Laramie or Cheyenne when attacked. The family's mutilated bodies were found near the road, but Briggs's remains were found some distance from the others. Authorities speculated that she received different—and harsher—treatment because of her race. Evidence suggested that the murderers were a group of white bandits and renegade Indians.

12. Rodman Wilson Paul, *Mining Frontiers of the Far West, 1848–1880* (Albuquerque: University of New Mexico Press, 1974), p. 178.

13. Brown and Willard, *Black Hills Trails*, pp. 419–20.

14. Paul, *Mining Frontiers*, p. 177.

15. Quoted from *Cheyenne Daily Leader*, 29 Mar. 1876, in Parker, *Gold in the Black Hills*, p. 72.

16. Sally Zanjani, *A Mine of Her Own: Women Prospectors in the American West, 1850–1950* (Lincoln: University of Nebraska Press, 1997), pp. 1–13, 209–10; Stokes and Driggs, *Deadwood Gold*, pp. 75–76; John G. Bourke, *On the Border with Crook* (New York: Charles Scribner's Sons, 1891), p. 384; Brown and Willard, *Black Hills Trails*, p. 472. On 8 August 1881, the *Black Hills Daily Times* noted that a "Mrs. John Kam, of Central City," was "staking off a claim . . . that she thinks is a bonanza," but she also wanted readers to know that she "kept a lodging house in Central City, where treasure seekers could find a good bed."

17. Klock, *Black Hills Ladies*, p. 12. The Mexican's spree ended a short time later when he was shot down in a bar by Brick Pomeroy, the man who had actually killed the Indian. Parker, *Deadwood: The Golden Years* (Lincoln: University of Nebraska Press, 1981), pp. 52–53. This tale, like the earlier one involving Wild Bill Hickok, probably needs to be taken with a grain of salt, but both stories illustrate the growth of Marchbanks's reputation and the way in which her story became intertwined with other Hills incidents and personalities. Klock's information on

Marchbanks is apparently based on L. J. O'Grady, "Old Aunt Lou in Hills Rush," *Sioux City Sunday Journal*, 3 Jan. 1926. As a child, O'Grady apparently knew Marchbanks and got the stories of her exploits directly from her.

18. Stokes and Driggs, *Deadwood Gold*, p. 76.

19. Parker, *Deadwood*, p. 74; Odell, "She Was Mother to All."

20. Quoted in Parker, *Deadwood*, p. 76.

21. Bourke, *On the Border with Crook*, pp. 384–85. Partitions between the bedrooms did not reach to the ceiling, so privacy was unheard of.

22. Odell, "She Was Mother to All." *See also* Parker, *Gold in the Black Hills*, p. 195.

23. Odell, "She Was Mother to All." *See also Black Hills Daily Times*, 15 Aug. 1879.

24. Odell, "She Was Mother to All"; Klock, *Black Hills Ladies*, pp. 12–13; Parker, *Deadwood*, pp. 74–75. Joseph R. Conlin's excellent book, *Bacon, Beans, and Galantines: Food and Foodways on the Western Mining Frontier* (Reno: University of Nevada Press, 1986), is devoted to the discussion of food acquisition, preparation, and consumption in mining camps.

25. *Black Hills Daily Times*, 8 May 1880.

26. Ibid., 11 Jan. 1881.

27. Ibid., 14 May 1881, 21 July, 10 Dec. 1882, 9 Aug. 1883.

28. Ibid., 8 Aug. 1881.

29. Ibid., 13 Sept. 1881. *See also* 16 Aug. 1881.

30. Ibid., 5, 12 June 1883. *See also* Klock, *Black Hills Ladies*, pp. 12–13.

31. Quoted in Odell, "She Was Mother to All."

32. Parker, *Deadwood*, pp. 81, 141–42; Thomas R. Buecker, "Confrontation at Sturgis: An Episode in Civil-Military Race Relations, 1885," *South Dakota History* 14 (Fall 1984): 242; Parker, *Gold in the Black Hills*, pp. 99–100; Christopher Hills, *Gold Pans & Broken Picks: The History of the Tinton Mining Region* (Spearfish, S.Dak.: By the Author, 1998), pp. 29–32. For more about the black community in the Hills, *see* Betti VanEpps-Taylor, *Forgotten Lives: African Americans in South Dakota* (Pierre: South Dakota State Historical Society Press, 2008), chap. 5.

33. *Black Hills Daily Times*, 2 Aug. 1879.

34. J. W. Smurr, "Jim Crow Out West," in *Historical Essays on Montana and the Northwest*, ed. J. W. Smurr and K. Ross Toole (Helena: Western Press & Historical Society of Montana, 1957), pp. 194–95.

35. Parker, *Deadwood*, p. 141.

36. Buecker, "Confrontation at Sturgis," pp. 238–61.

37. Odell, "She Was Mother to All."

38. Parker, *Deadwood*, p. 141.

39. Quoted in Odell, "She Was Mother to All."

40. Ibid. The information about her hair color came from the interview with Karen Glover, 12 May 1994.

41. *Black Hills Daily Times*, 27 Mar. 1885.

42. Odell, "She Was Mother to All"; Marchbanks Probate Files.

43. Karen Glover, "Rocky Ford, Crook County, Wyoming" (manuscript), n.d., p. 1, author's collection; Odell, "She Was Mother to All"; *Black Hills Daily Times*, 18 Oct. 1885. The legal description of her property was W/E, NE/SE, and E/NW/SE/SW of Section 8, Township 52 North, Range 61 West.

44. *Black Hills Daily Times*, 26 June 1885. *See also* 5 June, 3 July 1885.

45. Taylor, *In Search of the Racial Frontier*, pp. 135, 152; Sara L. Bernson and Robert J. Eggers, "Black People in South Dakota History," *South Dakota History* 7 (Summer 1977): 244. My research for Guenther, "At Home on the Range," indicates that the figure for black ranches in Wyoming in the 1900 census is too low. For more on Campbell, *see* VanEpps-Taylor, *Forgotten Lives*, pp. 129–32.

46. Odell, "She Was Mother to All"; Crook County Assessment Rolls, 1886, Crook County Assessor's Files, Crook County Courthouse; photograph of Lou Marchbanks, 1910, by Mrs. Armstrong, Williams Collection, Crook County Museum, Sundance, Wyo.

47. Crook County Assessment Rolls, 1887, p. 53, and 1888, p. 28.

48. Ibid., 1889, p. 45; 1890, p. 57; 1895, p. 98; 1902, p. 52; 1906, p. 80; 1908, p. 79.

49. Parker, *Deadwood*, p. 74; Postcard, Rocky Ford Inn, Crook County Library; Glover, "Rocky Ford, Crook County, Wyoming," p. 3; Interview with Glover, 12 May 1994.

50. Interview with Violet Smith, Sundance, Wyo., 12 May 1994; Interview with Glover, 12 May 1994. Smith's husband is a descendant of Marchbanks's neighbors, one of whom, Annie Lucretia Smith, was named for the woman who helped deliver her into the world.

51. Odell, "She Was Mother to All"; Marchbanks Probate Files.

52. "Burr and Ted Officer," in *Pioneers of Crook County*, p. 371; Interview with Glover, 12 May 1994; Crook County Assessment Roll, 1905. The Officers' homestead was located in Section 5, Township 52 North, Range 61 West. *See also* Hills, *Gold Pans & Broken Picks*, pp. 146–47.

53. Hills, *Gold Pans & Broken Picks*, pp. 146–48, 221; Cher Burgess, United States Forest Service archaeologist investigating the site of the Reynolds homestead, to author, 1 June and 28 Dec. 1998; Burgess, "Its About Time: The African American Experience in the Black Hills" (press release), 1 Dec. 1998, author's collection. Kate Reynolds's life in many ways paralleled that of Lucretia Marchbanks.

Born a slave in 1849 in Fayetteville, Arkansas, Reynolds, her husband Pleasant, and their infant son Clarence moved to the Black Hills in 1876. After she and her husband split up in 1883, Kate Reynolds operated a boardinghouse and cooked for a living, just as Marchbanks had. Reynolds also worked as a private nurse and midwife, though she had more training than Marchbanks, having been a nurse during the Civil War. Doing everything she could to keep the home together, she became known as "Aunt Kate." *See* VanEpps-Taylor, *Forgotten Lives*, pp. 134–35.

54. Klock, *Black Hills Ladies*, p. 13. *See also* O'Grady, "Old Aunt Lou in Hills Rush."

55. Marchbanks Probate Files. Knode's bill for services performed in March 1908 was submitted 1 June 1912. Clarenbach's bill was dated 12 February 1912 and itemized services he performed between February 1907 and November 1911. H. A. Lilly of Sundance Pharmacy submitted a bill dated 8 May 1912.

56. Quoted in Odell, "She Was Mother to All."

57. Ibid. *See also Belle Fourche Bee*, 30 Nov. 1911; *Deadwood Daily Pioneer-Times*, 24 Nov. 1911; *Lead Daily Call*, 24 Nov. 1911; and *Queen City Mail*, 29 Nov. 1911.

58. Petition for Sale of Personal Property, 29 Mar. 1912, Treasurer's Office Receipt, 26 Dec. 1913, Final Decree, Estate of Lucretia Marchbanks, 7 June 1918, Petition to Correct Final Decree, 26 June 1918, all in Marchbanks Probate Files.

59. Parker, *Deadwood*, p. 141; "Burr and Ted Officer," p. 371

60. Quoted in Taylor, *In Search of the Racial Frontier*, p. 134.

Wong Fee Lee

DEADWOOD'S PIONEER

MERCHANT

Edith C. Wong, Eileen French,

and Rose Estep Fosha

As word of gold in the Black Hills spread across the country in the wake of Lieutenant Colonel George Armstrong Custer's 1874 expedition of discovery, thousands of fortune-seekers rushed into western Dakota Territory. Among the throngs hoping to profit from the new discoveries were Chinese immigrants, many of whom were already adept at both mining gold and "mining the miners" by selling them goods and services. One of these individuals was Wong Fee Lee, who arrived in Deadwood in 1876 and over the next several decades became the most prominent member of the Black Hills Chinese community.[1] Three contiguous properties where he lived, raised a family, and carried on his mercantile business and mining interests were located on lower Main Street in the National Historic Landmark city of Deadwood. His store, built in 1885, and an adjoining structure, built in 1896, became historic properties known as the Wing Tsue (pronounced wing-SHWAY) buildings. From 1876 into the 1920s, three generations of the Wong family lived at the Wing Tsue complex, making for a continuous occupation of nearly forty-five years, a rare occurrence in the history of the Chinese in the West.[2] The premises were also rented to European Americans and other Chinese, some of whom conducted businesses from this same loca-

This essay originally appeared in slightly different form in *South Dakota History* 39 (Winter 2009): 283–335.

tion. In 2005, when new owners were preparing to renovate the last architectural vestige of Deadwood's Chinese district, both buildings collapsed, and the rubble was hauled away. Even though these structures are now gone, their history remains in the stories of the properties and the people who lived and worked there.

The History of the Wing Tsue Properties

The facts surrounding Wong Fee Lee's journey to the Black Hills and his first years in the region are vague.[3] Early newspaper accounts tell of groups of Chinese traveling by stagecoach and wagon from Cheyenne and Evanston, Wyoming, and Denver, Colorado, and of individuals with contrived names such as Bi-Dam, Ding Dong, and Heap Wash.[4] Wong family history and Wong Fee Lee's obituary from the 23 October 1921 issue of the *Deadwood Daily Pioneer-Times* relate that he first settled in the town of Custer, where he may have worked as a cook for a group of prospectors. Wong Fee Lee himself stated that he had previously been a well-known merchant in Montana. Sam Schwarzwald, a long-time furniture dealer on Main Street, arrived in Deadwood in August 1876 and testified that he met "Wing Tsue" that month, strongly suggesting that Wong Fee Lee had established himself in Deadwood by that time.[5]

Over the next several years, recorded evidence begins to accumulate regarding Wong Fee Lee's existence and the beginning of his Wing Tsue Bazaar, which sold Chinese groceries, clothing, and medicines, in addition to other dry goods and novelty items. The earliest known document pertaining to Wong Fee Lee is also the first documented instance of Chinese property ownership within the city. Discriminatory laws prohibited the Chinese from purchasing property in many places, but not in Deadwood. A quit claim deed dated 4 June 1877 granted Wong Fee Lee, in return for "one hundred and five dust dollars," a seventeen-by-one-hundred-foot lot with buildings on the west side of Main Street, further identified as "part of lots 68 and 69 in the town of Elizabeth."[6] By 1881, when Deadwood incorporated the neighboring camp of Elizabethtown, numerous Chinese-owned stores, restaurants, boarding houses, and laundries had sprung up in this section, earning it the name of "Chinatown."[7]

One of the first business directories for Deadwood, published in 1878, contained a single listing for a Chinese businessman, a "Wong Lee" who worked as a practicing physician.[8] This individual may or may not have been Wong Fee Lee, but Dr. F. S. Howe, who had arrived in

In 1877, frontier photographer F. Jay Haynes recorded this early view of Deadwood in its rugged gulch. State Archives Collection, South Dakota State Historical Society

Deadwood by 1880, wrote in his memoir *Deadwood Doctor*: "I became very well acquainted with practically all of the Chinamen of Deadwood, in fact, usually took care of them. Dr. Wing Tsue was one of the finest men I have ever known."[9] Numerous references to "Dr. Wing Tsue" appear in Deadwood newspapers throughout the years, likely due to the fact that he sold apothecaries in his store.

The earliest newspaper references to Wong Fee Lee, and among the first to identify any Chinese individual by given name, appeared in the *Black Hills Daily Times* and the *Black Hills Daily Pioneer* on 7 March 1878. Both newspapers carried columns noting the arrivals and departures of travelers and mentioned that Wong Fee Lee had left Deadwood on the Cheyenne stage. The following month, the newspapers proclaimed the arrival of freight for Wing Tsue via the Cheyenne and Black Hills Forwarding Company. This instance is also the first time the name "Wing Tsue" appeared in print. From April through June 1878, the Cheyenne and Black Hills Forwarding Company delivered eighty-seven packages to the Wing Tsue store, an indication that the business was thriving within a year.[10]

One of Wong Fee Lee's grandsons, Kam Leung Wong, explained the meaning of the store name in an interview conducted in 1992. "During that period of time," he noted, "no Chinese would name a company or a store by his own name. It [was] completely taboo. . . . It has come from the philosophy of Confucian modesty. You don't blow your own horn." He went on to relate: "'*Wing*' is like 'glory'; '*Tsue*' means 'getting together' or 'joining,' so the whole thing is 'getting together in glory.' It's kind of like, 'the people come together, the glorious people come together.'"[11]

Wong Fee Lee appears in the 1880 census as "Wing Touie" living in household 64 on Main Street in Deadwood. He was registered as a thirty-nine-year-old tea merchant. Living with him was his thirty-four-year-old brother, Wong Bong, also a tea merchant. Four others in the household included Wong Coon, age thirty, and Wo Mung Shing, age twenty-eight, who listed their occupations as "clerk in store." A. Toy, age twenty-five, was in the laundry business, and Mong Yue Wing, age forty-five, worked as a servant. All six were listed as single Chinese males. Extrapolating from other known locations, this household was situated at or near 566 Main Street, a few doors south of the Brison residence (household 59) at 554 Main and the Morris residence (household 61).[12] Amie Morris quitclaimed "Lot number Sixty-Nine . . . adjoining the store of Wing Tsue" to him and Wong Nung in 1883.[13]

The earliest-known historic photograph of lower Main Street in Deadwood was taken in the fall of 1877 by photographer F. Jay Haynes. The Wing Tsue store structure undoubtedly appeared in the image, but no representation of lower Main Street with businesses and residences accurately identified appears until 1891, when the Sanborn Map Company of New York produced a detailed planview for fire insurance purposes. One year later, Haynes returned to Deadwood, and his 1892 photograph documents the transformation of lower Main Street that took place after the devastating fire of 1879 and the destructive flood of 1883.[14] Many of these changes were not recorded in other historical documents, or the documents themselves have vanished.

Deadwood's location in a deep gulch through which Whitewood Creek flows made the rugged western community especially susceptible to both fire and flood. Fear of the "fire fiend,"[15] as it was called in early newspapers, became full-blown on 26 September 1879, when flames and explosions from stored mining materials raged from the south end of Deadwood to the north end, destroying most of the downtown section and part of Chinatown. The mining enterprise of Spencer, Norton & Company owned the bedrock title to a portion of land underlying the town. When the smoke cleared, investor Frank Norton objected to allowing any Chinese to rebuild and placed a high price on the property in an attempt to deter any Chinese buyers.[16]

The effect of Norton's stance on Wong Fee Lee's interests is not known, but the fire and resulting property losses taught Wong the same lesson others in town had learned: in order to protect investments, rebuilding should be done with stone or brick. "The best and most substantial looking fireproof in town is now being built in the middle of Chinatown," reported the *Black Hills Daily Times* in 1879. "The walls are stone, and are very thick and heavy. It is built on top of the ground and the rear end of it is built up against the rocky cliffs."[17] Following the flood of May 1883, the newspaper again noted, "Chinamen make the best fire-proofs in the world. The one at the rear of the store that is now being demolished had walls three feet thick, with a door on the outside and another one on the inside of the door passage, that, when closed, would be nearly air tight. A hopper on the top, filled with fine, dry sand, connected with the space between the two doors by a spout, with a slide, so that when the building was in danger, by pulling out the slide, the sand would run down and make the whole thing more than fire-proof."[18]

After the 1883 flood, Hi Kee, Wong Fee Lee's main competitor in the mercantile business, purchased and moved to property at 560 Main Street, close to the Wing Tsue store.[19] By midsummer, the *Black Hills Daily Times* reported, Hi Kee had "a number of his countrymen employed in building a fireproof in the bluff back of the house."[20] (Three fireproofs belonging to Wing Tsue and Hi Kee, along with all of the contents, would survive a fire in February of 1885). The city also took advantage of the need to repair water damage after the flood and widened the thoroughfare through Chinatown so that it could accommodate the large wagon trains that would often clog movement through this section of town. The street was raised three feet and widened, covering over one of Wong Fee Lee's fireproofs and forcing him to rebuild his frame store.[21]

On a frigid night in February 1885, flames originated in the Wing Tsue store and roared north on Main Street through ten mostly frame buildings until they were stopped at Brison's Bakery at 554 Main.[22] Again, the city seized the opportunity to enact improvements. The street through Chinatown was widened by another six feet, and Mayor Solomon ("Sol") Star supported extending the water main to the Wing Tsue store, thus enabling the fire department to "carry a stream to any part of Chinatown."[23] Finally, the city prohibited anyone from rebuilding with materials other than brick or stone without permission. On 6 April 1885, the Deadwood City Council granted a building permit to

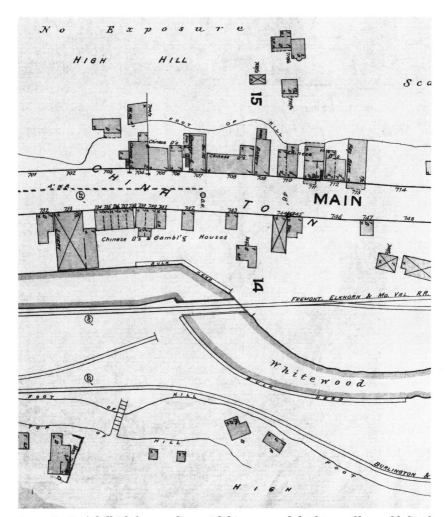

Wong Fee Lee's hillside house, along with his store and the fireproof located behind it, appear on the top side of Main Street at far left in this detail from an 1891 Sanborn map. State Archives Collection, South Dakota State Historical Society

"Wing Tsue."[24] As a result, Wong Fee Lee had workers construct the brick store at 566 Main Street that would survive for the next 120 years.

Over the decades, various advertising and identifying markings appeared on the Wing Tsue store. At some point, the date of the founding of the Wing Tsue Company, 1889, appeared on the structure.[25] A photograph taken in 1897 shows "Wing Tsue Chinese Bazar [*sic*]" painted on the front windows. In the course of an immigration interrogation conducted in 1915, the inspector asked about the meaning of the Chi-

*The sign painted on the window identifies the Wing Tsue Chinese
Bazaar in this 1897 photograph. Jeanette Thacker, Lead, S.Dak.*

nese characters on the storefront, to which Wong Fee Lee replied that
they represented the name of the firm, "Wing Tsue."[26] As late as 2005,
"Wing Tsue Chinese Groceries and Provisions" could still be deciphered
on the bricks of the second story.

A stone structure at 564 Main, also owned by Wong Fee Lee, appears
in photographs taken in 1892, 1900, and 1925. The front wall is on the
same line as the 1885 store, suggesting that it was constructed at the
same time, possibly to serve as a fireproof building for storing merchandise. It is shown still standing on the Sanborn map dated 1948, but its
origins remain a mystery in the history of the Wing Tsue complex.

Also unknown is the date of construction for the unassuming house
on the hillside at 568 Main that became the home of Wong Fee Lee
and his family, which eventually included a wife and eight children.
Sanborn maps reveal that sometime between 1897 and 1903, the home
was enlarged uphill to the back, granting more living space. Large ter-
raced gardens ran up the hillside, as well, providing fresh produce for
the family and, presumably, for store customers. In July 1888, the *Black*

Wong Fee Lee constructed this building next door to the bazaar in 1896. Adams Museum, Deadwood, S.Dak.

Hills Daily Times challenged Deadwood's European-American population to attempt a similar accomplishment.[27] These extraordinary gardens are clearly visible in the photograph taken by F. Jay Haynes in 1892.

The last major construction project Wong Fee Lee undertook was the two-story brick structure built in 1896 adjoining the older Wing Tsue building. Four short newspaper items provide information on what would also become a Deadwood landmark. The *Deadwood Daily*

*These two views depict the changes in Deadwood's Chinatown between 1892
and 1900. The 1892 photograph by F. Jay Haynes (above) shows the Wing Tsue
complex at the left end of the built-up area on the far side of Main Street. The
gardens extending up the hillside are those of Wong Fee Lee and his competitor,
Hi Kee. Visible in the 1900 photograph by William H. Jackson (opposite)
are the additions to the Wing Tsue buildings. Above, Montana Historical
Society Research Center, Helena; right, Colorado Historical Society, Denver*

Pioneer reported in early October that Wong Fee Lee was enlarging
the storeroom of his existing building and planned to rent out the new
building then under construction.[28] Two weeks later, the *Daily Pioneer*
noted that plaster work was progressing, and the premises were "nearly
ready to occupy."[29] In December, the newspaper reported, "Williams &
Son are painting the new business house recently built by Wing Tsue,
on lower Main street, and are also retouching the interior of Hi Kee's
store, expecting to finish the work today."[30] On New Year's Day 1897,
the *Daily Pioneer* gave more details, describing the new building as
twenty-eight by thirty-two feet and the addition at the rear of the old
building as seventeen by twenty-two feet. Like the new building, the
addition consisted of two stories, the top floor of which was "divided
into living and sleeping rooms."[31] The new structure was included on
the 1897 Sanborn map and first appears in a photograph taken in 1900

by William Henry Jackson.[32] Wong Fee Lee never relocated the Wing Tsue store to the new building but continued operations from 566 Main for the length of the company's existence.

Wong Fee Lee owned other properties in Deadwood, including two lots located directly across Main Street from his store. Early in the town's existence, pigpens were a source of displeasure to the European-American population, but because pigs and the consumption of pork were an integral part of Chinese culture, a prominent merchant like Wong Fee Lee would be certain to provide this necessity. Throughout the years, local newspapers listed roast pig as being served at all the Chinese celebrations, rituals, and burials.[33] Wong Fee Lee owned and paid taxes on property located in block 12, lots 22 and 24, for many years.[34] One deed refers to this strip as "owned by Wing Tsue, and occupied by him as a pig pen."[35] Charles Ham, who settled in Rapid City, told of driving the first six hundred squealing pigs across the South Dakota plains and up to Deadwood. In a 1938 interview, he described meeting a "wealthy Chinese merchant who came out with a servant holding an umbrella over his head [and] inspected and purchased several swine."[36] In all likelihood, the merchant with the aristocratic bearing was Wong Fee Lee.

The scope of Wing Tsue Company operations is apparent in documents generated as various partners or Wong family members prepared to visit China or return to the United States. Under the Chinese Exclusion Act of 1882, Congress prohibited the immigration of Chinese laborers, who were viewed as a threat to the jobs of American workers. In order to travel abroad and return, the law required Chinese residents to submit affidavits and other paperwork attesting to their status as non-laborers.[37] Immigration inspectors also commonly visited the business location to see the premises in person and to interview well-known local residents to confirm the legitimacy of a Chinese merchant's operations.

Documents collected under the Chinese Exclusion Act confirm that the Wing Tsue Company operated continuously from 1889 until at least 1915. Wong Fee Lee maintained a controlling interest in the amount of four to five thousand dollars, limiting his partners to shares of no more than one thousand to fifteen hundred dollars each. The number of partners, who also served as store clerks or traveling salesmen, varied from as few as five to as many as fourteen. Over the years, the value of company real estate ranged from seven to fifteen thousand dollars, and the stock of merchandise carried varied from four to six thousand dollars. One estimate of average yearly receipts, in 1911, was ten thousand dollars. In addition, Wong Fee Lee and several Chinese and European-American partners owned hard-rock mining claims in the northern Black Hills that were valued as high as twenty thousand dollars. Chinese immigrants on the western frontier often took part in placer mining, which required little investment in equipment. Their involvement in hard-rock mining, however, is less common and speaks to the business and leadership abilities of Wong Fee Lee.[38]

State and federal census figures from 1900 to 1920 provide yet another window on the Wing Tsue complex and its occupants. The United States census for 1900 shows Wong Fee Lee, his wife Hal Shek, and seven children ranging in age from four to fifteen years (all of whom were born in South Dakota and attended public school) living in the residence, which is recorded at 566 Main, although the house itself was on the hill behind the properties. The 1896 building at 568 Main was being rented to six Chinese males ranging in age from thirty-three to fifty-seven. They had lived in the United States for eighteen to twenty-nine years and included three cooks, a restaurant owner, a merchant, and a barber.[39]

The 1900 census also records quite a number of additional individuals as occupants at 566 Main. A total of fourteen Chinese males listed as partners, boarders, and heads of household were engaged in the occupations of restaurant keeper, cook, gambler, janitor, and general store clerk. The ages of the men ranged from thirty-one to fifty-six years. All spoke English and had resided in the United States from fifteen to thirty-eight years. One Chinese female, age forty-two, who had been in the country for thirty-two years, was listed as heading her own household. An apparent house of prostitution consisted of nine white females. One, age thirty-six, was listed as head of household with the occupation of "lodging housekeeper." She had eight "lodgers," aged twenty to twenty-seven, all of whom were single, widowed, or divorced.[40]

Testimony in immigration documents sheds additional light on the residents at 566 Main.[41] While Wong Fee Lee owned the commercial properties, he delegated the responsibility of renting and collecting monies to a local insurance man, C. O. Gorder, who underwrote the fire policies on the structures and kept the premises rented. Wong Fee Lee reportedly knew a "house of ill-fame" and a gambling house were being conducted but was unconcerned as long as these activities were not affiliated with the Wing Tsue name and income. These documents, however, place the gambling operations and the house of ill fame at 564 Main.[42]

The 1905 South Dakota state census offers less information, showing two Chinese males, Wing Tsue, age sixty, and a nephew, Wong Bing Quong, age nineteen, living at 566 Main. Three years earlier, Wong Fee Lee and his family had traveled to China. All four daughters remained there to marry, while other family members came back at various times. The 1910 federal census confirms that Wong Fee Lee, his wife, and three sons between the ages of fifteen and twenty-six were again residing at 566 Main. Also in the household was an eighteen-year-old woman who was betrothed to one of the sons and residing with the family while she obtained her education. The building at 568 Main was rented to four Chinese males, and 564 was rented to two.[43]

With the 1915 South Dakota state census, a new generation of the Wong family appears. Wong Fee Lee was again listed as Wing Tsue, a seventy-four-year-old merchant. His wife was not listed. Nephew Wong Bing Quong was now twenty-nine years old and married, and Wong Fee Lee's youngest son, age twenty, was single. Wong Fee Lee's three small grandsons, a six-year-old born in China and a one-year-old

Altered by time and barely recognizable in 2001, the 1885 bazaar (566 Main), at right, and the 1896 rental property (568 Main) were the last two buildings of the Wing Tsue complex. Eileen French and Dan Taylor, Rapid City, S.Dak.

and a one-month-old born in South Dakota, were the children of his oldest son, Wong Hong Quong, age thirty, and his twenty-six-year-old wife.[44]

The federal census for 1920 is the last one showing Chinese residents at the Wing Tsue complex. Wong Fee Lee's nephew, now thirty-four and a long-time resident of Deadwood, lived at 566 Main with his wife, two sons, and a daughter, ages six, four, and two, all born in South Dakota. Wong Fee Lee's oldest son was there too, now thirty-six and working in the Deadwood post office. A photograph of the Wing Tsue store building at 566 Main Street taken in the same year shows the iron shutters that Wong Fee Lee had mounted, now fastened, symbolizing the close of an era. Wong Fee Lee had returned to China in 1919, and his sons also either returned to China or relocated to other cities in the United

States. In 1921, according to the *Black Hills Pioneer*, W. G. Ross had taken over the 1896 building to use as a glove factory.[45]

Over the next several decades, various businesses occupied the old Wing Tsue buildings in Chinatown, and in their last years, they stood vacant and somewhat neglected. Beginning in 2001, however, Deadwood's Chinatown gained attention both locally and nationally as archaeologists began to excavate properties on lower Main Street, discovering pristine deposits of artifacts that helped to illuminate the lives of Chinese immigrants. Funded by the City of Deadwood and the State Archaeological Research Center, a program of the South Dakota State Historical Society, the excavations continued until 2004. Today, archaeologists from the center continue the work of analyzing the numerous features and thousands of artifacts uncovered so that they may serve as a window on Chinese culture in the Black Hills.[46]

The Wong Family in Deadwood

Although Wong Fee Lee has long been well known to those familiar with Black Hills history, most of his one hundred or so descendants throughout the United States have only recently become aware of his role as a prominent Deadwood pioneer and merchant. Neither Wong Fee Lee, his wife Hal Shek, nor their eight children left behind any personal accounts or records of their lives in South Dakota. In deference to Chinese tradition, the couple's descendants refrained from asking their elders about their lives. Young people were to gain knowledge only by listening; direct inquiries were not considered proper. Kam Leung Wong, a grandson of Wong Fee Lee and Hal Shek, recalled seeing American Indian arrows displayed on the bookshelf at his childhood home in Canton, China, in the 1930s and hearing his grandmother's stories of "Yin-Jins" coming into the store to try to buy "fire water." He also told of his surprise years later, in 1945, when his father, Som Quong Wong, revealed that his cooking skills extended back to his youth in Deadwood, where he helped to roast whole pigs in Wong Fee Lee's store.[47]

The task of researching Chinese-American families is a complicated one. In Chinese tradition, as opposed to Western practice, an individual's surname comes first, meaning that two versions of a name may appear in documents. Phonetic spellings of Chinese names can also produce several variants of the same name, depending on the tran-

Dressed in their best attire, Wong Fee Lee and his family sat for a formal portrait in Deadwood in 1894. From left are King Que, King Sowe, Hal Shek holding infant Fay Juchs, Fay King standing before maid Shu Lin Lau, Fee Lee and toddler son Som Quong, and Hong Quong. Adams Museum, Deadwood, S.Dak.

scriber, as seen in the "Fay" or "Free" that occasionally appeared in Wong Fee Lee's name.[48] The common Chinese practice of addressing older relatives by their familial titles, such as "Paternal Grandmother," means that in some cases, descendants do not even know their ancestors' names. Also confusing is the tradition of using different names throughout one's lifetime. In addition to a given name, individuals may have a childhood name, a married name, and a nickname or variation on a formal name. Wong Fee Lee's store name, Wing Tsue, became such a well-known moniker for him in Deadwood that he adopted it as a second name, allowing its use in legal documents with his signature. Kam Leung Wong related that he did not hear the name Wing Tsue until he was twenty-three years old and visiting one of his parents' former

Deadwood High School classmates. When she remarked on how intrigued she had been with the items in "Dr. Wing Tsue's store," Kam Leung replied, "Who was Dr. Wing Tsue?"[49]

Family oral history relates that Wong Fee Lee, the third of four sons, was born sometime in the 1840s in the village of Bak Saar, Taishan (Toi San) County, in Guangdong (Kwangtung) Province of southern China. No other details of his childhood, upbringing, or lineage are known.[50] Events in Guangdong, however, undoubtedly played a role in his decision to journey to the United States as a young man. Years of war, political corruption, overpopulation, and famine had ravaged the southern Chinese countryside and left the inhabitants impoverished. By contrast, the provincial capital, the old port city of Guangzhou (Canton) was a hub of international commerce with ready connections to the outside world. With the discovery of gold in California in 1848, men from the region seized the chance to flee to Gum Shan, or "Gold Mountain." Others followed during the 1860s as work to complete the transcontinental railroad across the western United States accelerated.[51]

According to census information, Wong Fee Lee emigrated to the United States in 1863, although in an interview he placed his arrival on the West Coast in 1870. No ship's record has been found to confirm either date.[52] Nor is it known whether he followed the common practice of signing with a labor agency to gain money for the passage. Like many other men, he married before leaving China, a custom that was encouraged to ensure the flow of income back home. His wife, Wong Woo Shee, died in China around 1866 while he was in the United States. According to family oral history, Wong Fee Lee had a first son in China, Wong Loung Quong, born to another woman. He also adopted one of his brothers' sons, Wong Yuen Yum of Yin Ping village, and supported this nephew until the boy was able to work. Yuen Yum never came to the United States.[53]

What type of work Wong Fee Lee engaged in upon arriving on the West Coast is not known. Like many other Chinese immigrants, he may have worked in a job related to railroad construction, possibly as a laborer or, more likely given what is known of his personality and preferences, as a launderer or cook. Family lore holds that Wong served as a cook for several wagons of gold prospectors headed for the Black Hills. The group reportedly fought attackers, possibly Indians or bandits, along the way. The men arrived in Deadwood via Custer in 1876 and staked out a number of claims, which they divided up by drawing lots. Even the "Chinaman" who served as cook received a share as compensation for the dangers encountered in reaching the Black Hills. Wong Fee Lee reportedly received two claims. When gold was discovered on property next to one of the claims, he sold it in 1877 and made a hefty profit. Written documentation of this transaction has not been found, but records do show that Wong Fee Lee began purchasing property and established the Wing Tsue mercantile store in 1877.[54]

During his early years in Deadwood, Wong Fee Lee also fathered a son, Wong Wing Hui, born in 1879 or 1880. Both the mother, Wo She, and the child left Deadwood for China in the early 1880s. In 1899, Wong Wing Hui, then nineteen, successfully applied for readmittance to the United States in order to gain an American education. No information has been discovered to indicate that he ever returned to Deadwood. The 1920 federal census, however, shows a thirty-eight-year-old Wing Hui Wong living in Los Angeles, California, married and heading a household with two Chinese single males, including his brother, a twenty-five-year-old man named Tung Quang Wong.[55] Wong Fee Lee's youngest son was named Tong Quong. Born in late 1895 or early 1896, he would have been twenty-five at the time of the 1920 census.

Wong Fee Lee made the first of three trips back to China in the fall of 1882, likely leaving the Wing Tsue Bazaar in the care of his brother, Wong Bong, who was living with him in Deadwood at the time of the 1880 federal census.[56] "Wing Tsue, the Chinese merchant of lower Main Street, starts this morning for China," stated the *Black Hills Daily Times* for 10 October 1882. "After visiting he will return to Deadwood with his wife and children."[57] Wong Fee Lee boarded the steamer *Arabic* bound for Guangzhou on 31 October. The ship's records describe him as five feet, five inches tall, with "a wart on the back of his neck, a scar under his right eye, and two round marks on his forehead." Interestingly, he is listed as a cook.[58] According to his statements in later immigration interviews, Wong's first wife was deceased. What "wife" was he planning to bring back to Deadwood? At that time, it would not have been unusual for a Chinese man to have more than one wife, but no records have been found to indicate that such was the case with Wong Fee Lee. Perhaps he had told his acquaintances in Deadwood that he was returning to China with the intention of marrying. If so, who were the "children" he would be bringing back?

In May 1883, the *Black Hills Daily Times* reported: "Wing Tsue, the Chinese merchant who went home on a visit last fall, has been heard from. He has purchased a new wife, first class in every particular, paying $300. She will come to Deadwood with him this fall."[59] While in China, Wong Fee Lee did marry a new wife, Haw Shoog Gain, in Guangzhou. Family oral history holds that an adopted son came back to the United States with the couple. This son, Wong Loung Quong, was commonly referred to as "First Uncle" by the second generation of Wong Fee Lee's descendants, even though he was not considered a member of the immediate family. It was believed that he never went to Deadwood and later lived in San Francisco, where he worked in a pawnshop. The federal census for 1900 reveals a Quong Wong Leung, age twenty-seven, single, a salesman, residing in San Francisco. He had been born in China in 1872 and immigrated to the United States in 1883, the same year Wong Fee Lee returned. Family history also holds that Wong Loung Quong later married in China and had at least two sons there.[60] The *Black Hills Daily Times* for 19 August 1884 noted the arrival from Sidney, Nebraska, of "Wing Tsue, wife and child and two Chinamen."[61] Could this child be the adopted son Wong Loung Quong? If so, he would have been about twelve years old. The true identity of the child who arrived in Deadwood, however, remains a mystery.

Yet another mystery arises with the newspaper's 29 August announcement that "Wing Tsue, who recently arrived from China with a sure enough wife and family, enjoys the distinction of being the first Mongolian to add to the population of the Hills. . . . A son and heir was presented him by his better half yesterday morning. The little shaver is something of a curiosity, and as such attracts great attention."[62] This child is never mentioned again in either the newspaper, Wong Fee Lee's immigration interviews, or census data. In fact, the birth of a child to Wong Fee Lee and Haw Shoog in December, just four months later, is repeatedly documented in all three sources, indicating a probable case of mistaken identity in the newspaper's report of the August birth.

Haw Shoog, whose name was most often rendered as Hal Shek but also as Ho Sek, Haw Shee, Hoo Shee, and Hoy Toy, was twenty-one and pregnant when she arrived in Deadwood. Little has been written about her aside from a description in *Old Deadwood Days* by Estelline Bennett, who grew up in Deadwood as the daughter of Judge Granville G. Bennett. Recalling a visit to the Wong Fee Lee household on Chinese New Year, Bennett described the merchant's wife as "the loveliest bit of exquisite china I ever saw. . . . Her black hair was built in a high pyramid with gorgeous pins and combs. Her brilliant silk jacket and trousers were heavy with embroidery, and her tiny useless little feet were encased in embroidered satin shoes with wooden soles."[63] Bennett wrote that Hal Shek "spoke no English, but her gentle gracious manners and her courteous solicitude made us feel as if we had talked over all the polite topics of the day." As a married woman who appears to have followed the customs of Chinese society, she most likely led a protected life that revolved around the family.[64] Commenting on Hal Shek's visit to the Bennett family a few weeks later, Bennett wrote, "I am sure it was the only time she ever left her rich, close rooms."[65]

In December 1884, Hal Shek gave birth to the couple's first child, Wong Hong Quong, who was mistakenly identified as a girl. "The wife of Wing Tsue, the Chinese merchant and doctor, has presented him with a celestial girl baby," the *Black Hills Daily Times* reported, "the first one born in the Hills. The mother is the first respectable China woman in the Hills, and the only one."[66] As the child of a "respectable" Chinese pioneer family, Hong Quong could be acknowledged in polite society, where he became something of a novelty. The *Times* noted an outing taken when the child was three years old: "The first Chinese baby of the Hills, son of Wing Tsue, lower Main street merchant, walked up town yesterday, led by his sire. The biography of this family when written in English, will be interesting reading."[67]

Wong Hong Quong grew up attending the Deadwood public schools. After his father took the entire family to China in 1902 so that they could obtain a Chinese education, Hong Quong attended Queen's College in Hong Kong. He was married in Guangzhou in 1903 and in 1905 became the first of his siblings to return to Deadwood.[68] "Quong is a Deadwood boy, born and raised here," bragged the *Daily Pioneer-Times.* "He is 21 years old and an unusually bright young man. It is his father's intention now to send the boy to the state School of Mines at Rapid where he will learn the industry for which the Black Hills is famous." Hong Quong appeared to be a confident young man, voicing his opinion about the Chinese Exclusion Act and commenting on the Chinese boycott of American goods then underway, "The only way to break the boycott that I can see is to allow free Chinese immigration and that I am sure America could not or would not consent to."[69]

Wong Hong Quong enrolled at the South Dakota School of Mines and Technology for the 1907–1908 academic year, but family oral history holds that a bout with meningitis forced him to quit college. Over the next few years, he made other trips to China, where his wife had remained. In 1912, he was back in South Dakota, working in the Canton Bazaar in Hot Springs.[70] His wife and a son who had been born in China soon joined him, and the first of the second generation of Wong family members to be born in South Dakota appeared shortly thereafter. In March 1914, the *Deadwood Daily Pioneer-Times* announced: "Wing Tsue for the third time, became a grandfather Friday morning, when there was born to his son, Wong Hong Quong and the latter's wife, an eight pound son. The pioneer Deadwood Chinese merchant is properly happy and proud and yesterday handed out a bunch of fine cigars to his friends. His son, who was born in Deadwood thirty years ago, was married in China on one of his several visits there, to Chew Men, who is now known as Wong Chang See, who is 29 years old and the mother of his three sons, two of whom were born in China. She herself is a native of Canton, China, and a very estimable little lady. The new baby's name is Wong Yun Cherk."[71]

There is no indication that Hong Quong eventually took over the Wing Tsue business, although he remained in Deadwood after Wong Fee Lee returned to China permanently in 1919. In 1920, the federal census listed Hong Quong as living at 566 Main Street and working in the local post office. In 1922, he left Deadwood for El Paso, Texas, where he worked for the United States Immigration Service.[72]

The next two children born to Wong Fee Lee and Hal Shek were daughters: Wong King Sowe (also known as King Shiu or King Sue), born in March 1886, and Wong King Que, born in August 1887.[73] Both girls attended public school in Deadwood, accompanied the rest of the family to China in 1902, and were married there. They eventually returned to the United States but never settled in Deadwood.

Wong Fee Lee appears to have been a protective father, as revealed in a newspaper article written when his son and two daughters were all under the age of four. One of the children was invited to the house of playmate Jessie Belding, but, the newspaper reported, "Wing Tsue, thinking that the child would not go, consented, but when he discovered his mistake, endeavored to persuade it to return, but it would not, so to keep peace in the family he accompanied the young folks to Mr. Belding's residence, where the little Mongolian was so thoroughly entertained that the father could not induce it to leave, every attempt at taking resulting in a howling disturbance. So winsome was Jessie that her visitors were held the entire day, to the intense annoyance of Wing Tsue who would not leave his child alone."[74] Wong Fee Lee could

From left in this image of five of the Wong children taken around 1899 are King Sowe, Hong Quong, King Que, Tong Quong, and Som Quong. The boys appear to be wearing their hair in the traditional style, with the front of the head shaved and the rest gathered into a braid, or queue, at back. Centennial Archives, Deadwood Public Library, Deadwood, S.Dak.

be indulgent with his children, as well. When the narrow-gauge Deadwood Central Railroad began operations, Estelline Bennett recalled that Wong took his three small children on the initial run, "and they were so enchanted of the journey that they insisted upon going every day. Whereupon he detailed an old Chinaman to take them back and forth until they tired of the sport, but that wasn't for weeks."[75]

A second son, Wong Som Quong, was born in the summer of 1889.[76] "This makes four of this well-to-do and respected family born in Deadwood," stated the local newspaper in announcing the birth. "Wing Tsue is the principal Chinese Merchant and head of the strongest faction in Deadwood. He carries a $50,000 stock of goods, and in every particular is an excellent resident if not a full fledged citizen."[77]

In fact, Wong family members became well integrated into the Deadwood community even while maintaining their Chinese identity. At one point, Wong Fee Lee and Hal Shek appear to have considered a Catholic education for their children. "The two little boys of Wing Tsue's, the Chinese merchant, are attending the public school in this city," stated one item in the local newspaper. "It was at first intended to send them to the convent, but the Sisters refused to receive them unless they wore regular American trousers. The younger child was so small that no trousers could be found to fit him, and he was sent to school arrayed in his Chinese finery." Estelline Bennett also recalled that the Wong children went to Sunday School.[78]

Like his older siblings, Som Quong attended public school in Deadwood and went to China with the family in 1902. Six years later, in 1908, he became the second Wong child to return to the United States. Due to the Chinese Exclusion Act, reaching Deadwood proved to be more difficult than the ocean voyage from China. Som Quong had completed the paperwork he needed to enter the country through the port at Seattle, Washington, but had changed his plans upon learning that rooms in the city were in short supply. Instead, he disembarked at San Francisco, California, where immigration officials refused to admit him. By the time his father enlisted the help of Eben W. Martin, a Deadwood attorney and United States congressman from South Dakota, Som Quong had developed an eye infection that provided officials with additional grounds to decline his reentry. The following week, an immigration inspector from Denver arrived in Deadwood to investigate the young man's background and determined that he was indeed entitled to return. Wong Fee Lee, in turn, guaranteed that his son's eyes would be given immediate treatment.[79]

Within two weeks, Som Quong was back in Deadwood along with the young woman he would later marry—Yuet Ha Tang, "a very pretty little lady [who] seemed to be impressed with great wonder at every strange scene that presented itself," reported the *Daily Pioneer-Times*.[80] At the time of the 1910 federal census, both young people were living with Wong Fee Lee at 566 Main Street and attending Deadwood High School.[81]

In 1912, the newspaper carried the story of a "brutal assault" upon "one of the most popular and gentlemanly young men in the Deadwood high school." Som Quong had been beaten by "two half-intoxicated burlies from Lead" as he walked down Main Street on a Sunday night in April. According to the newspaper report: "Sam weighs about 100 pounds and the lightest of his assailants weighs no less than 160 pounds. The assault was absolutely without provocation." The pair later pled guilty to assault and battery, and each man was fined fifty dollars plus twenty-nine dollars in costs. The attack left Sam Quong confined to bed with a broken rib and numerous bruises about his head.[82]

Despite his injuries, Som Quong graduated from Deadwood High

Wong Fee Lee sold an impressive array of apothecaries in the Wing Tsue store. The two girls are likely Wong's daughters. Adams Museum, Deadwood, S.Dak.

School that spring. Yuet Ha Tang, or Anna, as she had become known, graduated in 1914.[83] Som Quong went on to study civil engineering and architecture at the University of Michigan in Ann Arbor, and Anna attended Oberlin College in Ohio followed by graduate studies in education at Columbia University in New York City. The pair married in New York in 1918. Within a few years, they returned to China, where Som Quong would head an engineering corporation and Anna would superintend a high school for girls.[84]

The next two children born to Wong Fee Lee and Hal Shek were daughters Wong Fay King, born in April 1891, and Wong Fay Juchs (Juck), born in October 1893. Both girls attended Deadwood public school before leaving with the family in 1902 for China, where they grew to adulthood and married their husbands. Fay King returned to the United States, but never to Deadwood. In December 1894, Wong

Fee Lee and Hal Shek had another baby who lived for approximately one month before dying on 30 January 1895.[85]

The couple's last son, Tong Quong, was born in Deadwood on 1 February 1896.[86] His birth prompted a lengthy newspaper article headlined "AN ORIENTAL EVENT. Chinese Quarters Growing—One of Deadwood's Curiosities Is an Exceptionally Americanized Chinese Family." The report provides insight into the family's everyday lives and their standing in the community:

> Deadwood numbers among her residents a most remarkable Chinese family. Wing Tsue is a Chinese merchant and doctor. He carries a large stock of costly Chinese fancy goods, teas, etc., does a good business and is making money. He is a peaceable, law-abiding man and is respected by the community. Eleven years ago Wing Tsue went to China and married one of Hong Kong's fair daughters and returned to Deadwood, where they have since resided and have a comfortable little frame house on the hillside back of his store, in Chinatown. The place is neat and has the appearance of the habitation of an American family of refined taste rather than of a heathen family. They have chickens, ducks, magpies, pigeons, pigs, dogs and cats about the premises, and all are given careful attention. Mrs. Tsue has house plants which she nurses with great care, and from them she derives pleasure. When Wing Tsue and his bride arrived in Deadwood they were given a very hospitable reception, in fact an American would consider it an ovation. Their Chinese friends gave them a big banquet, and made a big fuss over the bride, who was considered very pretty. During their eleven years of married life eight little Tsues have come to bless their happy home, the last one putting in an appearance yesterday morning. It was a boy. The last child before this one, which was born less than a year ago, died when a few days old. They now have seven children, and they range down in height like stairs with very narrow steps.
>
> The children appear to be the joy of their parents and are indulged to a greater extent than some of our American families, while at the same time they are carefully trained and taught. They are all exceedingly nicely behaved and some of the American children of this or any other city would do well to emulate them. Four of the children, the oldest ones, attend the public school and are prompt and punc-

tual. They can talk, read and write English fairly well and are quick to learn and remarkable for memory. They take a deep interest in their studies, even the smaller ones, and show a desire to learn. Their deportment is splendid and in this they always stand among the best in school. They have a very mild and rather retired disposition, never talk loud nor quarrel and we have never known them to be impudent nor be guilty of naughty tricks which as a rule young Americans are the originators of.

It is an interesting and novel sight to see these four Chinese children going to school. They walk along slowly, hand in hand, ranging down in size from the largest, a boy, strung out sort of obliquely, trudging along attending to their own business. Visitors to the city are very much amused at this odd sight, to them, though to the residents it is common and uninteresting. The children are always neatly and warmly dressed. The oldest boy is dressed in modern American clothes from hat to shoes and could scarcely be distinguished from some American boys excepting for his pig tail which is closely wrapped around his head, his flat face, almond-shaped eyes and yellow complexion. The smaller ones usually wear the garb of their native land, with blouse of blue, black or a dull purple China silk.

This family is one of the features of grotesque Deadwood, and it is a wonder to us that some magazine writer hasn't made it the subject of an interesting article. Wing Tsue and his happy little family are worthy people, and we congratulate him and his wife on the advent of their latest acquisition.[87]

A description of the christening of Tong Quong, who, like his eldest brother, was mistakenly identified as a girl, appeared in the newspaper the following month. The "momentous event in celestial society" took place at the elaborately decorated home of "Dr. and Mrs. Wing Tsue, the aristocratic couple of Deadwood's Chinese contingent." More than one hundred Chinese from throughout the Black Hills partook of an array of "the most costly and dainty dishes" and, in return, presented "elegant gifts" that included about four hundred dollars in gold coin.[88]

Tong Quong went to China with the rest of the family in 1902 and returned to Deadwood in 1912.[89] He appears to have worked for a time with his father. The Deadwood city directory for 1916 lists "Wing Tsue" as a physician affiliated with "Wing Tsue Lung & Co." and carries another listing for "Wong Tong Quong proprs, Chinese and Japanese Goods 566 Main."[90]

Following the birth of Tong Quong, another unnamed child was born to Wong Fee Lee and Hal Shek in April 1898; this child died eleven months later.[91] The couple's fifth daughter and last child, Wong Fay Lan (Lon), was born in January or February 1902.[92] Later that year, the family took her to China. Like her sisters, she never returned to Deadwood.

The two Wong children who died as infants in 1895 and 1899 were buried in Deadwood's Mount Moriah Cemetery. The first, listed as "Wing Tsue Child" in the cemetery records, was interred in lot no. 254 in South Potter's Field. The five-by-eight-foot lot cost five dollars. The Lawrence County mortuary records give no gender but indicate that the child was one month old; the undertaker was W. W. Osborn; no clergyman performed a service; the interment took place in Chinese ground; and the cause of death was bronchitis.[93] The second child, listed only as "Wing Tsue's infant," died at eleven months of age and was buried in lot 3 of section 6.[94] The newspaper noted only that the child had died following a short illness and was buried with "no funeral, the remains being taken in charge by C. H. Robinson and conveyed to the cemetery."[95] Although the practice of disinterring the remains of deceased individuals for return to China took place in Deadwood, it is not surprising that no records have been found to indicate that such was the case with the two children of Wong Fee Lee. Foremost, neither child was yet one year old. According to Chinese tradition, the death of one so young would not have called for any formal funeral or death rituals.[96] Furthermore, both children were born and died in Deadwood, where the family lived; there would have been no significance in returning disinterred remains to a village in China.

Wong Fee Lee and the Deadwood Community
As a businessman in the United States, Wong Fee Lee enjoyed a higher social standing than he would have in China, where, according to historian Iris Chang, merchants were relegated to the bottom of a "social hierarchy that valued the scholar, the official, and the farmer, but not the merchant." In the United States, by contrast, "financial success in business was worshipped." Throughout the American West, merchants occupied the most prominent positions in Chinese communi-

ties. Usually literate and bilingual, they often served as intermediaries between Chinese and European Americans. Their stores sold goods that appealed to both groups, providing meeting places for the cultures in addition to serving as social centers for the Chinese population of an area.[97]

Wong Fee Lee often played a leading role in organizing Chinese participation in Deadwood events as well as accommodating European Americans in Chinese cultural celebrations. The monetary contributions of Wing Tsue and other Chinese individuals to the 1879 Fourth of July fund earned recognition in the *Black Hills Daily Times* along with the comment, "Our heathen residents are not such a bad crowd after all, when there is a deficiency to be made up for any patriotic purpose." The Chinese donations continued over the years.[98] Wong Fee Lee, in turn, capitalized on the American holiday, as evidenced in an 1885 newspaper advertisement for "WING TSUE, DEALER IN Chinese Fireworks!" The advertisement promised "Special Prices given on 4th of July FIREWORKS" in addition to promoting "Silk Handkerchiefs, Ladies' Shawls, FRESH TEAS, Paper Napkins, China Clothes, Chinese Drugs and Medicines, Hanging Panels Hand Painted, Hand Painted Pictures, And everything usually kept in a Chinese Store."[99]

In 1888, Deadwood's Fourth of July celebration for the first time included Chinese participants in the parade and fire-hose competition. The Chinese parade entry, according to the *Black Hills Daily Pioneer*, was "certainly unique and interesting under the leadership of Wing Tsue, the Stewart of Chinatown, who carried aloft the flag of the Flowery Kingdom. Hi Kee, a rival in trade, also supported an elaborate banner of the distant realm. With the outfit appeared a Chinese 'band' capable of discordant sounds to a degree not thought possible."[100] The 1888 fire-hose race between the teams of Wing Tsue and Hi Kee for a fifty-dollar purse today remains a well-known event in Deadwood's Chinese history. The team of Hi Kee emerged victorious,[101] and the following year brought another race in which the "Laundrymen" won over the "Wing Tsue" team.[102]

The Chinese residents of Deadwood put much time and effort into their celebration of the Chinese New Year, an occasion occurring between late January and mid-February and one that European Americans viewed with great curiosity. Dwellings and stores were decorated for the event, guests feasted at New Year's Eve banquets, candles burned all day, and firecrackers exploded. The Chinese opened their

On 4 July 1888, the hose teams of Wong Fee Lee and Hi Kee, reputedly the only two Chinese hose teams in the United States, competed in a hub-and-hub race. State Archives Collection, South Dakota State Historical Society

homes and businesses to visitors who partook of the assorted "candies, nuts, fruits, cigars, liquors, and gifts" that loaded tables.[103] In 1881, the *Black Hills Daily Times* described the preparations being made in the store of Wong Fee Lee, where an "immense amount of wax candles are being manufactured for the occasion, of every conceivable size and appearance, ranging in price from a few dimes to dollars. An artist was busily engaged decorating them with beautiful rivers and transparent landscapes. All kinds of curious smelling fish, imported from the kingdom, were arranged around the room."[104]

The following year, the *Daily Times* ran a detailed description of the New Year closing ceremonies, an event "much fraught with roast pork, stew, rice, whisky and other Chinese delicacies," that Wong Fee Lee hosted to thank his customers for their patronage. "A Chinese orchestra consisting of four pieces turned out music, and oh, such music, too!," wrote the reporter, who was accompanied by interpreter Coon Sing. "Seventeen cats, ten dogs and a wagon load of coyotes all yelling at once couldn't equal it for noise. To add to the confusion, whole packages of firecrackers were being shot off, while a couple of Chinamen in the harshest of falsetto voices were singing songs, to which the "hiyahs" of the Sioux are as the sweetest of sounds." A lively game of forfeits, "in which a good deal of yelling was done," added to the hubbub:

> The players were divided into pairs facing each other across a table, on which stood vessels of Chinese whisky and eatables. At a signal each bared his arm and began to yell something which sounded to us as follows: "Faht suck, gad yah, ge-o-g, h-o-a-se, shack sow good." As each word was pronounced the players brought down their fists as though striking a blow, and opened one, or sometimes two or more fingers. This was kept up until some one made a mistake, when he was compelled to take a drink. Should a drop be spilled or left in the cup he was, as a forfeit, compelled to take three additional drinks. As their tanglefoot, made out of rice, is strong enough to take care of itself, the result was that many a poor Celestial was soon in a condition heretofore thought to be attainable only by his more civilized brethren. The racket was kept up until late into the night and a string of white men and ladies were continually going and coming from the strange sight.[105]

The colorful, exotic nature of Chinese funerals also turned these occasions into public events. As Estelline Bennett recalled in *Old Deadwood Days*, mourners "marched up Main Street and Sherman, and around up the steep Ingleside way that led to the cemetery on Mount Moriah, scattering little red pieces of paper with Chinese characters on them. They were intended to distract the attention of the devil away from the dead, some one told us, and we gathered them up with much interest."[106] In 1896, the local newspaper covered the ceremonies held for Ki You (Li How), who was buried in the Chinese section of Mount Moriah Cemetery. As a member of Deadwood's Chinese Masons, the deceased man

> was given all the elaborate ceremony and shown all the respect due one of his degree. The lodge and his countrymen observed their usual ceremony, which took place out in Main street, in front of Hi

Kee's place, before starting to the cemetery. The ceremony is in accordance with their ritual and consists of feeding the dead, prayers, singing, etc., and is very interesting if not impressive. The procession was headed by the Deadwood band, followed by the hearse, then the Masonic lodge in full regalia, headed by Wing Tsue and Hi Kee. About 20 Masons were in line and among them was Dr. H. A. L. von Wedelstaedt, who is said to be the only English speaking member of the Chinese Masonic lodge in this country. The cortege was quite formidable and was followed to the cemetery by probably 500 curious people while the sidewalks were crowded with men, women and children as the procession passed along.[107]

The Chinese Masons were well known in Deadwood as a benevolent society whose members took care of their countrymen, as demonstrated in the later case of Mak Gib, an elderly Chinese laundryman from the Portland mining camp who was clubbed to death during a robbery. Although the murdered man did not belong to the local chapter, Wong Fee Lee and his fellow masons from Deadwood nevertheless saw to it that he was buried at Mount Moriah Cemetery with his plot paid for by "Friends of Mac Gib."[108] The Chinese Masons were never listed as a purchaser of lots in the Mount Moriah Cemetery records, but the name of Wing Tsue, whether acting on his own or, possibly, as a representative of the masons or another group, is the most frequently listed Chinese purchaser of lots. He is listed eleven times as paying for burial plots for Chinese individuals, including Ki You, between 1895 and 1918. The majority of the lots are located in section A and section 6, as well as section 2 and South Potter's Field.[109]

Mount Moriah was also the site of two annual cultural traditions that are still practiced in China. On Qingming, or Tomb Sweeping Day, typically held in early April, the Chinese visit the graves of family members to clear away any underbrush or weeds that have grown up in the preceding months. Offerings of food, spirit money, and joss sticks (incense) are placed at the site to keep the deceased happy in the spiritual world, thus ensuring the ancestor's blessing for the family's continued growth and prosperity. Similar ceremonies mark the Hungry Ghost Festival, held in the seventh month of the lunar year, usually August. During this period, ghosts are said to wander the earth in search of food. Satisfying them with offerings of food, joss sticks, and the burning of fake money is meant to ensure good fortune.[110] One Sunday in

Will Make Your Eyes Dance!

The BARGAINS in
CHINESE GOODS
At WING TSUE'S STORE
Lower Main Street, Deadwood,

SURPASS EVERYTHING Ever offered in this country. All goods have been marked down to almost actual cost owing to overstock and the elegant and costly goods in his stock are being offered to the public very cheap. This stock consists of the very best

Ornamental Chinaware
Toilet and Perfume Cabinets
Embroidered Banners

SILK SHAWLS and **HANDKERCHIEFS** In various shapes, sizes, colors, and designs, guaranteed hand embroidered and superior to any other in this market.

CHOICE IMPORTED TEAS. These goods are going cheap and the public is invited to call and inspect them.

WING TSUE, Deadwood, So. Dak.

Wong Fee Lee and his partners advertised their business extensively.
This advertisement appeared in the 22 December 1894 Black Hills Daily
Times. *State Archives Collection, South Dakota State Historical Society*

August 1887 "was observed by the Chinese of this city by feeding the spirits of their deceased brethren," stated an account in the Deadwood newspaper. "Seven or eight hack loads of them went up to the cemetery and went through their peculiar ceremonies. Five roast hogs were taken and placed at the heads of the graves. Colored paper was burned, tea spilled on the ground, the priests bowed and shook themselves around for a time and then all came home, of course, bringing with them the roast hogs. There were two factions led by Wing Tsue and High Kee, each party keeping entirely aloof from the other, roast pigs and all."[111]

Hi Kee, the other prominent merchant in Deadwood's Chinatown, resided at 560 Main Street, not far from the Wong Fee Lee family and the Wing Tsue establishment.[112] The men's open opposition to each other, whether due to business competition or personality conflict, was well known and, perhaps, dramatized in the print media. In 1885, Hi Kee filed suit against Wong Fee Lee for credit owed in the amount of seventy dollars. Both men retained attorneys, and the court "swarmed with Chinamen as the suit progressed."[113] In the end, Justice Hall awarded ninety dollars in Hi Kee's favor. Wong gave notice that he planned to appeal.[114] In 1910, two Colorado newspapers carried an article claiming that rivalry between the two men was believed to have been behind the destruction of Deadwood's thirty-year-old Chinese Masonic Lodge, or Joss House, as well as the laundry business of Sam Wah. The fire that destroyed the structures began in some adjoining haymows and appeared to have been deliberately set.[115]

Despite their conflicts, Wong Fee Lee and Hi Kee were able to set differences aside and cooperate when doing so proved advantageous or profitable. The men invested in at least one mining enterprise together. In 1898, along with Hi Hop and Hi Young, they explored a claim on Sheeptail Divide. "The syndicate is well backed financially and mining operations are conducted after the most improved American methods," noted the *Engineering and Mining Journal*.[116] Wong Fee Lee and Hi Kee were also involved together in gambling enterprises. On 4 January 1892, both men were among several Black Hills Chinese arrested in a nighttime raid for illegal activities associated with games of chance. Hi Kee was listed as one of the sureties for Wong Fee Lee, and both men were released from jail on a five-hundred-dollar bond. They faced charges of sending and receiving lottery literature through the mail, an offense that carried a potential five-hundred-dollar fine and punishment of one year in prison. The men retained W. H. Parker and Granville G. Bennett as counsel, pled guilty, and paid fines of one hundred dollars each.[117]

Gambling was not the only vice with which Wong Fee Lee's name became associated. As early as 1877, the local newspaper reported on the prevalence of opium smoking in Deadwood,[118] and three years later Wong and a fellow Chinese, Quong Soon, were arrested for keeping opium smoke houses. Rumors also circulated that the pair had been charged with conspiring to have another Chinese man, Coon Sing, murdered for allegedly informing the authorities. Wong Fee Lee and Quong Soon refuted the stories in a letter to the editor of the *Black Hills Daily Times*: "Although Chinamen, we are not indifferent to the good opinion of the people of Deadwood. . . . The whole story about Coon Sing is a pure fabrication. It is true that we have been arrested on the unfounded charge of selling opium for smoking purposes, but this is all. . . . Until the trial is had, the law presumes that we are innocent of the charge, and we know that this presumption in our case is also true in fact. The public press ought not to seek to prejudice our case with the public in advance of the trial." Clearly not hesitant to assert their rights, the men concluded the letter with some insinuations of their own: "It may be that future events will show that some of the officers whom you commend for their zeal, are engaged in practices connected with this asserted sale of opium that would make any ordinary Chinaman a gentleman by comparison with them, even if everything they say were true."[119] In the trial that took place on 27 January 1880, Wong Fee Lee was found guilty and assessed a fine of twenty-five dollars plus costs.[120]

Opium continued to be a concern for Deadwood throughout the 1880s. Two years later, "Wing Tone" (Wing Tsue) and "Kong Soon" again faced charges of selling opium for smoking purposes, but the charges were dismissed on motion of the district attorney.[121] The prevalence of opium use contributed to negative sentiment against the Chinese during this period. "Recently the Chinamen have again commenced the open sale of the drug," reported the *Black Hills Daily Times* in late 1883. "If the sale of the drug to white people cannot be stopped, we will advocate and insist that these Chinamen will have to go. They are a curse to our people, and if they will not obey our laws they no longer have any rights among decent people. . . . [W]hen they assume their present attitude, we say 'they must go.'"[122]

In 1895, under revised city ordinances,[123] the Deadwood chief of police led a special force in raids on five "opium joints" in Chinatown, arresting eighteen Chinese and two white men. Attorney W. L. McLaughlin was retained by ten of the Chinese, with Wong Fee Lee posting bail for the men at two hundred dollars each. In the end, only the owners of four "smoke houses" went to trial, where they were convicted and fined up to seventy-five dollars plus costs. Officials hoped the raids and convictions would set an example and "cause the violators of the law in such cases to at least be more cautious about their business and not conduct [it] so open and bold."[124]

Although an opium den existed on Wong Fee Lee's property, his reputation as an upstanding Deadwood citizen remained largely intact. In fact, he may have been more closely associated in the public mind with opium as a medicinal rather than a recreational drug.[125] In any case, his associations with vice activities do not appear to have affected his ability to travel to or from China under the Chinese Exclusion Act. Nor do they appear to have restricted his ability to bring in the various business partners from China who worked for him over the years.

Historian Iris Chang has noted that, during the late 1800s and early 1900s, "the principals and shareholders in a Chinese business were relatives or were from the same district. They created a chain migration pattern as original settlers sent for relatives and neighbors to assist them in the continuation of businesses in specific areas."[126] An article in the *Deadwood Daily Pioneer-Times* in 1907 illustrates both this migration network and what the newspaper called "the peculiarity of the workings of the present immigration laws of this county." One of Wong Fee Lee's business partners was growing old and had a son whom he wanted to bring from China to take his place. With the help of Sol Star, then clerk of courts for Lawrence County, the man filed the necessary paperwork and sent for his son. At port in Washington State, immigration officials "plied him fast with questions which the boy answered as best he could understand. When asked whether he was the son of Wing Tsue's partner, he evidently did not comprehend the question and said 'no.'" He was then told that he could not enter the country, but he managed to get a wire sent to Wing Tsue, who "invoked the aid of his white friends," the newspaper continued. "The result was that the government had the boy held on the coast which is costing Wing Tsue 75 cents per day board, ordered an inspector and an interpreter to come here and investigate, their expenses to be paid by Wing Tsue or his partner and even yet there is no assurance that the boy will reach his destination."[127]

Wong Fee Lee had firsthand experience with the vagaries of the Chinese Exclusion Act beginning in early 1902. His brother and business partner, Wong Bong, had a son who had been born in Deadwood but had lived in Guangdong Province, China, since the age of three. When the young man, Wong Bing Quong (Wong Quinn), was seventeen, he returned to the United States but was detained in Port Townsend, Washington, on the grounds that neither the information on his passport nor his photograph matched his appearance. Authorities held Wong Bing Quong for several weeks while they conducted an investigation that involved interviewing Deadwood citizens, the submission of affidavits, and, ultimately, the intervention of Congressman Eben Martin. Wong

Bing Quong was finally released and allowed to return to Deadwood, where he attended school and lived and worked in Wong Fee Lee's store for several years.[128]

Wong Fee Lee's interventions did not always lead to the desired end. When one of his partners, Wong Yick Lai, traveled to China for a visit in 1910, he neglected to file the paperwork needed to facilitate his return to the United States.[129] Despite having lived in Deadwood for the previous twenty-one years, Wong Yick Lai was ultimately deported. The inspector sent to Deadwood to investigate the case reported: "There is a wide discrepancy on material points between the statements made by the applicant and those made by the manager (Wing Tsue) and assistant manager (Wong Mow). While the firm of Wing Tsue Co. is one of the best known in Deadwood, and I doubt if any man, white or Chinese, has a better standing among the business circles than Wong Fee Lee, when it comes to a matter of friends or relatives seeking admission to this country he is seemingly no better than the average Chinaman." Wong Fee Lee did not help matters when, according to the inspector, he "evidently had a suspicion that all was not well with the case and asked me if I could not fix the testimony in some way so that his partner could be admitted, saying that he would make it all right with me."[130]

In September 1902, Wong Fee Lee took his entire family back to Guangdong. The local newspaper reported that the parents and six children boarded the Burlington passenger train at the Deadwood depot, but, in fact, all eight children made the journey. According to the newspaper article, Wong Fee Lee, Hal Shek, and the youngest child were to remain abroad for a year before returning to Deadwood. "The two oldest girls will remain in China and take care of the other children," the article stated. "It may be several years before they again see their Deadwood friends. The young ladies have been favorites ever since they attended the public schools of Deadwood, and number their friends only by the list of their acquaintances, and all of them are sorry to see the young ladies leave. Both are bright girls, and both are just as charming as they are bright, while their brothers are well liked by all who know them."[131] Wong Fee Lee returned alone to Deadwood the following year, while the rest of the family remained in China, where the children were educated in Chinese language and history. Little is known about how they adjusted to their new homeland, but family oral history suggests that the older children, having grown up in Deadwood, had a

IN THE MATTER OF THE APPLICATION OF WONG FREE LEE,
sometimes known as Wing Tsue, for permission to go to China and return to the United States.

STATE OF SOUTH DAKOTA ）
                 ） SS
COUNTY OF LAWRENCE. ）

                             Wong Free Lee being first duly
sworn deposes and says that he is a resi-
demt of Deadwood, South Dakota, United States
of America, and has resided in said city for
more than twenty years last past; that he
is engaged in business as a Chinese merchant,
on Lower Main Street, in the City of Deadwood, being the presidemt of the Chinese
Mercantile firm known as the Wing Tsue Co.,
and that he is sometimes known as, and called
Wing Tsue, by reason of his being a member of
said firm; that he is a married man, and
his family, besides his wife, includes eight
children, all of whom are citizens of the
United States, having been born in the City
of Deadwood; that he is making this application at the present time, intending to
take his wife and children back with him to
China, and leave them in China for some
time so as to have them educated in the
Chinese language; that he himself desires
to be absent for about two years, when he
desires to return to the United States, and
resume charge of his business as the head of the Wing Tsue mercantile firm; that he is a merchant and recognized as such by the citizens of Deadwood, and that he has not performed any manual labor
for more than ten years past, his time having been given to the
management of his mercantile business; that he is also registered

*Under the Chinese Exclusion Act, Wong Fee Lee and Hal Shek were required
to submit their photographs with this application for their 1902 visit
to China. National Archives, Pacific Alaska Region, Seattle, Wash.*

difficult time. All of the sons, but none of the daughters, would eventually return to Deadwood, although none settled there permanently.

Wong Fee Lee departed for the United States from the Port of Hong Kong aboard the SS *Shawmut* and arrived at the Port of Tacoma, Washington, on 11 December 1903. Before departing for China the previous year, he had prepared for his return by filing paperwork with the collector of customs in Port Townsend, Washington. Testifying on his behalf were several prominent Deadwood citizens: attorney William S. Elder, circuit court clerk Sol Star, postmaster John Baker, hardware merchants John Wilson and George V. Ayres, furniture dealer Sam Schwarzwald, American National Bank cashier N. E. Franklin, wholesale grocer W. E. Shluws, Mayor E. McDonald, and First National Bank cashier D. McPherson.[132]

Despite these preparations and his previous experience with the Chinese Exclusion Act, Wong Fee Lee found himself detained at Port Townsend for nearly two months while a special investigator visited Deadwood to verify that he was, in fact, a merchant and not a common laborer. Among the documents generated by the special inspector's investigation were additional sworn statements from seven Deadwood citizens, including general insurance agent C. O. Gorder, attesting to Wong Fee Lee's honorable character and the fact that he owned and managed legitimate business interests valued at between ten and fifteen thousand dollars. As a partner in the Wing Tsue firm and the keeper of the store, Wong Bing Quong, Wong Fee Lee's nephew, was also interviewed. He verified that the mercantile business occupied the first floor, cellar, and back storehouse at 566 Main Street, as well as the adjoining properties of 564, 564½, 568, and 568½ Main Street. Finally, three Chinese renters of Wong Fee Lee properties were interviewed: Sen Lee, who ran his own gambling business out of 568 Main Street; Di Sing, who had a house of ill-fame at 564 Main Street; and Wong Hoi, who conducted a gambling business at 564½ Main Street.[133] The inspector concluded that Wong Fee Lee had a "legitimate mercantile business" and "in view of the statements made by the white witnesses" was indeed a "bona fide merchant."[134]

During Wong Fee Lee's detention, the *Deadwood Daily Pioneer-Times* kept residents apprised of the case and offered its own assessment of the situation. "The Chinese are the only people in the world to whom the United States is not a free country," stated one editorial. "To every other nation on earth we open our doors and extend a welcome.

But, nearly seventeen years ago, a cry arose along the Pacific coast that the 'Chinese must go.' It was a cry so loud, so vehement, that all the other states in the Union listened. . . . If there have been any good effects from the Geary law, they are not apparent. The bad ones are numerous."[135] The writer went on to chronicle Wong Fee Lee's contributions to the community over the previous quarter century and to condemn a system that would allow "a Kamschatan or a Fiji Islander or any other old nationality [to] come into the country and make himself generally obnoxious. He could send all his money back to the old country if he wanted to, and he could spend his time stirring up riot and rebellion, but he could still come and go as he pleased." In contrast to depictions of Chinese immigrants written earlier in Deadwood's history, the writer concluded: "The Chinaman is always a law-abiding citizen. The only crime he is ever arrested for is running an opium joint and this is not often. He doesn't murder or steal and is never guilty of disorderly conduct. He is always a competent man in his business whether that be running a restaurant, a laundry, or a Chinese bazaar. If he says he can cook and do general house work, the maid-weary house-keeper knows before she tries him that she has secured a jewel. Yet he alone of all the world, is made the object of an exclusion act."[136]

On 5 February 1904, the *Daily Pioneer-Times* reported that Sol Star had received word of Wong Fee Lee's release, due, in part, to pressure from both Star and Congressman Martin.[137] Wong immediately left for Deadwood, where he arrived on 7 February. The newspaper reported that the merchant was happy to be back and "says that he was not afraid of being deported as he had too many good friends in Deadwood." Wong related that he had been one of approximately one hundred Chinese held at the Port Townsend customs house, where the agents "run things about to suit themselves," but that he had been treated courteously. At the time he was freed, all but thirty had been given their passports and allowed to proceed.[138]

In the years after he returned to Deadwood, Wong Fee Lee continued to operate his business enterprises with the help of his sons, members of his extended family, and other partners. By 1910, the Chinese population of Deadwood had declined to forty,[139] and Wong Fee Lee and the Wing Tsue Bazaar were becoming remnants of an earlier era. In the spring of 1912, the community marked the seventieth birthday of the "pioneer Chinese merchant of Deadwood" with a celebration. "He will receive the congratulations to which a good citizen, a devoted father and an industrious booster for the Black Hills is entitled," stated the *Daily Pioneer-Times*. "He is a member of the Society of Black Hills Pioneers,[140] having come to Deadwood in 1876, [and] he has stuck to the town through all its varying fortunes and has devoted much of his wealth to the development of the mining industry of the Black Hills. His children have been educated in the public schools of Deadwood and are a credit to their parents and the city." The newspaper also made note of Wong's support for the Chinese Revolution, which had overthrown Manchu rule the previous year: "Always a believer in the United States and its institutions, Wing Tsue has been an advocate of revolution in his native land. He is an upholder of the newly created republic there and has been a liberal contributor to the funds that made the revolt successful."[141]

By 1915, due to the declining economy and dwindling population of Deadwood, Wong Fee Lee faced a troubled financial situation. He defaulted on his mortgage, and the First National Bank purchased the Wing Tsue properties for a total of $1055.10.[142] The merchant continued, however, to carry on with his business at the same location, renting the buildings he had formerly owned.

In January 1918, Wong Fee Lee suffered a "slight stroke of paralysis" while attending the annual meeting of the Society of Black Hills Pioneers, but he was reportedly doing well, "thanks to the many friends who visited him."[143] Within days, his sons Som Quong, attending the University of Michigan, and Hong Quong, in business in Mobridge, South Dakota, along with Som Quong's fiancée Anna Tang, attending Columbia University in New York, returned to Deadwood to attend to Wong Fee Lee's recovery.[144] The following year, friends of Wong Fee Lee gathered at the Deadwood train depot "to bid him goodbye and to wish him a pleasant time" as he left to spend the summer in Los Angeles in the hope of regaining his health.[145] He then planned to make a short visit to China and return to the United States. Two and a half years after leaving Deadwood, however, Wong Fee Lee passed away in Guangzhou.[146]

The *Deadwood Daily Pioneer-Times* eulogized Wong, who had arrived with the gold prospectors and stayed to build a life in the Black Hills, as "a man of many accomplishments, shrewd in business and a patriotic citizen of his adopted country. . . . He was a man whose word was his bond, scrupulously honest, a contributor to every charity which appealed to him, free and generous, a heavy purchaser of liberty bonds and a contributor to every enterprise that would help Deadwood. He was held in high esteem by everyone of the old time residents of Deadwood and the Hills, and there will be many who will regret to learn of his passing."[147]

Wong Fee Lee was buried in Guangzhou, where his grave was marked with the name Fe Ming Wong. According to family oral history, the site was later destroyed by members of the Communist Party. Today, the only memorial to the Chinese merchant who arrived with the gold prospectors and stayed to become an integral part of the Deadwood community lies in the written record of his life and of the Wing Tsue properties that once stood on lower Main Street.

NOTES

1. Several works have treated the Chinese in the Black Hills, including, most recently, Liping Zhu and Rose Estep Fosha, *Ethnic Oasis: The Chinese in the Black Hills* (Pierre: South Dakota State Historical Society Press, 2004). *See also* Mildred Fielder, *The Chinese in the Black Hills* (Lead, S.Dak.: Bonanza Trails Publications, 1972); Bob Lee, ed., *Gold, Gals, Guns, Guts* (Pierre: South Dakota State Historical Society Press, 2004); Watson Parker, *Gold in the Black Hills* (Pierre: South Dakota State Historical Society Press, 2003); Joe Sulentic, *Deadwood Gulch: The Last Chinatown* (Deadwood, S.Dak.: By the Author, 1975); Daniel Liestman, "The Chinese in the Black Hills, 1876–1932," *Journal of the West* 27 (Jan. 1988): 74–83; and Grant K. Anderson, "Deadwood's Chinatown," *South Dakota History* 5 (Summer 1975): 266–85. For Wong Fee Lee specifically, *see* Gregory J. Nedved, "Wong Wing Tsue and Deadwood's Chinatown in the Gold Rush Years," *Chinese American Forum* 5 (Apr. 1990): 8–14, and Beatrice Wong and LeRoy Wong, "Fee Lee Wong: Adventurer, Sojourner, Prospector, Businessman, Physician, and Family Man," in *Society of Black Hills Pioneers, Volume 2, 1876–2004* ([St. Onge, S.Dak.]: Society of Black Hills Pioneers, 2004), pp. 41–56.

2. For example, A. Dudley Gardner et al., "Women and Children in the Evanston Chinatown," *Wyoming Archaeologist* 48 (Fall 2004): 21, note that Chinese communities in the West were overwhelmingly male, and opportunities for studying locations where women, children, and families lived are rare.

3. Deadwood experienced several disasters, especially fires and floods in the early years, that robbed historians of valuable documentation. Census records have also been lost, leaving a twenty-year void between 1880 and 1900, a critical period in the development of Deadwood and its Chinatown.

4. *Black Hills Daily Times*, 14 Apr. 1877; *Black Hills Pioneer*, 26 May 1877; *Black Hills Champion*, 13 Aug. 1877; *Cheyenne* (Wyo.) *Leader*, 6 Feb. 1876; *Black Hills Weekly Pioneer*, 30 June 1877.

5. *Deadwood Daily Pioneer-Times*, 23 Oct. 1921; Statement of Wong Fee Lee, 23 Mar. 1909, Chu Hip Chinese Exclusion Act Case File, RS 2439, Records of the District Courts of the United States, Record Group (RG) 21, National Archives and Records Administration (NARA)-Pacific Alaska Region, (PAR), Seattle, Wash.; Interview of Sam Schwarzwald, 14 Jan. 1904, Wong Free Lee Chinese Exclusion Act Case File, Box 12, File RS 406, Records of the Immigration and Naturalization Service, RG 85, NARA-PAR.

6. Lawrence County, S.Dak., Record of Deeds, vol. 4, p. 232, Lawrence County Courthouse, Deadwood, S.Dak. Elizabeth, Elizabethtown, and Chinatown are all references to lower Main Street prior to its incorporation into Deadwood's city limits.

7. Liping Zhu, "Ethnic Oasis: Chinese Immigrants in the Frontier Black Hills," in *Ethnic Oasis: The Chinese in the Black Hills*, p. 10. Also located on lower Main Street were numerous saloons, gambling houses, brothels, and theaters, earning this section of Deadwood the nickname "Badlands."

8. J. M. Wolfe, *Wolfe's Mercantile Guide, Gazetteer, and Business Directory of Cities, Towns, . . .Located upon the Lines of the Following Named Railroads: Union Pacific, Omaha & Northwestern, . . . and Towns in the Black Hills* (Omaha, Nebr.: Omaha Republican Book & Job Printing House, 1878). The business listings for Deadwood, transcribed by Joy Fisher, are available at *USGenWeb*, files .usgwarchives.net/sd/lawrence/business/deadwood-1878.txt.

9. Frank Stewart Howe, *Deadwood Doctor* ([Deadwood, S.Dak.: By the Author, 1944]), p. 37.

10. *Black Hills Daily Times*, 7 Mar., 29 Apr., 15 June 1878; *Black Hills Daily Pioneer*, 7 Mar., 11 Apr., 16 June 1878.

11. Interview of Kam Leung Wong and Kam Cheung Wong, Deadwood, S.Dak., by Raul Ponce de Leon, 22 May 1992, unpaged transcript, Deadwood Public Library, Deadwood, S.Dak. Kam Leung Wong also explained the meaning of his grandfather's given name: "'*Fe*' means something of a 'shining light.' '*Lee*' is something like 'profitable.' That's his name. '*Wong*' means 'yellow.' Yellow color."

12. Manuscript Population Schedule (MPS), Deadwood, Lawrence County, D.T., in U.S., Department of the Interior, Office of the Census, *Tenth Census of the United States, 1880*, National Archives (NA) Microfilm Publication (MP) T9, roll 113, sheet 248.

13. Lawrence County, Record of Deeds, vol. 19, p. 505.

14. Haynes's 1877 view of Chinatown can be found in the Haynes Foundation

Collection, Montana Historical Society, Helena. For the various maps of Deadwood produced throughout the years, *see* Deadwood, S.Dak., 1885, 1891, 1897, 1903, 1909, 1948, Sanborn Fire Insurance Maps, State Archives Collection, South Dakota State Historical Society, Pierre.

15. *Black Hills Daily Times*, 13 Feb. 1885.

16. Ibid., 2, 15 Oct. 1879. Organized anti-Chinese sentiment had flared briefly in the Black Hills in 1878, prompted by decreasing placer-mine yields and growing sentiment nationally against Chinese workers. A local branch of the anti-Chinese Caucasian League and Miners' Union committed a few acts of violence in 1878, but the movement quickly faded in the Black Hills. *Black Hills Daily Times*, 26 Feb., 5, 7 Mar. 1878.

17. *Black Hills Daily Times*, 14 Nov. 1879. A "fireproof" could be a cellar or warehouse, attached to or detached from another structure. It was typically made of brick or stone and could be covered with dirt to protect the contents from fire.

18. Ibid., 24 May 1883.

19. Lawrence County, Record of Deeds, vol. 19, p. 492.

20. *Black Hills Daily Times*, 25 July 1883. Two of the stone fireproofs are evident on the 1891 Sanborn map, one behind the Wing Tsue store.

21. Ibid., 13 Feb. 1885; *Black Hills Pioneer*, 5 June 1883.

22. *Black Hills Daily Times*, 13 Feb. 1885.

23. Ibid., 25 Mar. 1886. *See also Black Hills Daily Times*, 14 Feb. 1885. The water-main extension to Chinatown was significant to Wong Fee Lee. He handed the story down to his son Som Quong, who then passed it on to his son Kam Leung, who had his photograph taken next to the fire hydrant in front of the Wing Tsue building in 1992.

24. *Black Hills Daily Times*, 14 Feb., 7 Apr. 1885.

25. Statement of Wong Yick Lai, 19 Aug. 1915, Wong Yick Lai Chinese Exclusion Act Case File, 14586/8-30, RG 21, NARA-Pacific Region (PR), San Bruno, Calif.

26. Ibid.

27. *Black Hills Daily Times*, 8 July 1888.

28. *Deadwood Daily Pioneer*, 3 Oct. 1896. A clue to the identity of the contractor is gleaned from testimony in the immigration records of Wong Fee Lee, where Sam Schwarzwald, known as "Hoodoo Sam" in the Chinese community, claims, "I recommended [the] contractor who did the work." Schwarzwald Furniture Company on Main Street had a new two-story brick structure built in 1895, and the same builder may have constructed the Wong Fee Lee building. Interview of Sam Schwarzwald, 14 Jan. 1914.

29. *Deadwood Daily Pioneer*, 16 Oct. 1896.

30. Ibid., 9 Dec. 1896.

31. Ibid., 1 Jan. 1897.

32. Jackson's photograph of Deadwood in 1900 (CHS.J3218) can be found in the William Henry Jackson Collection, Colorado Historical Society, Denver.

33. Statement of Wong Fee Lee, 7 May 1898, Chee Hip Chinese Exclusion Act Case File, 14297, RG 21, NARA-PAR; *Black Hills Daily Times*, 1 June 1878, 12 Sept. 1879, 7 Sept. 1882, 22 Mar. 1883, 2 Sept. 1884, 30 Aug. 1887, 5 Apr. 1891.

34. *Black Hills Daily Times*, 5 Aug. 1890; *Deadwood Daily Pioneer-Times*, 13 Oct. 1905.

35. Lawrence County, Record of Deeds, vol. 75, p. 444.

36. *Rapid City Daily Journal*, 15 Jan. 1938.

37. For an in-depth examination of the Chinese Exclusion Act, *see* Andrew Gyory, *Closing the Gate: Race, Politics, and the Chinese Exclusion Act* (Chapel Hill: University of North Carolina Press, 1998).

38. Statement of Wong Fee Lee, 7 May 1898; Statement Exhibit A, 23 Mar. 1909, Chu Hip Chinese Exclusion Act Case File; Interview of Wong Fee Lee, 13 Dec. 1912, Wong Tong Quong Chinese Exclusion Act Case File, Box 441, File 7030/992, RG 85, NARA-PAR; Statement of Wong Yick Lai, 19 Aug. 1915; *Black Hills Mining Review* 4 (15 Aug. 1898): 4; Lawrence County, Mining Deed Record, bk. 160, p. 534, Lawrence County Courthouse.

39. MPS, Deadwood, in *Twelfth Census* (1900), NA, MP T623, roll 1551, sheet 13. The census taker likely collected the information from Wong Fee Lee at his store.

40. Ibid.

41. Ironically, while these documents were collected for the purpose of discrimination, the information they contain is now considered a historical and genealogical treasure.

42. Interviews of C. O. Gorder, 15 Jan. 1904, Wong Hoi, 15 Jan. 1904, and Di Sing, 15 Jan. 1904, all in Wong Free Lee Chinese Exclusion Act Case File.

43. South Dakota, Second State Census, 1905, State Archives Collection, SDSHS; MPS, Deadwood, S.Dak., in *Thirteenth Census* (1910), NA, MP T624, roll 1483, sheet 3B. In contrast to census information, Wong family history holds that Wong Fee Lee's wife did not return to the United States after the 1902 trip to China. She died in Hong Kong in 1940 at the age of seventy-eight. Wong and Wong, "Fee Lee Wong," p. 56.

44. South Dakota, Third State Census, 1915, SDSHS. According to other sources, the two oldest boys were born in China. *See Deadwood Daily Pioneer-Times*, 1 Mar. 1914; Interview of Wong Hong Quong, 19 Dec. 1918, Cheung Siu Man Chinese Exclusion Act Case File, Box 1206, Case 55100/886, RG 85, NARA-PAR.

45. MPS, Deadwood, S.Dak., in *Fourteenth Census* (1920), NA, MP T625, roll 1721, sheet 2A; *Deadwood Daily Pioneer-Times*, 16 Aug. 1921.

46. For a summary of the Deadwood Chinatown excavations, *see* Zhu and Fosha, *Ethnic Oasis*, pp. 330–62.

47. Recollections of Kam Leung Wong (untitled), n.d., Edith C. Wong Collection, San Luis Obispo, Calif.

48. Ironically, Wong's Chinese Exclusion Act file carries the name "Wong Free Lee." Throughout this article, common variant spellings appear in parentheses.

49. Recollections of Kam Leung Wong.

50. No documentation of Wong Fee Lee's birth in China has been found. All United States records are based on Wong's own reports, which list his birth anywhere from 1841 to 1846. For example, his year of birth appears as 1841 in the 1880 census (*Tenth Census*, roll 113, sheet 248), 1846 in the 1900 census (*Twelfth Census*, roll 1551, sheet 13), 1845 in the 1905 South Dakota census, 1842 in the 1910 census (*Thirteenth Census*, roll 1483, sheet 3B), and 1841 in the 1915 state census. The *Deadwood Daily Pioneer-Times* report of Wong's seventieth birthday celebration in its 6 April 1912 issue indicates a birth date of 1842. In 1903 immigration interview, Wong gave his birth year as about 1845, while another interview in 1912 gave the date as 1842, specifying his place of birth as Yen Ping village, Canton, China. Interview of Wong Free Lee, 11 Dec. 1903; Interview of Wong Fee Lee, 13 Dec. 1912.

51. Iris Chang, *The Chinese in America: A Narrative History* (New York: Viking, 2003), pp. 10–19.

52. The 1900 federal census lists Wong Fee Lee as immigrating to the United States in 1870. He later claimed that he had traveled alone from China to San Francisco in July–August 1863. *Twelfth Census*, roll 1551, sheet 13; Interview of Wong Fee Lee, 13 Dec. 1912.

53. Chang, *Chinese in America*, pp. 18–19; Interview of Wong Fee Lee, 13 Dec. 1912.

54. Chu Hip Chinese Exclusion Act Case File; Interview of Wong Free Lee, 11 Dec. 1903.

55. Wong Wing Hui Chinese Exclusion Act Case File, 15001, Wong, Wing Hui (6008), RG 21, NARA-PAR; Los Angeles Assembly District 65, Los Angeles, Calif., in *Fourteenth Census*, roll 109, sheet 34A. Family history also acknowledges a first son who did not have the same mother as the other eight children who were born in Deadwood.

56. *Tenth Census*, roll 113, frame 216.

57. *Black Hills Daily Times*, 10 Oct. 1882.

58. Nedved, "Wong Wing Tsue and Deadwood's Chinatown," p. 10.

59. *Black Hills Daily Times*, 3 May 1883.

60. Interview of Kam Leung Wong and Kam Cheung Wong; San Francisco, San Francisco County, Calif., in *Twelfth Census*, roll 107, sheet 5B.

61. *Black Hills Daily Times*, 19 Aug. 1884.

62. Ibid., 29 Aug. 1884.

63. Bennett, *Old Deadwood Days* (New York: J. H. Sears, 1928), pp. 29–30. In his 13 December 1912 interview, Wong claimed that his wife did not have bound feet.

64. Chang, *Chinese in America*, pp. 89–92.

65. Bennett, *Old Deadwood Days*, p. 30.

66. *Black Hills Daily Times*, 15 Jan. 1885. While the newspaper reported a January birth date, the 1910 federal census lists Wong Hong Quong's date of birth as December 1884. *Twelfth Census*, roll 1551, sheet 13. Confusion over the birthdates of all of Wong Fee Lee's children also arises from the difference in the Chinese solar/lunar calendar and the Gregorian calendar. In his 13 December 1912 interview, Wong stated that Hong Quong was born in "KS 10-11th month," translated there as Dec. 1884–Jan. 1885.

67. *Black Hills Daily Times*, 24 July 1887.

68. *Deadwood Daily Pioneer-Times*, 9 Feb. 1904, 16 Dec. 1905.

69. *Deadwood Daily Pioneer-Times*, 22 Dec. 1905.

70. Letter from William W. Jones, Registrar, South Dakota School of Mines & Technology, Rapid City, S.Dak., n.d., Edith C. Wong Collection; *Deadwood Daily Pioneer-Times*, 17 July, 17 Aug. 1909, 20 May 1911; interview of Wong Hong Quong, 13 Dec. 1912, Wong Tong Quong Chinese Exclusion Act Case File.

71. *Deadwood Daily Pioneer-Times*, 1 Mar. 1914.

72. *Fourteenth Census*, roll 1721, sheet 2A. The second generation of Wong family members referred to Hong Quong as "Second Uncle" (Wong Fee Lee's adopted son Loung Quong Wong was "First Uncle). The siblings born after Hong Quong were then known as "Third Uncle," "First Aunt," and so on.

73. *Twelfth Census*, roll 1551, sheet 13. In his 13 December 1912 interview, Wong Fee Lee stated that "King Sow" was born in "KS 12-4th month," translated as May 1886, and "King Gue" was born "KS 13-8th month," translated as September–October 1887.

74. *Black Hills Daily Times*, 22 Apr. 1888.

75. Bennett, *Old Deadwood Days*, pp. 288–89. The *Black Hills Weekly Times* for 16 March 1889 corroborates Bennett's account, noting: "Wing Tsue's trio of children have become infatuated with the steam cars. For the curiosity of the thing he

took them to Lead one day, and now they want to go every day. A dry nurse in the form of a superannuated Chinaman took them up yesterday."

76. The *Black Hills Daily Times* for 21 July 1889 announced the birth date as 16 July, but family history holds that Som Quong was born 20 June 1889. In his 13 December 1912 interview, Wong Fee Lee stated that his son was born "KS 15, 6th month" translated as June–July 1889. *See also Twelfth Census*, roll 1551, sheet 13.

77. *Black Hills Daily Times*, 21 July 1889.

78. *Deadwood Daily Pioneer*, 15 Sept. 1891. *See also* Bennett, *Old Deadwood Days*, p. 30.

79. *Deadwood Daily Pioneer-Times*, 29 Aug. 1908.

80. Ibid., 11, 12, Sept. 1908. According to family history, Yuet Ha Tang was born 17 October 1895 in Maui, Hawaii. Her father, Yum Nam Tang, left China for Maui in 1860. He remained there until he joined the Chinese revolution against the Manchus, under the leadership of Sun Yat-sen. Yuet Ha Tang was a godchild of Sun Yat-sen.

81. *Thirteenth Census*, roll 1483, sheet 3B.

82. *Deadwood Daily Pioneer-Times*, 30 Apr. 1912.

83. Ibid., 5 June 1914; *Deadwood Weekly Pioneer-Times*, 27 Oct. 1921.

84. *Deadwood Daily Pioneer-Times*, 23 Oct. 1921; *Deadwood Weekly Pioneer-Times*, 27 Oct. 1921.

85. *Twelfth Census*, roll 1551, sheet 13. In his 13 December 1912 interview, Wong Fee Lee stated that "Fee King" was born "KS 17, 3rd month" translated as April–May 1891, and "Fee Juk" in "KS 18, 8th month," translated as September–October 1892.

86. *Deadwood Daily Pioneer*, 2 Feb. 1896. The birth date listed in *Twelfth Census*, roll 1551, sheet 13, is December 1895. According to Wong Fee Lee's 13 December 1912 interview, Tong Quong was born "KS 21, 12th month, 20th day," translated as 3 Feb. 1896.

87. *Black Hills Daily Times*, 2 Feb. 1896.

88. Ibid., 3 Mar. 1896.

89. Interview of Wong Tong Quong, 13 Dec. 1912.

90. Joy Fisher, "Deadwood, Lawrence Co., SD–1916 Business Directory," transcribed from *Northwestern Gazetteer and Business Directory*, vol. 20 (R. L. Polk Co.), files.usgwarchives.org/sd/lawrence/business/dead1916.txt.

91. *Black Hills Daily Times*, 20 Mar. 1899.

92. In his 13 December 1912 interview, Wong Fee Lee stated that "Fee Lon" was born "KS 27, 12th month," translated as January–February 1902.

93. Record Book of Deadwood Cemetery Association, Microfilm 1825, p. 218, State Archives Collection, SDSHS; Lawrence County, Mortuary Records, 30 Jan. 1895, Lawrence County Courthouse; *Black Hills Daily Times*, 31 Jan. 1895. Entries in the Record Book are handwritten, with variable legibility; what appears as lot no. 264 is actually lot no. 254, as verified in Lawrence County, Record of Deaths, Dakota Record of Deaths, Lawrence County Courthouse, as well as the cemetery lot map. South Potter's Field ends with lot no. 254; lot no. 264 is nonexistent. Note that Sulentic's *Deadwood Gulch*, p. 85, errs in reporting the cause of death for this child as typhoid fever, with the body removed 14 September 1904.

94. Record Book of Deadwood Cemetery Association, p. 218.

95. *Black Hills Daily Times*, 20 Mar. 1899.

96. Roberta S. Greenwood, "Old Rituals in New Lands: Bringing the Ancestors to America," in *Chinese American Death Rituals: Respecting the Ancestors*, ed. Sue Fawn Chung and Priscilla Wegars (Lanham, Md.: AltaMira Press, 2005), p. 246.

97. Chang, *Chinese in America*, p. 77.

98. *Black Hills Daily Times*, 11 July 1879. *See also* 4 July 1883, 6 July 1889.

99. *Black Hills Daily Pioneer*, 1 July 1885.

100. *Black Hills Daily Times*, 6 July 1888.

101. Ibid., 4, 6 July 1888.

102. Ibid., 6 July 1889. No record has been found of a Chinese team officially going hub-to-hub against a non-Chinese team.

103. Zhu and Fosha, *Ethnic Oasis*, p. 35.

104. *Black Hills Daily Times*, 18 Jan. 1881.

105. Ibid., 27 Feb. 1882.

106. Bennett, *Old Deadwood Days*, p. 30.

107. *Black Hills Daily Times*, 24 Jan. 1896. The lone non-Chinese member of the Chinese Masons was Henrich Alexander Leopold von Wedelstaedt, whom Estelline Bennett described as "a tall, straight, dignified Prussian, family physician to half of Deadwood. . . . He had jet black hair and whiskers and when he marched with the Chinese he wore his high silk hat, swung his goldheaded cane, and threw his head and shoulders back, proud of being the only man of his race among the Chinese masons" (*Old Deadwood Days*, pp. 30–31). *See also* Liestman, "Chinese in the Black Hills, 1876–1932," p. 79.

108. *Deadwood Daily Pioneer-Times*, 26 Sept. 1905; Record Book of Deadwood Cemetery Association. According to Liestman, "Deadwood had one of the eight Chinese Masonic Lodges in the United States." The Chinese Masons were a tong, one of the fraternal associations Chinese immigrants brought to the United States to provide one another with business and benevolent assistance. The Chinese Masons, or Chee Kung Tong, also "had the political objective of seeking the

overthrow of the Manzhu dynasty" (Liestman, "Chinese in the Black Hills," p. 79). There are numerous historical references to two tongs in Deadwood, one headed by Wong Fee Lee and the other by Hi Kee. *See*, for example, Howe, *Deadwood Doctor*, p. 37.

109. Record Book of Deadwood Cemetery Association. The public cemetery in Deadwood was established in 1877, with site selection in 1878. "Historical Overview Mt. Moriah Cemetery, 1878–1938," *City of Deadwood*, www.cityofdeadwood.com/index.asp?Type=B_BASIC&SEC=%7BA0DB4AD3-F0E9-4EAC-8E22-995D27A3329B%7D&DE=%7BB193AD02-3E69-4EAE-8D51-D2441F28C456%7D. The first public Chinese burial was of Yang Set in September 1878. *Black Hills Daily Times*, 2 Sept. 1878. According to the cemetery record, the first Chinese burial occurred on 8 March 1879, and the first Chinese individual listed as purchasing a lot was Wing Tsue in 1895, for his child.

110. *Black Hills Daily Times*, 1 Apr. 1884; "The Hungry Ghost Festival," ChineseCulture, www.chinese-culture.net/html/hungry_ghost_festival.html.

111. *Black Hills Daily Times*, 30 Aug. 1887. According to a family story, Wong Fee Lee once told his son Som Quong that if a non-Chinese person ever asked when the Chinese dead would arise to eat the offerings of food left at their gravesites, he should, in turn, ask when their dead would arise to smell the flowers. Som Quong said he was always ready with such a response but never had the question posed. Much to the surprise of Wong family members, a variation of this anecdote appeared in Watson Parker's *Deadwood: The Golden Years* (Lincoln: University of Nebraska Press, 1981), p. 146.

112. *Twelfth Census*, roll 1551, sheet 14.

113. *Black Hills Daily Times*, 12 July 1885.

114. Ibid., 12, 14 July 1885.

115. *Longmont* (Colo.) *Ledger*, 14 Oct. 1910; *San Juan Prospector* (Del Norte, Colo.), 15 Oct. 1910.

116. "General Mining News," *Engineering and Mining Journal* 65 (21 May 1898): 622.

117. *Black Hills Daily Times*, 5 Jan., 14 Feb. 1892; U.S. District Court, District of South Dakota, No. 41, *United States v. Wing Tsue*, Jan. 1892, NARA-Central Plains Region, Kansas City, Mo.

118. *Black Hills Daily Times*, 2 Aug. 1877.

119. Ibid., 26 Jan. 1880.

120. Ibid., 28 Jan. 1880.

121. Ibid., 12 Apr. 1882.

122. Ibid., 23 Nov. 1883.

123. Ordinance No. 17 related to keeping a disorderly house, as related to opium

smoking, and Ordinance No. 45 prohibited the selling or supplying of opium for smoking purposes on Main Street. The crime was considered a misdemeanor, punishable by a fine of between five and one hundred dollars plus court costs. Deadwood, S.Dak., *Ordinances of the City of Deadwood, Revised* (1892), pp. 33–34, 65–66.

124. *Black Hills Daily Times*, 6, 7 Feb. 1895.

125. *See*, for example, *Deadwood Daily Pioneer-Times*, 28 Mar. 1899.

126. Chang, *Chinese in America*, p. 77.

127. *Deadwood Daily Pioneer-Times*, 4 Jan. 1907.

128. Ibid., 15 Mar. 1902; South Dakota, State Census, 1905.

129. Ibid., 2 Sept. 1915.

130. Wong Yick Lai, No. 14586/8-30, arriving 08-17-15 on the Steamer Mongolia into Port San Francisco, Wong Yick Lai Chinese Exclusion Act Case File, 14586/8-30, RG 21, NARA-PR.

131. *Deadwood Daily Pioneer-Times*, 2 Sept. 1902.

132. Interview of Wong Free Lee, 11 Dec. 1903; Affidavit [July 1902], Wong Free Lee Chinese Exclusion Act Case File.

133. Interviews of C. O. Gorder, 15 Jan. 1904, George Ayres, 14 Jan. 1904, Sam Schwarzwald, 14 Jan. 1904, W. E. Shluws, 15 Jan. 1904, Wong Bing Quong, 14 Jan. 1904, Sen Lee, 15 Jan. 1904, Wong Hoi, 15 Jan. 1904, and Di Sing, 15 Jan. 1904, all ibid.

134. Office of Chinese Inspector, Portal, N.Dak., to Commissioner-General of Immigration, Washington, D.C., 21 Jan. 1904, ibid. At Port Townsend, Wong underwent a physical examination. On 14 December 1904, a representative of the United States Public Health and Marine-Hospital Service wrote the port inspector: "Sir: You are hereby notified that I have this day examined the Chinaman, Wong Fee Lee, whom I find to be free from contagious or loathsome disease, and from mental defect, and not likely to become a public charge."

135. Yet another in a series of laws restricting Chinese immigration, the Geary Act (1892) required all Chinese living in the United States to apply for a certificate of residency. Zhu and Fosha, *Ethnic Oasis*, p. 355n.12.

136. *Deadwood Daily Pioneer-Times*, 5 Feb. 1904.

137. Ibid.

138. Ibid., 9 Feb. 1904.

139. Zhu and Fosha, *Ethnic Oasis*, p. 9.

140. Like the Prussian von Wedelstaedt among the Chinese Masons, Wong Fee Lee was the lone Chinese member of the original Society of Black Hills Pioneers, a "moral, benevolent, and literary association" formed to memorialize those "whose sagacity, energy and enterprise induced them to settle in the wilderness, and be-

come founders of a new State." At the time, membership was limited to those who arrived in the Black Hills before the end of 1876. *Some History of Lawrence County* (Deadwood, S.Dak.: Lawrence County Historical Society, 1981), p. 1. Beginning with Wong Fee Lee's grandson Kam Leung Wong in the 1990s, numerous descendants have joined the modern Society of Black Hills Pioneers.

141. *Deadwood Daily Pioneer-Times*, 6 Apr. 1912. Wong Fee Lee had long supported the overthrow of the Qing dynasty, a corrupt and ineffective regime dominated by the Manchu ethnic minority. In February 1912, revolutionary forces succeeded in deposing the emperor and establishing the Republic of China. In 1905, during the Russo-Japanese War, Wong stated: "The many Chinamen who have lived in America and have gone back to China are the ones who will have great effect upon the future of China. They know what a free government is and they are all ready and anxious for a change in that direction" (*Deadwood Daily Pioneer-Times*, 30 July 1905).

142. Lawrence County, Foreclosure Record, 219, Sheriff's Certificate of Sale No. 154355, 29 June 1915, pp. 172–73, Lawrence County Courthouse.

143. *Deadwood Daily Pioneer-Times*, 29 Jan. 1918.

144. Ibid., 1. Feb. 1918.

145. Ibid., 30 Apr. 1919.

146. *Rapid City Daily Journal*, 23 Oct. 1921.

147. *Deadwood Daily Pioneer-Times*, 23 Oct. 1921; Wong and Wong, "Fee Lee Wong," p. 56

5

The Bower Family

A PHOTOGRAPH ALBUM OF THE

"GENUINE ORIGINAL FAMILY BAND"

compiled and annotated by Maxwell Van Nuys

EDITOR'S NOTE: The Walt Disney movie *The One and Only Genuine Original Family Band*, with its all-star cast of Hollywood notables, drew excited crowds when it opened in South Dakota in 1968. In fact, the production had two premiers—one at Radio City Music Hall in New York City and the other in Rapid City, South Dakota. It was a uniquely South Dakota story based on the real-life experiences of the Bower Family Band, composed of seven of the eight children of John Calvin ("Cal") Bower and Keziah Bower. Soon after giving its first concert in Vermillion, Dakota Territory, in 1884, the family migrated to the Black Hills, where it achieved a measure of local fame during the 1880s and 1890s.

Nearly sixty years later, the band's youngest member, Laura Bower Van Nuys, recorded her family's story in a book entitled *The Family Band: From the Missouri to the Black Hills, 1881–1900* (University of Nebraska Press, 1961). She had been encouraged to preserve the stories by her son, Maxwell Van Nuys, who also harbored "a faint hope that such a book might appeal to Walt Disney as the basis for a musical." That dream became a reality, but Van Nuys remained disappointed that his mother's book had been published without illustrations. Several years later, he assembled an album of photographs of the places and

This album originally appeared in a different format in *South Dakota History* 31 (Summer 2001): 113–45.

people she had mentioned, gathering them from family members and archival collections. Van Nuys also wrote an accompanying narrative, basing it on *The Family Band* and his own recollections and observations. Adapted here to fit the format of this book, the album adds yet another dimension to the story of the Bower Family Band and the people of the Black Hills.

Bower Family Album

John Calvin Bower and Keziah Huntington Bower

Calvin and Keziah Bower set out from Lodi, Wisconsin, in a covered wagon bound for Vermillion, in the southeast corner of Dakota Territory, in 1870. With them were their four youngsters, Alice, Sidney, Mayo, and Lulu. The family was one of the earliest to settle in Dakota Territory, preceding the Great Dakota Boom by several years. In Vermillion, the Bowers occupied a two-story house (marked with a white cross in the photograph of Vermillion) just up the street from the grocery store (marked "C.I.K." for "Cash Is King"). The town, as the Bowers and others would learn to their sorrow, was located too low and too near the banks of the marauding Missouri River. Not far in the distance residents could see the bluffs across the river in Nebraska.

Cal Bower worked as a stonemason, bridge-builder, and house-mover and ran a ferry across the Missouri. At left in the photograph of the Vermillion river front is the flat boat he used in bridge building, and his crew appears to be laying a willow mat for a steamboat landing. In addition to his other jobs, Bower conducted a singing school and

Vermillion, Dakota Territory

Vermillion river front, with Bower flatboat

Alice ("Od") Bower

played the fife and snare drum. In a few years, the family was joined by Cal Bower's parents, Rensselaer and Christina Camack Bower, staunch abolitionists who became active in the county Bible society. They brought with them their youngest children, Willis and Mary Lida.

Cal and Keziah Bower's oldest child, Alice (nicknamed "Od"), was soon playing the organ for church and the piano for dances, although she and the rest of the family never danced themselves. Alice supported herself from age fifteen by giving piano lessons and teaching in the town's log schoolhouse, where she spanked a future South Dakota governor, Carl Gunderson. Her driving ambition was to become a journalist, and she defied convention to learn the printer's trade while working for the local newspaper, the *Standard*. As the years passed, the oldest boy, Sidney, found himself "struck" for a schoolmate, Agnes ("Aggie")

Vermillion schoolhouse

Sidney Bower   *Agnes Walker*

Walker, whom he would love for the rest of his life. By 1881, four more children, all girls, had been added to the Cal Bower family: Rose and Nettie (twins), Quinnie, and Laura.

In the spring of 1881, flooding caused by huge ice jams on the Missouri River nearly wiped out the town of Vermillion. Among the casualties were numerous steamboats, houses, and businesses, including the *Vermillion Standard* newspaper office. As for the Bowers' house, the voracious Missouri swallowed it up, and the family lost everything except some cows, two pigs, and one load of goods hurriedly piled onto Cal Bower's flatboat. The forlorn family of ten moved in with his parents, whose small log house sat just out of reach of the floodwaters. A close look at the flood-ravaged *Standard* office reveals a bill announcing "Montanio and Liberman's New York Show and Comet Band." This performance, if not flooded out, would certainly have been attended by the musical Bowers and may well have provided inspiration for the Bower Family Band.

At any rate, Vermillion's town band welcomed anybody with musical talent. Sidney and Mayo, seventeen and fifteen years of age, joined up the year after the flood. Their five younger sisters all wanted to play horns, too, but in those days, bands were not for girls. Nevertheless,

Bower girls: (from left) Quinnie, Nettie, Lulu, Rose

Standard *office, with show bill*

Vermillion main street, with Standard *printing office*

Steamboat Helena *in ice gorge*

Laura Bower

Bower Family Band: (standing from left) Mayo, Rose, Lulu, Nettie, Sidney; (seated) Quinnie, Laura

the boys soon had each sister playing a band instrument—even Laura could play a baritone horn at the age of four—and a family band became practically inevitable. The Bower Family Band made its first public appearance at a Christmas concert given by the Vermillion band. The local newspaper praised the performance of the Bower children, "who all played upon brass instruments with a melody and precision in time that completely took the audience by storm."

Intent on her journalistic career, Alice did not join her brothers and sisters as a family band member. Word of her unusual ambition had traveled west to the Black Hills, where Joseph R. Gossage, an eligible bachelor, had established the *Black Hills Journal* at Rapid City. He sought to make Alice's acquaintance, and after corresponding for some time, the couple exchanged pictures. "In commenting on your photograph," Alice wrote Joe, "I omitted speaking of your moustache. You would never forgive me if I did not tell you it was grand, perfectly lovely, too nice for anything, etc." She, in turn, gave him a tintype of herself holding a card case he had sent her as a gift. A diary entry she had recorded two years earlier proved prophetic: "My future husband must be; A strong temperance man; . . . If possible, I want him to be an editor of a *Republican* newspaper. By the way, he *must* be a republican in politics." Joe Gossage passed the test with flying colors. After sixteen months of corresponding, the two met for the first time. (Their letters can be found in the book *Sunshine Always: The Courtship Letters of Alice Bower and Joseph Gossage of Dakota Territory.*) They wed in June 1882 and left immediately for the Black Hills, arriving in Rapid City by stagecoach from Sidney, Nebraska.

The sight of wagons heading west shook Cal Bower's determination to remain in Vermillion, and both he and his wife missed their eldest daughter. The Bower Family Band gave a farewell concert in Vermillion in May 1885, and two days later, a vanguard consisting of Sidney, Rose, and Cal Bower's sister Lida left for the Black Hills. The rest of the family followed a month later, traveling by covered wagon up the east bank of the Missouri River to the dusty frontier town of Pierre. Crossing to Fort Pierre, they took a trail across the Great Sioux Reservation, following the Bad River for much of the way. After about two weeks of traveling at an average of eighteen miles a day, they at last saw the dark profile of the Black Hills.

As the party crossed a ridge, the village of Rapid City suddenly came into view. They soon found the Gossages' little white house (at cen-

Vermillion band, with Sidney (third from right) and Mayo (far right)

*Joseph
R. Gossage*

Alice Bower

Fort Pierre, Dakota Territory, with Bad River (foreground)

Rapid City, Dakota Territory, with Gossage house (center)

Bower ranch, French Creek

ter, between the long white building and the larger white house in the photograph of Rapid City). There, while the trail-weary group rested, Alice played for them on her new piano.

The reunion was brief, for the family had to build their new home on lower Battle Creek, located about midway between the Black Hills and the Badlands. Later, they took claims on French Creek, not far from the Pine Ridge Indian Reservation. At both places, Cal Bower and the boys built log cabins, which could be put up more quickly than a frame house and were cooler in summer and warmer in winter. Once again, the Bowers were on the leading edge of a wave of homesteading. Small farms and ranches where families raised their own cattle, pigs, and chickens would soon dot the landscape, helping put an end to the open range. Among their French Creek neighbors would be the Bales of Norfolk, England. "Gentleman farmers," they lost their landholdings in England and sought better fortune in America. George Bale would take notice of Nettie Bower, and she of him.

In the spring of 1886, the Fremont, Elkhorn & Missouri Valley Railroad was laying tracks from western Nebraska into Dakota along the eastern edge of the Black Hills. Anticipating its arrival in Rapid City on the Fourth of July, officials planned a great parade and celebration.

In hopes of being invited to participate, the Bower Family Band gave a concert on 5 June at Library Hall, the center of theatrical and musical entertainment in Rapid City. The band also had Joe Gossage's *Black Hills Journal* working for it, and the invitation was forthcoming.

When the Fourth arrived, the Bower Family Band was seated in the grandstand, with the Fort Meade military band posted in the balcony above them. General George Crook was the guest of honor among a host of other dignitaries. At the close of each oration, the chairman waved for music, and the military band took it for granted that it should respond. During the closing speech, Sidney Bower told his band members to be ready the instant the speaker finished. This time, the chairman had hardly risen from his seat when Sidney did his own waving and the Bower Family Band struck up "Hail Columbia." The stirring tune brought the audience to its feet, clapping and shouting, while the disgruntled Fort Meade band folded up their music racks and left the platform.

Library Hall, Rapid City

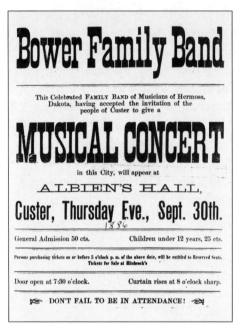

Bower Family Band

This Celebrated FAMILY BAND of Musicians of Hermosa, Dakota, having accepted the invitation of the people of Custer to give a

MUSICAL CONCERT

in this City, will appear at

ALBIEN'S HALL,

Custer, Thursday Eve., Sept. 30th.

1886

General Admission 50 cts.   Children under 12 years, 25 cts.

Persons purchasing tickets on or before 5 o'clock p. m. of the above date, will be entitled to Reserved Seats. Tickets for Sale at Hitchcock's

Door open at 7:30 o'clock.   Curtain rises at 8 o'clock sharp.

☞ DON'T FAIL TO BE IN ATTENDANCE! ☜

Handbill, Custer concert, 1886   *Mit Everly*

Other engagements followed. In September 1886, the Bower Family Band gave a concert in Custer, site of the first gold discovery in the Black Hills. On the long trip through the Hills, the Bowers camped out overnight, getting out their horns to rehearse before sundown. Unbeknownst to the band, a lone sheepherder stood spellbound some distance away, listening to the strains of music echoing over the hills. Years later the shepherd, Mit Everly, learned the reason for the serenade from Quinnie, the woman who became his wife. On returning from another concert tour, the band discovered that fire had ravaged the main street of Hermosa, the town nearest their ranch. The people of Hermosa gladly accepted Sidney's offer to put on a concert the next day and donate the proceeds to those most in need.

As its renown grew, the band played many engagements in the next few years, including Fourth of July celebrations, political rallies, county fairs, weddings, and school entertainments. At the annual Custer County Stock, Mineral, and Agricultural Fair at Hermosa in September 1888, the band was at its best, sporting new outfits. Besides the usual games and races, an added attraction was a group of Oglala Lakota

LIBRARY HALL

FRIDAY EVENING, DEC. 11.

GRAND

CONCERT

GIVEN BY THE

Bower Family Band!

ASSISTED BY

LOCAL TALENT!

Music by the Band and Arion Orchestra.

The Evening's Entertainment will conclude with a
Laughable Farce, entitled

THAT RASCAL PAT!

ADMISSION, - - 5o CENTS.

Seats Reserved without Extra Charge

Tickets for Sale at Postoffice.

AT PUBLIC HALL

On - Thursday - Evening,

SEPTEMBER 20, 1888.

GRAND CONCERT

BY THE

BOWER FAMILY BAND.

PROGRAMME.

PART 1.

1.	Overture—Dispatch.	Southwell.
	Family Band.	
2.	Vocal Quartette—Hunter's Chorus.	Leslie.
	Lulu, Nettie, Rose and Quinnie.	
3.	Guitar Duett—Medley Overture.	Selected.
	Lulu and Rose.	
4.	Cornet Duett—Fraternity.	H. Bellstedt Jr.
	Sidney and Mayo.	
5.	Song—I'm Going to Write to Papa.	Westendorf.
	Laura.	
6.	Brass Quartette—Cebella.	Pettee.
	Lulu, Rose, Nettie and Quinnie.	
7.	Imitation Caliope.	Selected.
	Sidney and Mayo.	
8.	Vocal Duett—The Hunter's Song.	Kucken.
	Lulu and Rose.	
9.	Baritone Solo—Highland Polka—with Band accompaniment. Lulu.	—Southwell.

PART 2.

10.	Trombone Solo—Song of the Roses—with Orchestral accompaniment. Rose.	—Rollinson.
11.	Vocal Solo—Rock a Bye Baby.	Barker.
	Lulu.	
12.	Ocarina Duett—Enchanted.	Southwell.
	Rose and Sidney.	
13.	Brass Trio—Thoughts of Twilight.	Pettee.
	Nettie, Quinnie and Laura.	
14.	Song—We'll Have to Mortgage the Farm.	Lockwood.
	Family.	
15.	Guitar Solo—Sebastapol.	Warrall.
	Lulu.	
16.	Tuba Solo—Home Sweet Home.	Selected.
	Laura.	
17.	Recitation—The Sisters.	Whittier.
	Lulu.	
18.	Cornet Solo—Lizzie Polka.	J. Hartman.
	Mayo.	
19.	Kazoo Chorus—Sweet Violets.	Emett.
	Lulu.	
20.	March—Ivanhoe Commandery.	Blake.
	Family Band.	

GRAND CONCERT,

— GIVEN BY —

THE BOWER BAND

ASSISTED BY LOCAL TALENT,

Library Hall, Friday Evening, Dec. 11, 1891

ADMISSION, 50 CENTS.

Section..............

Row..............

Seat..............

Hermosa concert, 1887

BENEFIT
ENTERTAINMENT
TO-NIGHT.
at 7:30 Sharp.

The BOWER FAMILY BAND
WILL GIVE ITS
CONCERT
This Evening at Stenger's Hall for the
benefit of the most serious sufferers from last
night's conflagration.

EVERYONE SHOULD ATTEND.

A Committee will be appointed to distribute
the proceeds.

Admission of Adults 25 cents.
Children 15 cents.

*Oglala dancers
at Custer County
Stock, Mineral, and
Agricultural Fair*

(Sioux) Indians from the Pine Ridge Indian Reservation. Sidney Bower posed for a photograph with the group (he is standing beneath the "X" to the left of center), which performed dances at the fair. Two years later, many Oglalas joined the messianic Ghost Dance movement, which promised to do away with white people but instead culminated in the massacre of Indians at Wounded Knee.

In May of 1889, Sidney wrote his sister Lulu, who was teaching school in Pactola, that he and a friend were planning to work in a logging camp. "We are trying to get some oxen broken to haul logs but they are so dumb that I don't know whether they will ever learn 'Gee' from 'Haw,'" he quipped, adding, "We played some tunes on our horns today." Lulu wrote back to inquire whether the band had a booking for the Fourth of July. "I wish that we could go to Rapid," she wrote. "I see by the paper that they talk of celebrating. . . . Try to get some place to play." Instead, the Bowers ended up performing for the holiday celebration at Whitewood, north of Rapid City. Their uncle Willis Bower contributed the oration for the day, filling in for a speaker who did not show up, and Sidney sang "Sherman's March to the Sea."

The following day, a patient photographer recorded the last picture of the entire Bower family. He had quite a time arranging a satisfactory grouping, and when Quinnie ripped her tight sleeve bending her elbow to place in her mother's lap, he had to make suggestions that would keep the rent from showing. Upon seeing the finished image, Quinnie told Sidney, "Papa's picture is just splendid, he has his heavenly smile, but Od [Alice] is holding Cleveland's Grand March. She must have been in a terrible hurry when she grabbed that piece of music!" Lulu called it "the one-eyed band" picture because everyone was tired out from the previous day's activities.

The day after the picture was taken, Sidney went back to his work in the logging camp near Hill City, where his oxen presumably learned "gee" from "haw." The younger girls, in turn, all went home to the ranch where, not long afterwards, a traveling photographer came by. Nettie wrote to Sidney: "We five girls had our pictures taken, just our five heads in one group. Mama was not home and we are not going to let her know it until they are done."

Late in August 1889, Sidney Bower told his Aunt Lida of his plans to marry Agnes Walker, whom he had left behind in Vermillion, and showed her a letter he had just received from Aggie. But the next letter he received from his childhood sweetheart was one in which she

Bower family:
(back, from left)
Sidney, Nettie, Lulu,
Rose, Mayo; (front,
from left) Alice, Laura,
Cal, Keziah, Quinnie

Logging camp, with Sidney (left)

asked for the return of her correspondence, for her heart now belonged to another. The disappointment was too great for Sidney. Taking fever and lacking the desire to fight it, he died within a week. Leaderless, the band might have died with him, but it carried on for many more years in the spirit in which Sidney had created, trained, and led it.

With the arrival of the "Gay Nineties," the enterprising and influential Fred T. Evans promoted Hot Springs in the southern Black Hills as a rival to Hot Springs, Arkansas, and other spas. Among his creations was Evans Plunge, the largest enclosed natural warm-water pool in the country. During the summer of 1891, Evans engaged the Bower Family Band to play at the plunge, housing them in a cottage along the creek on the Chautauqua grounds. The engagement, unfortunately, was a qualified success, but lots of building activity in Hot Springs kept Cal Bower busy and made the venture worthwhile.

Teaching at a difficult school the winter before had nearly broken Lulu's health, but by summer she had exciting news—a beau ideal was coming to visit her. His name was Ed Barthold, and one glance made it clear why Lulu had fallen in love with him. He had an easy manner and wore his well-cut clothes as though he were accustomed to strolling on Pall Mall, but his hands showed that he knew how to work. Before long, Ed, who ranched near Newcastle, Wyoming, wrote Lulu that he would be the happiest man in the Black Hills "if only I had your consent, for

*Laura, Lulu, Rose, Nettie,
Quinnie (clockwise from top)*

Sidney Bower

Hot Springs Chautauqua grounds

my dear Lulu, you are everything to me." He added that he would wait while she thought things over, but Lulu replied the next day: "I did not stop to consider matters for to me they needed no considering. My mind was made up as soon as I learned the object of your letter." They were married at the end of 1892.

Mayo Bower had an eye for the girls, but with six prim and proper sisters, he was looking for something quite different, and he found her at a Methodist church social. Carrie Millis was already on her own, having left her family in the East, and was among the first females to break the Victorian tradition that, in town, nice girls rode sidesaddle only. In a parade led by the Bower Family Band, Carrie boldly rode her pony down Main Street in Rapid City sitting astride a man's saddle. Everyone was shocked, none more so than the Bower girls. Over their protests, Mayo fell more in love with her than ever.

In the fall of 1892, the Bower Family Band did its share for South Dakota's contribution to the World's Columbian Exposition at Chicago by touring the Black Hills to raise money for the women's exhibit. The girls sewed new uniforms and, swallowing their pride, took their pro-

Ed Barthold

spective sister-in-law Carrie into the band. Rose had dedicated herself to mastering Sidney's trumpet and brought in another musician, Nina Eggleston, to take over her trombone. Lulu was on the drums. Her doctor, fearing she had consumption, had advised her not to blow a horn. Mayo directed the band, which now bore the name "Bower Family Concert Company and Ladies' Cornet Band." Mayo, who needed more money in order to get married, spent the summer of 1893 working as a

Mayo Bower

cowboy in Montana. In one letter to Lulu he wrote, "Tonight I will com-
mence to night hawk the horses. . . . The other morning I got thrown
higher than a kite." At the end of summer, he came home and married
Carrie.

Alice Bower Gossage, meanwhile, was spending more time at the
Black Hills Journal office, working as both reporter and typesetter.
Her husband had finally resigned himself to the arrangement, which
saved the wages of a compositor. Thus, business sense as well as her

PROGRAMME.

The Bower Family Concert Company AND Ladies' Cornet Band.

Pretty as a Picture,...............Overture, E. N. Catlin.
Band.

Sleep, Darling, Sleep,.. ....Female Trio, H. S. Perkins.
Nettie, Rose and Quir nie.

The Vision,.................Trombone Solo, E. Brooks.
Nettie.

When de Bell Rings,..................Song, Max Vernor.
Mayo.

The Patriot Polka,.........Cornet Solo, W. P. Chambers.
Rose.

Medley Overture,.................Guitar Duett, Selected.
Lulu and Nettie.

Indian Club Swinging................Rose and Quinnie.

Hearts Desire......Orchestra Bells, band accompaniment.
Nina Eggleston.

Love's Old Sweet Song.............Contralto, L Molloy.
Quinnie.

Columbian Exposition, Medley arranged by Quinnie Bower.
Rose.

Iva,.......... ....Brass Quartette, Pettee,
Nettie, Rose, Quinnie and Laura.

Sebastopool,.................Guitar Solo, Henry Worrell.
Lulu.

Beelzebub,...Tuba Solo, band acompaniment, A. Cattozzi.
Quinnie.

Bower Family Concert Company and Ladies' Cornet Band: (back, from left) Mayo, Nina Eggleston, Rose, Carrie Millis, Lulu; (front, from left) Quinnie, Laura, Nettie

own ambition had combined to make Alice an all-around newspaper-woman, just as she had planned. When Joe Gossage traveled back east to buy a press, the *Deadwood Pioneer-Times* reported admiringly, "The publisher's wife prepared the entire copy, including editorial and local matter for yesterday morning's daily." In time, she would eclipse her husband in the management of the newspaper, and her byline, "A.G.," would become a byword in the Black Hills.

Rose was determined to make a career of playing cornet and struck out on her own. She found great success in putting on benefit concerts for churches and societies in and about the Black Hills. Quinnie accompanied her on at least one trip (program reproduced here). The sisters

worked up an Indian club-swinging act, and with Rose's whistling and Quinnie's tuba solos and mellow contralto, they needed to recruit little local talent in the towns they visited to make up a good entertainment.

That winter, while everyone concerned appeared or tried to appear happy, all were worried about Lulu. The cough she had developed while teaching school had never entirely left her and, in fact, became much worse. Unable to carry the burden of her own household, she sought refuge at the family ranch on French Creek, where Rose helped care for her. With spring came an end to her suffering. In but a couple of years, a broken-hearted Ed Barthold lay beside her in death. The loss of Lulu so deeply affected Rose that she believed the "white plague" of tuberculosis had marked her as its next victim. Much distressed, she gave up the cornet and went to Georgia to find a new life.

In the mid-1890s, news of an 1892 strike not far from a great granite outcrop later known as Mount Rushmore rekindled gold fever in the Black Hills. The resulting Keystone gold mine gave its name to the town

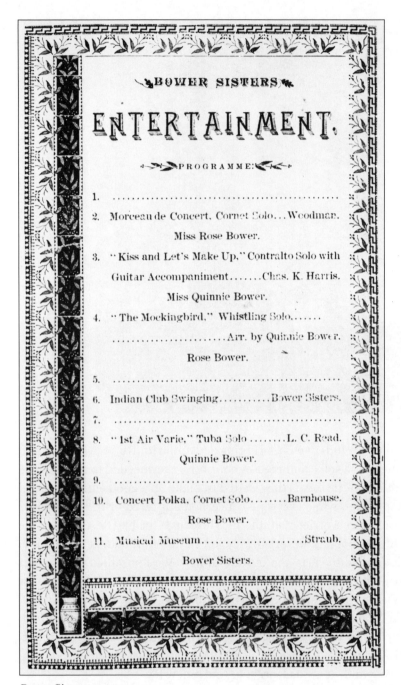

Bower Sisters program

Lulu Bower

Keystone, with Holy Terror Mine (right) and Mount Rushmore (horizon)

that soon grew up around it. Two years later, the young daughter of a William B. Franklin discovered an even richer vein. Legend has it that her father named the lode the "Holy Terror" for the reaction his wife exhibited when he returned home following some heavy celebrating. Cal Bower was excited, too—not by gold, but by the demand for house-builders. So, in the spring of 1895, most of the close-knit Bowers congregated in Keystone. Uncle Willis Bower joined them, becoming Keystone school superintendent and teaching the upper grades. Quinnie became teacher of the primary grades. That fall, fire erupted in the Keystone Mine. All the schoolchildren joined the rest of the town in forming a bucket brigade and helping to save several lives. In appreciation, so the story goes, Mrs. Franklin of Holy Terror fame took the pupils down to the photography shop and had their picture taken. Willis, with the moustache, is in the second row, with Quinnie on his left. Laura appears second from the right in the third row.

Nettie was not entirely happy about living in Keystone, for she could not see as much of her attractive young neighbor, Englishman George Bale, as she could at the ranch. Before long, however, she found a job clerking in the town's general merchandise store, where she loved talking to customers. Mayo and Carrie had been staying on the ranch, but Carrie wanted to join the excitement at Keystone. Although he preferred ranching, Mayo relented and soon found himself working in the mine. Rose, meanwhile, had gradually recovered her spirits in Georgia and, learning that her health never had been in danger, she returned to her family in Keystone and to her cornet.

Together again, the Bower Family Band became the nucleus of the

Keystone band leading July Fourth parade

Keystone band, which may well have been among the first marching bands in the West to admit women to its ranks. If eyebrows were raised at this turn of events, they were about to rise higher at the sight of Carrie, whose time was drawing near for presenting the family with its first grandchild. The 1896 Fourth of July parade was coming up, and nothing was going to keep Carrie from marching with the band. As the Keystone band struck up a tune and swung down the dusty street at the head of the parade, a photographer recorded the last glimpse we have of the Bower Family Band. Nettie is in front, with Mayo and Laura behind her. Carrie, whose baby Marguerite was born less than three weeks later, is just out of sight.

As the Holy Terror lode ran out, the members of the Bower Family Band dispersed. Quinnie became the third Bower daughter to marry, wedding Mit Everly, the sheepherder who had gone on to become shift boss at the Holy Terror Mine in 1899.

Nettie turned down several Keystone suitors in favor of George Bale two years later. Rose, whom some considered the beauty of the family, rejected all suitors. In later years, she enlisted herself and her cornet in the causes of woman suffrage and temperance. Mayo and Carrie, Nettie

Keystone general store, with Nettie behind counter

Mayo and Carrie Millis Bower, with Marguerite

Mit and Quinnie Bower Everly

George Bale   Nettie Bower Bale

and George, and Quinnie and Mit all went into ranching. Their parents, Cal and Keziah Bower, returned to the French Creek ranch. Alice and Joe Gossage continued to make the *Black Hills Journal*, now the *Rapid City Daily Journal*, the leading newspaper of western South Dakota.

Laura, the youngest Bower child, went on to attend South Dakota Agricultural College at Brookings. Returning to Rapid City, she taught school and succeeded her sister Rose as city librarian. In 1910, she married Claude Van Nuys, a professor at the South Dakota School of Mines. Following publication of her book *The Family Band* in 1961, producers from Walt Disney Studios agreed to produce it and assembled a stellar cast. Laura, the only surviving member of the band, and other family members enjoyed watching the filming of "her" movie in the Disney studios in Los Angeles, California. All of the band members were accurately represented in the film with the exception of Quinnie, who was depicted as a boy, an adaptation that changed Mayo's role as well. Laura Bower Van Nuys enjoyed her fame in South Dakota to the fullest. In Rapid City, a writers' group and contest were named for her. She died in Denver, Colorado, in 1979 at the age of ninety-eight.

Rose Bower

Cal and Keziah Bower

Alice Bower Gossage

Cast of The One and Only Genuine Original Family Band: *(back, from left) Walter Brennan (Grandpa Bower), Debbie Smith (Lulu), Kurt Russell (Sidney), Leslie Ann Warren (Alice), Janet Blair (Keziah), Buddy Ebsen (Cal); (front, from left) Bobby Riha (Mayo), Pamela Ferdin (Laura), Smitty Worden (Nettie), Heidi Rook (Rose), John Walmsley (Quinnie). Not pictured is John Davidson, who portrayed Joe Gossage.*

Joe Gossage

Laura Bower

Thomas J. Grier

AN IRON HAND IN A VELVET GLOVE

THE MANAGEMENT OF THE

HOMESTAKE MINE, 1885–1914

Susan L. Richards and Rex C. Myers

Thomas Johnston Grier—square-stout, tobacco-chewing, Canadian-born—superintended the Homestake Mining Company headquartered in Lead, South Dakota, for nearly thirty years. Under his management, which combined both benevolence and firm control, the company grew from a fledgling enterprise into one of the largest producers of gold in North America. After Grier's death in 1914, mine workers erected a heroic statue on Main Street in honor of his memory, and to this day, the Lead Chamber of Commerce gives a public-service award bearing his name. The citizens of Lead remembered Grier's good will, but it was the superintendent's strong grip on Homestake's operations and employees that kept the company profitable. Indeed, inside the velvet glove of Grier's paternalism, an iron fist controlled all aspects of Homestake's operation.

Lead may have been just another mining camp during the heady days of the Black Hills gold rush of the mid-1870s, but within a decade, it became a one-mine community and took on the accouterments of a company town. The Homestake presence permeated life in Lead as thoroughly as the pounding of the ore-crushing stamps that dropped twenty-four hours a day. Under Grier's management, Homestake bought out adjacent mining claims,

This essay originally appeared in *South Dakota History* 38 (Summer 2008): 95–124.

assumed ownership of the land on which workers built their homes, and paid miners through a company-owned store that sold food and goods and extended credit for purchases between paydays. The company also owned the area's first railroad and kept a constant eye on the bottom line, paying regular monthly dividends that made the predominantly absentee owners extremely rich. At the same time, Grier cooperated with the local miners' union and facilitated industrial socialism at a level unheard of in other western mining camps. Miners and their families benefited from free medical care as well as a free library, kindergarten, and state-of-the-art recreation center, excellent schools, disability and life insurance, stock options, year-end bonuses, and an eight-hour day. Grier, however, made it clear that what was good for the Homestake Mine came first. As long as the company remained unthreatened, a benevolent paternalism prevailed; when challenged, however, Grier manipulated life in Lead like a despot.[1]

The discovery of gold in the Black Hills dated officially to Lieutenant Colonel George A. Custer's 1874 expedition to the region. Immediately after news of mineral wealth reached the outside world, determined prospectors swarmed the pine-covered hillsides. George Hearst, in partnership with others, bought the Homestake claim from its discoverers in 1877 and moved deftly to consolidate his holdings and acquire the water and lumber resources needed to mine effectively. In an era when "infrastructure" had not entered corporate language, Hearst built the framework that would make the Homestake Mining Company profitable.[2] In fact, the Homestake mine became the mother lode of prosperity.

Samuel McMaster joined Homestake as its first superintendent. Savvy and experienced, he did Hearst's bidding. Also working with McMaster's management team was twenty-nine-year-old telegrapher and bookkeeper Thomas J. Grier. Known as "T. J." to his friends, he had a broad smile, a quiet laugh, an eye for detail, and a tremendous capacity for work. Shortly after arriving on the job on 21 September 1878, Grier purchased a three-and-one-half-by-six-inch notebook with cross-lined pages to carry in his vest pocket. In a meticulous, cramped but clear hand, he penned entries about all aspects of Homestake operations, diagramming claims, noting profit and loss data for corporate activities, and keeping personal accounts. Little missed his attention.[3]

Discreetly, Grier worked his way into Hearst's confidence. When McMaster died in December 1884, Grier's name rose to the top of the

Thomas J. Grier was Homestake Mining Company
superintendent for twenty-nine years. State Archives
Collection, South Dakota State Historical Society

list as a potential replacement. Homestake owners mulled over the selection of candidates for several months before the board of directors gave Grier their unanimous support as the new superintendent on 9 July 1885. The decision was a bold one. Hearst, McMaster, and all the other prospective superintendents had practical mining experience. Grier, on the other hand, excelled as a manager and looked beyond simply extracting ore to addressing the "big picture" issues of a complex corporation, such as worker relations and technological innovation.[4] Historians Richard H. Peterson in *The Bonanza Kings* and Michael P. Malone in *The Battle for Butte* both discuss mine owners and managers who came to play prominent roles in the politics and economies of their communities, noting that those who had risen through the ranks themselves shared a sense of camaraderie and displayed benevolence toward their workers.[5]

Hearst affirmed his faith in Grier face to face. Beginning 31 July, he spent twenty-three days checking out his interests in the Black Hills. More importantly, he checked out the man chosen to oversee them. Hearst left satisfied.[6] Grier went on to make the mine work efficiently and pay well throughout his years as superintendent. No evidence in either the Hearst papers or the Homestake records suggests that Grier ever submitted his management decisions to the directors for prior approval. He notified them, often in advance, but they never second-guessed him and overrode a decision. Grier also set a clear ethical standard for himself by choosing not to own Homestake stock. "Having no shares of stock, . . . I was in a stronger position," he later stated. "The door was not open for any criticism."[7] Grier had no vested, owner-based interest in the Homestake. His aim was to manage profitably for others.[8]

Homestake's new superintendent continued to fill his notebook with operational details. Grier tirelessly acquired adjacent claims, solidifying the company's exclusive access to the ore vein. "Patented," he wrote over a claim deed once the Homestake owned it.[9] Underground, better timbering and the backfilling of stopes improved miner safety. Above ground, the Homestake Mercantile Company, housed in a large brick building in Lead and known as the "Brick Store" or simply "The Brick," took over payroll management to make it more efficient. A two-story frame company hospital and drugstore replaced the original four-room cabin, and Homestake entered the hotel business. In both the mine and the mills, experimentation with mechanical dry drills, electricity,

Hearst Mercantile Company, also known as the Brick Store,
opened in 1879. Adams Museum, Deadwood, S.Dak.

and steam power took place.[10] Within five years of Grier's assuming stewardship of the Homestake, fifteen hundred men processed up to seven hundred tons of ore from eighty claims through 650 stamps every working day. Homestake furnaces burned one hundred cords of wood daily, part of the one million board feet harvested annually in a process the *Black Hills Daily Times* characterized as "more scientific and more systematical" than previously.[11]

At the same time, Grier sought to develop a positive relationship with workers. When representatives of the Knights of Labor and the Lead City Miners' Union requested 1 September 1888 as a Labor Day holiday, Grier closed the Homestake, made the company's railroad available for picnic excursions, and personally spent the day "looking after the comfort and safety of the crowd."[12] In May 1890, the superintendent decided to modify shift times in order to have more men underground at all times as a safeguard against fire. Miners objected, crowded Union Hall in Lead, and organized a delegation to meet with

Grier, who went to Union Hall in person. His willingness to compromise paid off, and on 6 June, both sides agreed to a new schedule.[13] While Grier's approachability became the hallmark of his successful relationship with labor, he did not, however, let it interfere with his success in getting what he wanted. The superintendent broadened his influence in the wider community, as well. He joined civic organizations, invested in other Black Hills mines, properties, businesses, and banks, and generally used his personal stature and corporate position to better Lead and surrounding communities, including helping to rebuild the neighboring town of Central City after a fire in April 1888.[14]

Grier had some rebuilding of his own to do in 1891. In that year, his notebook contained a stark entry recorded at the end of February, "Geo. Hearst died."[15] Hearst's entire twenty-one-million-dollar estate (approximately four and one-half billion dollars today) went to his widow, Phoebe Apperson Hearst. Grier's allegiance transferred seamlessly. "I want to thank you most especially," Phoebe Hearst wrote in 1893, "for all your kindness & promptness . . . when I have asked for information of any kind, and for your loyalty to my interests."[16] Hearst tapped her cousin Edward Clark to handle many of her business affairs, and both came to appreciate the expertise and vision of Grier, who was unhesitatingly forthcoming with his employers.[17]

Outsiders often saw Homestake as Phoebe Hearst's company, but in reality, she controlled only 36 percent of the stock, or fifty-one thousand shares. California investors James B. A. Haggin and Lloyd Tevis held 31 and 21 percent, respectively, while others held smaller amounts. Shortly after Hearst inherited her husband's empire, miners, mill workers, and others on the Homestake payroll were offered the opportunity to purchase company stock. Given Grier's influence and understanding of what corporate stock ownership could mean for worker loyalty, it may be logical to assume that he played a part in the decision. "We were interested to have as much stock there [in Lead] as we could," Edward Clark later recalled, "because it makes people friendly." Over the next twenty years, employees purchased about ten thousand shares, all in small blocks of less than fifty shares.[18]

In the quest to ensure profits for shareholders, efficiency mattered most. Grier determined that mining and processing the entire ore body would prove more profitable for the company in the long term than picking out only the most valuable ore pockets. Better drills and better mills meant sustained yields, and the superintendent sought out innovative methods to improve the company's bottom line. Grier continued to acquire adjacent mine properties, as well. In 1876, the Homestake consisted of a single mountaintop claim; by 1901, Homestake Mining Company owned the entire mountain. In the interest of efficient management, Grier also brought the formerly freestanding Brick Store into the corporate structure. The region's largest, best-equipped all-purpose mercantile proved extremely profitable. Phoebe Hearst received 100 percent of the store's net profit, while Grier used the mercantile to dispense pay to workers and Hearst's largesse to the community.[19]

Because the town of Lead owed its existence to the Homestake, company lawyers were able to leverage an agreement with Lead town fathers concerning the land on which the community sat. Homestake officials wanted perpetual access to the underlying minerals, while townspeople desired lots, streets, and other framework for growth. Grier had retained as company attorney Gideon C. Moody, a former federal judge and prominent Republican politician, who consummated a deal with civic leaders on 18 March 1892. Plain and simple, Homestake owned the land. Lead residents received company-issued permits to occupy the property, but if, at some future moment, Homestake desired the land, it could evict any resident or business by giving ninety days' notice. The company paid all property taxes, while residents and businesses paid taxes only on their homes and other improvements.[20]

By 1893, Grier had the distinction of working for the country's richest woman and managing the nation's richest gold mine. The next two years, however, would truly test his management skills. On 13 April 1893, fire broke out on the three-hundred-foot level of the Homestake Mine. Grier had miners and mules evacuated and then sent teams of men down to fight the burgeoning conflagration. The company's mine and mills ceased production for the first time ever. Men struggled in the suffocating smoke and gasses for just fifteen minutes at a time before they had to be evacuated to fresh air. Grier labored alongside the miners and was overcome several times. According to the *Black Hills Daily Times*, the superintendent sent "no one where he dare[d] not go himself."[21] Grier's personal risk-taking, like his openness, created a bond between manager and men that would pay dividends for the remainder of his tenure.[22] The firefighting efforts failed, and on 24 April, Grier ordered the mine flooded. He learned from the disaster. Initial reporting about the fire's location had been in error because the men had no idea where they were in the extensive labyrinth of shafts and tunnels. Grier subsequently had signs made to identify all levels of the mine clearly.[23]

In the aftermath of the fire, the superintendent also had to deal with the effects of the 1893 depression. Officially, Grier maintained the standard $3.50 daily wage, but he reduced expenses by converting some underground mining to contract bids. Such savings failed to make the Homestake mines around Central City profitable, however, and Grier closed down those operations, putting hundreds out of work. Amid the resulting discontent, the normally staid Lead City Miners' Union (LCMU) sent a five-member delegation to Butte, Montana, where the Lead union joined with their Copper City brethren to create the Western Federation of Miners (WFM). The Lead miners formed the number two local of this radical union, which was dedicated to the cause of worker solidarity in achieving better pay and working conditions at mines throughout the West. The Panic of 1893, the collapse of silver prices, and broad unrest further depressed the labor market and left workers with little to celebrate at the grand opening of the new Miners' Union Hall on Christmas Eve in 1893.[24]

Depression deepened throughout 1894. As labor unrest spread from Pullman sleeping cars to western mines, the LCMU went on record opposing what spokesmen called the "ill gotten gains" of corporations determined to "crush out organized labor" and "rob the laboring class at will."[25] Philosophically, the out-of-work Central City miners agreed, but in practice they took antithetical action, proposing on 19 July to accept a decrease in wages from $3.50 to $3.00 per day if Grier would reopen their mines. Unions in Lead and Terry Peak declined to support or oppose the gambit. Grier met with union members in late July at their initiative, not his, and agreed to reinstate the jobs at the lower wage. The distinction was important, for it portrayed Grier as willing to extend the velvet-gloved hand of compassion rather than tightening the iron grip of profitability in the midst of depression. Miners signed on at $3.00 per day and returned underground on 8 August. Stamp mills resumed pounding ore.[26] Miners held a "resurrection ball" to celebrate the reopening and danced until after midnight.[27]

Grier invited both Phoebe Hearst and James Haggin to visit Lead in the late summer and fall of 1894. Hearst made her first visit to the community on 18 August; Haggin followed on 25 October. Both owners left impressed with Grier's work. Haggin, in particular, praised the superintendent's "perfectly systematized routine" for operating the Homestake and expressed unqualified "confidence in his judgment and integrity" in conducting mine "improvement, enlargement, and investment."[28] The superintendent discussed both a free library and a kindergarten with Hearst, who gave him permission to move forward immediately with the first institution. Grier used the library as an opportunity to help the LCMU, which was struggling to make payments on its new seventy-thousand-dollar hall. He rented three rooms on the top floor, had them refitted, ordered books and a piano (Phoebe Hearst liked music in the library), hired a piano-playing librarian, and gave the facility to Lead as a Christmas present from Hearst.[29] The dedication events were a "grand success," Grier wired her.[30]

Grier continued to institute corporate and community improvements, such as expanded electrical lighting and the construction of a new schoolhouse, which he facilitated by arranging for Hearst to purchase thirty-one thousand dollars in bonds. The superintendent himself awarded cash prizes to the top students from each class. At the same time, Hearst began her lifelong practice of giving Christmas presents to employees of the Brick Store, the library, and, later, the kindergarten. To every church in Lead, she gave two hundred dollars annually. Such acts further endeared her to Lead residents as more a benefactor than a capitalistic owner. Grier endeared himself to the new librarian, Mary Jane Palethorpe. Following her divorce, he married her on 8 August 1896.[31]

Grier's next challenges came from Washington, D.C. The Homestake Mining Company consumed vast amounts of wood for mine timbering, general construction, and smelter fuel. In 1894, the United States government sued the company for ignoring federal restrictions governing the cutting of timber on public land, contending that it had illegally taken approximately seven million trees over nearly two decades. Homestake fought the charge and lost a four-year court battle but paid only seventy-five-thousand dollars in fines, a small sum compared to the value of the timber taken. To help prevent the complete destruction of forests in the Black Hills and elsewhere throughout the country, President Grover Cleveland set aside 21 million acres of forest reserves nationwide—967,680 in the Black Hills—before he left office in 1897. Grier and mining company officials elsewhere complained about the loss of free timber, but newly elected president William McKinley did not rescind the order. National forests became a reality.[32]

Mining companies throughout the West, including the Homestake, viewed the reserves, which came with new restrictions on timber cutting, as a threat to their profitability and resorted to fraud in order to continue cutting timber. Gifford Pinchot, a special agent for the secretary of the interior who went on to become chief of the United States Forest Service, sought a solution that would both conserve the resource and satisfy the needs of industry. He proposed a plan that allowed for government-regulated timber cutting at a minimal cost. Grier understood compromise and recognized the need to ensure that the timber resources vital to Homestake's future operation would continue. On 3 November 1897, he and company counsel Gideon Moody held a three-hour meeting with Pinchot, during which they agreed to a process that became the blueprint for the next century of timber cutting on federal land. Under Timber Case No.1 (1899) Homestake began the first regulated harvest of trees from public land. Over the next nine years, the company cut fifteen million board feet of timber. Grier became the Forest Service's cause célèbre for progressive resource management.[33]

The Homestake superintendent continued to push the company forward technologically, as well. In 1899, it became one of the first large-scale mining operations in the world to use cyanide successfully to process ore and waste concentrates. Grier had cut a deal with the developer of the process, Charles Merrill, who bore all of the costs of experimentation in return for a percentage of profits if the process worked. It did. The innovation made the Homestake operation even more efficient, allowing the company to recover 94 percent of the gold present in its mixed ores.[34]

On the morning of 8 March 1900, fire, the nemesis of mining communities, swept Lead, destroying homes and businesses in one-quarter of the town. Firefighters and Homestake employees made a stand at the Brick Store and stopped the conflagration. Homestake lost nothing to the blaze.[35] At Grier's suggestion, Hearst and Haggin thanked the community by donating five thousand dollars to Lead's fire companies and another one thousand dollars to the firemen of Deadwood. The *Lead Evening Call* effused about Grier, characterizing him as "kind-hearted, generous, brainy . . . [a] truly great man . . . doing many acts of kindness and charity in a quiet way."[36]

With Hearst's help, Grier accomplished a pet project the two had discussed years earlier—the creation of a kindergarten in Lead. Grier arranged for Hearst to attend its dedication in the spring of 1901 and hosted a reception on the evening of 27 May at which mine employ-

By the turn of the twentieth century, the Homestake was largely self-sufficient in all of its mining and milling operations. It generated its own electricity, ran its own railroad, and logged and milled its own timber. State Archives Collection, South Dakota State Historical Society

ees and community residents had an opportunity to meet their benefactor personally. Between two and three thousand people attended. Thomas and Mary Jane Grier, along with Phoebe Hearst, stood in a reception line for hours and shook every hand. "The soft white hands of ladies, the uncalloused hands of the office man or clerk, the hard brown hand of the laborer, received the same warm clasp," reported the local newspaper.[37] Phoebe Hearst exulted, "I was glad to see them and it was right."[38] A mutual appreciation characterized the relationship between the mine owner and the community. In 1903, children and residents of Lead collected nickels and dimes to purchase a silver loving cup for Hearst. She thanked them and returned for another visit in the fall of 1905.[39]

Grier also demonstrated a purposeful kindness, presenting himself in a manner as friendly to workers as he wanted them to be toward the company. Homestake carpenters fixed the Miners' Union Hall on several occasions.[40] He had the Brick Store buy advertisements in the pro-labor *Lead Register* and Deadwood's socialist *Lantern*. Grier and the store contributed aid to victims of an earthquake in Italy, the native country of many Homestake miners. In 1897, the superintendent granted company employees a half day off to hear WFM president Edward Boyce speak in Lead, where he denounced the capitalist exploitation of labor but expressed "delight" with local worker conditions.[41] The LCMU had helped to form the WFM in 1893 but dropped out almost immediately when the organization refused to pay costs for their representatives to attend a convention. Back in the WFM fold by late 1896, LCMU members were well aware of the federation's visible and defiant stance elsewhere. Even though the LCMU was more a benevolent and protective association than an active labor union and never staged a strike, local members gave financial support to their WFM brethren who were locked in industrial conflict outside of the Black Hills.[42]

Grier characterized his work force as "responsible, decent people, . . . bread-winners, and not loafers" and publicly recognized them as an important component in Homestake's profitability.[43] In some ways, he treated labor much like a fraternity, supporting the formation in 1898 of the Homestake Veterans Association, a social organization for employees with at least twenty-one years of service. Grier belonged, as did other members of management and the union alike. Fraternal "good feelings" had their limits, however, and did not address some of the larger issues that concerned the mine's rank-and-file workers. Periodically during the 1890s, the LCMU tried to expand its influence and increase its membership, which varied between 30 and 50 percent of eligible miners. In early 1901, the union resorted to intimidation and the placing of recruitment signs on Homestake property. Grier met the organizers head on and personally removed the placards. Any employee was free to join the union, he stated, but no one should be forced to do so. Grier clenched his iron fist, and the union backed off.[44]

Lead's miners worked ten-hour days but were well aware that eight-hour days had become a reality in California and the Comstock during the 1860s, throughout Utah by 1896, and in the copper camps of Montana in 1900.[45] Discussion of a reduced workday surfaced as early as 1890 and reappeared periodically. Officially, however, miners did

*Miners worked and ate by candlelight in the dark tunnels of the
Homestake for ten hours a day until 1906, when Grier granted
the company's workers an eight-hour workday. State Archives
Collection, South Dakota State Historical Society*

not ask for the adjustment, and management did not offer to bring it
about. That situation changed on 9 December 1906, when a union committee met with Grier to make the request. Clearly not surprised, the
superintendent recognized the opportunity to keep the workers' good
will and prevent further union inroads. He dealt with the request two
days later. "EIGHT-HOUR DAY GRANTED MINES," a headline in the
Lead Daily Call exclaimed. In truth, miners worked a nine-hour day,
counting time for preparation and cleanup, but only spent eight hours
underground. The Homestake also maintained its basic wage of $3.50
per day, effectively giving workers a pay increase of approximately 10
percent. Grier then acted even more expansively, extending the eight-
hour day to all Homestake employees, whether in mills, Brick Store,
library, or kindergarten, beginning 15 December 1906.[46] By the summer of 1907, most other Black Hills mines had also embraced the eight-
hour day.[47]

Fire broke out underground once more on 25 March 1907. Again, miners descended into gas and smoke in a vain effort to contain disaster; again, Grier worked long hours to meet and care for the men as they came out of the shafts. Both the *Lead Daily Call* and *Deadwood Pioneer Times* went to great lengths to compliment Grier's personal attention to employee safety. All the same, the fire proved intractable, and Grier ordered the mines flooded. On 30 May, dewatering began. Eighty-five million gallons had to be pumped from a mine that was much larger and deeper than it had been at the time of the 1893 fire.[48] Full mining operations resumed in October, coinciding with a celebration sponsored by the Homestake Veterans Association that drew five thousand happy people. "Let us all," Grier observed, "as in the past, see to it that for the future no harm comes to the good old goose that lays for us the golden egg."[49]

Grier continued to do his part to keep the goose profitable, but other factors complicated the task. In 1909, the WFM launched a campaign to accomplish what the LCMU had not been able to do—increase union membership. Organizer William Tracy arrived in February, intent on bringing every Homestake miner into the WFM fold. Labor Day brought reinforcements in the form of Emma Langdon, editor of the union's *Miners Magazine*, James Kirwan of the executive board, and Mary Harris ("Mother") Jones, a fiery orator and agitator. Nearly two dozen different unions marched in Lead's Labor Day parade, assembling afterward for a picnic and Mother Jones's two-hour speech, which "drifted very strongly into socialism," from the perspective of the *Lead Daily Call.*[50]

Grier was less concerned with a drift into socialism than with the miners' bold march toward a closed shop. Through a series of resolutions, the WFM made it clear that if, by 25 November 1909, all Homestake miners were not union members, the federation would call a strike.[51] Nothing of the sort would happen on Grier's watch. He knew the extent to which the closed shop restricted management in other western mining districts. Union forces may have become accustomed to Grier's velvet gloves, but he would not have them bind his iron fists. In response to the union threat, Grier notified the company's board of directors and Phoebe Hearst that he intended to shut down operations at Lead for "a few weeks" until miners came to their senses. Furthermore, when the mine reopened, he would make it strictly non-union.[52]

On 10 November 1909, Grier had Homestake's corporate counsel

Chambers Kellar sue the LCMU for ten thousand dollars in damages resulting from the union's intimidation of miners. One week later, on 17 November, Grier took out an advertisement in the *Lead Daily Call* stating that after 1 January 1910 Homestake would "engage only non-union men."[53] For the first time ever, editorials attacking Grier personally appeared in the *Lead Register* and Deadwood's *Lantern*. Freeman Knowles, the *Lantern* editor, foamed over corporate "parasites" like Grier, who posed as a "friend of labor" but assessed miners a mandatory $1.10 per month for medical coverage. Furthermore, asked Knowles, what had Grier ever done for a single Homestake widow? "DRAW CLOSER TOGETHER," the editor warned; Grier and all other Black Hills mine owners were simply waiting "to strike you under the fifth rib."[54]

Tempers flared on the night of 18 November 1909. Speaking in a packed Union Hall, William Tracy worked miners to fever pitch and then invited Grier to come and speak. The superintendent arrived to applause, but as he began to talk, Freeman Knowles interrupted with an anticorporate harangue. Grier left. The WFM next sent a delegation to plead its case with Phoebe Hearst. She declined to hear it, leaving everything in Grier's hands. The superintendent did not give miners an opportunity to strike on 25 November; he closed all Homestake operations on the twenty-fourth, locking out workers before they could strike.[55] If the miners guessed that a closed shop would come as easily as the eight-hour day, they had guessed wrong.

The lockout split Lead into pro-union and pro-Homestake camps. Rhetoric flashed in the press and spewed from pulpits.[56] The Reverend Marshall F. Montgomery, rector of Christ's Church, waxed most eloquent on behalf of Homestake in his Thanksgiving message. "The outward and visible sign of [the] bountiful providence of God is the Homestake mine," the pastor intoned. "God's goodness and mercy is seen in every activity pertaining thereto; . . . every wish for the common good granted, every contrivance for the common welfare inaugurated, everything that . . . the betterment of humanity could suggest has been undertaken."[57]

Grier became a vengeful angel, closing the company hospital and pulling advertising for the Brick Store from both the *Register* and the *Lantern*. Notice went out that miners who wanted to return to the Homestake had until 15 December to renounce all union ties and register with the company's general office.[58] The Lead city council, yielding to Grier's pressure, agreed to pay for "special policemen" to keep order. Armed Pinkerton "detectives" arrived immediately thereafter.[59] Grier also played the trump card of Homestake's land ownership, warning that troublemakers with property "upon any lands belonging to my superintendency . . . will lose their improvements."[60] In accordance with the Homestake action, the owners of all of the smaller mines in the Black Hills agreed to shut down and hire only non-union labor upon reopening.[61]

Twenty-four years of good will paid off for Grier. The WFM relied on threats of strikes and violence to leverage change. Grier simply outmaneuvered the union's tactic at Homestake, where longtime miners had too much respect for the superintendent to resort to violence. Cracks appeared quickly in the union façade as miners quietly signed Homestake's non-union pledge. On 15 December, the WFM organized a parade of "non-signers," but Grier had eight hundred and fifty names on his list ("the horde of lickspittles," Freeman Knowles called them).[62] The WFM helped Grier's cause when it announced strike benefits of only two meals per day (for members only, not families) and $3.50 per week.[63]

To bolster his position further, Grier orchestrated the formation of the Loyal Legion, composed of men who wanted to return to work, on 6 January 1910. Legion organizers passed out red, white, and blue buttons and immediately signed up five hundred men, who were loyal to Grier as much as to the Homestake. In return, Grier promised to reopen the mine on 13 January. That morning, the Ellison hoist's big whistle called Loyal Legion and non-union members back to work.[64] The sound was "the choicest music" Lead had enjoyed in nearly two months, according to the *Daily Call.*[65]

Despite this success, Grier had one piece of unfinished business—breaking the miners' union structurally and financially. As promised, the other Black Hills mine owners—thirteen of them—went non-union and took out an ongoing advertisement in the *Lead Daily Call* asking all businesses to give "vigorous" support for "Non-Union labor conditions" everywhere. At the Homestake, Grier instituted background checks on men and rejected those with WFM or Industrial Workers of the World (IWW) records. In the spring of 1910, vandalism flared up in connection with an unsuccessful effort by the WFM to influence Lead city elections. Animosities lingered for the next couple of years, but in 1912, the LCMU went bankrupt and lost its charter.[66]

The Homestake hospital was built in 1889. Adams Museum, Deadwood, S.Dak.

The Homestake resumed full production on 3 March 1910, but Grier had felt the sting of employee criticism during the lockout. Immediately, he dropped the $1.10 per month hospital assessment and opened the facility free of charge to all employees and dependents. On 1 August, he initiated the Homestake Employee Aid Fund, a generous workmen's compensation program. An employee-dominated board exercised control over sick and disability pay, setting disability payments that ranged from two hundred dollars for insanity to eight hundred dollars for total disability. In addition, the fund included an eight-hundred-dollar death benefit to be paid to the widows Freeman Knowles had lionized during the lockout. Grier also upgraded mine facilities to make employees safer. He improved "dry" rooms, where miners cleaned up after work; instituted a "First Aid and Mine Rescue" program to identify dangerous conditions, correct them, and train rescue crews; gave out awards to employees who worked a year without injury; and added a year-end pay bonus of 7 percent of wages earned for all employees.[67]

The crown jewel among the benefits Grier provided workers was the recreation building he announced on 13 November 1911. The multipurpose structure would house the library, a swimming pool, bowling alley,

From the lobby of the Homestake Opera House and Recreation Building, pictured here, visitors proceeded to the auditorium, library, gymnasium, bowling alley, billiard room, or swimming pool. Adams Museum, Deadwood, S.Dak.

game and exercise rooms, and a large auditorium. Use of the facilities would be free to the community.[68] Construction had just begun in the spring of 1912 when the sixty-two-year-old Grier had a heart attack, followed by surgery in mid-October. He returned to Lead in early 1913, but company physician D. K. Dickinson laid out a stark ultimatum and prognosis: reduce stress, leave Lead's high elevation, and live ten, maybe twenty, more years; return to work and live three. Phoebe Hearst sought to smooth the way for Grier, offering to allow him to retain his salary and position while superintending *in absentia* and visiting Lead once or twice annually. Grier declined. He did, however, make out a will in May of 1913 and begin construction of a second home in Los Angeles, California.[69]

As Grier recovered, Congress was instigating an inquiry into industrial working conditions throughout the country and designated Lead as a site for public hearings. From 2 to 4 August 1914, four members of the Congressional Committee on Industrial Relations walked Lead streets, prowled area mines, and solicited formal testimony. Grier spent most of two days on the stand defending his twenty-nine years as Homestake superintendent. He did not face a friendly audience. Chairman John R. Commons, a vocal progressive and professor of economics at the University of Wisconsin, had founded the American Association for Labor Legislation. Austin B. Garretson, a longtime member of the Order of Railway Conductors, had risen to the presidency of the union. John B. Lennon had unionized Denver tailors in 1883 and in 1914 served as national treasurer of the American Federation of Labor (AFL). James P. O'Connell, a machinist, had belonged to the Knights of Labor in the 1890s and was now vice-president of the AFL.[70]

In his testimony, Grier spelled out every benefit Homestake employees enjoyed, some of which even company counsel Chambers Kellar called "socialistic and . . . progressive." At the end, Chairman Commons sat back, impressed. First, however, he took Grier to task for having "crushed out all opposition, not only labor opposition but all business opposition, in so far as you cared to do it, during the lockout."[71] Commons then marveled, "You have here the most remarkable business organization that I have come across in the country. You have developed welfare features which are beyond anything that I know of, and are given with a liberal hand." Committee members Garretson and O'Connell worried that such features were only a heartbeat away from chang-

Two years after Grier's death, the Homestake Veterans Association erected this bronze statue on the grounds of the Opera House and Recreation Building to honor the superintendent. State Archives Collection, South Dakota State Historical Society

ing. When Garretson characterized Grier's administration as "a despotism, benevolent though it may be," the Homestake superintendent pled "guilty to the charge of benevolence in a high degree," but he took exception to the charge of despotism.[72]

On 31 August 1914, the symbol of Grier's benevolent despotism, the Homestake Opera House and Recreation Building, opened. Grier made a "neat little address" and then turned the facility over to company employees for the benefit of everyone in Lead.[73] On Saturday night, 5 September, Thomas and Mary Jane Grier walked through the building one last time. The next day, they left by train for Los Angeles, where Grier's second heart attack killed him on 22 September.[74]

"Today Lead is mourning," the *Daily Call* grieved upon learning of the superintendent's death.[75] Businesses and schools in Lead and Deadwood closed on Monday, 28 September, the day of Grier's funeral. His body lay in state that morning in the new recreation building before being taken to the Episcopal church for services. Grier was then laid to rest in the West Lead cemetery, on a knoll overlooking the greater part of Lead and the Homestake works. To commemorate his contributions to the company and the community, members of the Homestake Veterans Association raised funds to erect a statue of Grier at the entrance to the Opera House and Recreation Building on Main Street in 1916.[76]

The throngs that turned out for the dedication of Grier's statue two years after his death testified to his large and lingering presence. Miners admired his willingness to face the same dangers they did in battling fires underground and appreciated his humane interest in their welfare. They also came to respect Grier's strong, efficient corporate management—always achieved on his own terms—that made people like Phoebe Hearst and James Haggin rich but also gave employees well-paying jobs in an environment that was livable for themselves and their families.[77] While Hearst's broad-ranging philanthropy was well known, it was Grier who focused her generosity on Lead to soften and enrich the lives of Homestake workers. The iron hand of his efficient management flexed itself within the velvet glove of his own benevolent socialism and Hearst's noblesse oblige. In combination, they formed a corporate milieu that was unique among western mining towns.

NOTES

1. Three histories of the Homestake provide context for Grier's career. Joseph H. Cash's *Working the Homestake* (Ames: Iowa State University Press, 1973) focuses on labor issues; Mildred Fielder's *The Treasure of Homestake Gold* (Aberdeen, S.Dak.: North Plains Press, 1970) is a newspaper-based social and anecdotal history; and Duane A. Smith's *Staking a Claim in History: The Evolution of the Homestake Mining Company* (Walnut Creek, Calif.: Homestake Mining Co., 2001) is panegyrical, marking the end of company mining.

2. For biographical information on George Hearst, *see* Judith Robinson, *The Hearsts: An American Dynasty* (Newark: University of Delaware Press, 1991), and Fremont and Cora M. Older, *George Hearst: California Pioneer* (Los Angeles, Calif.: Westernlore, 1966).

3. *Black Hills Daily Pioneer*, 21, 22 Sept. 1878; Thomas J. Grier, Notebook, Mar. 1879, Thomas J. Grier File, Black Hills Mining Museum, Lead, S.Dak. Born in Peckingham, Ontario, on 18 May 1850, Grier was the fourth of James and Annie Patterson Grier's ten children. He learned telegraphy at age seventeen and started his career in Montreal before economic booms in the western United States enticed him to Utah in 1871. For an enthusiastic but not always accurate family genealogy, *see* William M. Grier, Jr., *The Griers: Pioneers in America and Canada, 1816–*

1991 (Denver, Colo.: Grier & Co., 1991). Biographical information also appears in George W. Kingsbury, *History of Dakota Territory*, and George Martin Smith, ed., *South Dakota: Its History and Its People*, 5 vols. (Chicago, Ill.: S. J. Clarke, 1915), 4:16–21; Doane Robinson, *History of South Dakota, Together with Personal Mention of Citizens of South Dakota*, 2 vols. ([Logansport, Ind.]: B. F. Bowen & Co., 1904), 2:1248–49.

4. Grier Notebook, July 1885; *Black Hills Daily Times*, 18 July 1885; Harry M. Gregg File, Miscellaneous Historical Documents and Papers, Homestake Mining Company Records (HMCR), Phoebe Apperson Hearst Public Library, Lead, S.Dak. The *Black Hills Daily Times* contains numerous items about Grier's early activities and the search for McMaster's successor, see 25 Apr., 30 May, 29 Dec. 1883, 4 Jan., 10 Aug., 7 Sept., 11 Oct., 8, 19, 26 Nov., 12, 14, 30 Dec. 1884, 12 July 1885.

5. Malone, *The Battle for Butte: Mining and Politics on the Northern Frontier, 1864–1906* (Seattle: University of Washington Press, 1981), pp. 77–79; Peterson, *The Bonanza Kings: The Social Origins and Business Behavior of Western Mining Entrepreneurs, 1870–1900* (Norman: University of Oklahoma Press, 1991).

6. *Black Hills Daily Times*, 1, 23 Aug. 1885.

7. U.S., Congress, Senate, Commission on Industrial Relations, *Industrial Relations: Final Reports and Testimony*, S.Doc. 415, 64th Cong., 1st sess., 1916, 4:3656–57.

8. This statement is not to suggest that Grier did not benefit financially from his involvement in the Black Hills. Homestake paid him well—twenty-five hundred dollars per month by the time of his death in 1914. He also secured financial interests in other regional enterprises. *See Industrial Relations: Final Reports and Testimony*, 4:3657, and Richmond L. Clow, "Wasp No. 2: 'The Wonder Mine of the Black Hills,'" *South Dakota History* 15 (Winter 1985): 278.

9. *See* Grier Notebook, Mar. 1879–early 1909; *Black Hills Daily Times*, 18, 27 Mar., 22 Dec. 1887.

10. Fielder, *Treasure of Homestake Gold*, pp. 142–43, 147, 153; Thomas J. Grier to George Hearst, 25 May 1888, MS 57, File 2, Box 37, Phoebe Apperson Hearst Papers (PAHP), Bancroft Library, University of California, Berkeley. Although Hearst Mercantile was a company store, Homestake paid workers in cash, not scrip. The store did, however, advance employees interest-free loans for purchases, collecting by prearrangement on payday. For a history of the Hearst Mercantile, *see* Steven R. Kinsella, "Company Store: The Hearst Mercantile, 1879–1942," *South Dakota History* 20 (Summer 1990): 96–119.

11. *Black Hills Daily Times*, 1 Jan. 1890. *See also* 1 Jan. 1889.

12. Ibid., 2 Sept. 1888.

13. Ibid., 25, 27–29 May, 7 June 1890.

14. R. E. Driscoll, *Seventy Years of Banking in the Black Hills* (Rapid City, S.Dak.: Gate City Guide, 1948), pp. 30–31, 60, 62; Cash, *Working the Homestake*, pp. 63–64; *Black Hills Daily Times*, 20, 24 Oct. 1885, 18 Feb., 17 Dec. 1887. Grier used First National Bank as his agent in purchasing mining claims when he did not want the Homestake name initially associated with the transaction. Driscoll, *Seventy Years of Banking*, p. 61. For the effort to rebuild Central City, *see Black Hills Daily Times*, 30 July 1887, 26–28 Apr. 1888, 19 Apr. 1890, 3 Sept. 1891.

15. Grier Notebook, Feb. 1891.

16. Phoebe A. Hearst to T. J. Grier, [n.d.] 1893, MS 57, File 1, Box 37, PAHP.

17. Fielder, *Treasure of Homestake Gold*, p. 154; Robinson, *History of South Dakota*, 2:1248–49; Edward Hardy Clark, "Reminiscences of the Hearst Family" (oral-history transcript), 1967, PAHP. Hearst arranged for Clark to serve on the Homestake board of directors beginning in 1894. When James B. A. Haggin died in 1914, Clark became company president until his own death in 1944.

18. Edward H. Clark, Testimony, 7 July 1920, HMCR. In stock dividends alone, Phoebe Hearst realized approximately $14 million from the Homestake mine during her lifetime. She also received all net revenues from the company store, which averaged between three-quarters of a million and one million dollars per year.

19. Fielder, *Treasure of Homestake Gold*, pp. 152–54, 156–57.

20. Ibid., pp. 151–52; Cash, *Working the Homestake*, pp. 58–59, 73, 75, 77. Nothing in the Lead press indicates any acrimony in the negotiation process, but Homestake officials clearly did not hesitate to exercise the company's economic clout when it came to developing new properties.

21. *Black Hills Daily Times*, 18 Apr. 1893. Coverage of the fire in the *Black Hills Daily Times* appeared in every issue from 15 April through 26 April 1893.

22. Historian Gunther Peck argues that, while risk-taking on the mining frontier was class-based (owners/managers assumed financial risk, while miners shouldered physical risk), it produced a sense of masculine bonding. Peck, "Manly Gambles: The Politics of Risk on the Comstock Lode, 1860–1880," in *Across the Great Divide: Cultures of Manhood in the American West*, ed. Matthew Basso, Laura McCall, and Dee Garceau (New York: Routledge, 2001), pp. 73–96. Grier's actions in the fire exemplify risk-taking at the miners' level and created a long-lasting bond.

23. *Black Hills Daily Times*, 25 Apr. 1893.

24. Mark Wyman, *Hard Rock Epic: Western Miners and the Industrial Revolution, 1860–1910* (Berkeley: University of California Press, 1979), pp. 172–73; Cash, *Working the Homestake*, p. 39; *Black Hills Daily Times*, 14 May, 26, 30 Aug., 27 Dec. 1893.

25. *Black Hills Daily Times*, 12 July 1894.

26. Ibid., 21 July, 1 Aug. 1894. Numerous articles in the *Black Hills Daily Times* between 21 July and 16 August 1894 chronicle the negotiations and resumption of work.

27. Ibid., 12 Aug. 1894.

28. Ibid., 27 Oct. 1894. *See also Lead Evening Call*, 18 Aug. 1894.

29. *Black Hills Daily Times*, 24 Nov. 1894; *Lead Evening Call*, 19, 23, 26 Dec. 1894; Alexandria Marie Nickless, "Phoebe Apperson Hearst: The Most Powerful Woman in California" (Ph.D. diss., University of California-Davis, 1994), pp. 120–21.

30. Telegram, Thomas J. Grier to Phoebe Apperson Hearst, 26 Dec. 1894, PAHP.

31. *Lead Evening Call*, 8 Apr., 1, 20 Aug., 7 Nov. 1895, 21 Jan., 10 Aug., 16 Oct. 1896, 12 Oct. 1899; *Lead City Daily Tribune*, 7 June 1901; Lawrence County, South Dakota, Marriage Records, 1895–1898, Book 3, p. 241, Lawrence County Courthouse, Deadwood, S.Dak.

32. Smith, *Staking a Claim*, p. 96; Richmond L. Clow, "Timber Users, Timber Savers: Homestake Mining Company and the First Regulated Timber Harvest," *South Dakota History* 22 (Fall 1992): 220–23; *Lead Evening Call*, 25, 26 Feb., 1 Mar. 1897.

33. Clow, "Timber Users, Timber Savers," pp. 224–34; Smith, *Staking a Claim*, p. 99; William M. Grier, *The Griers*, pp. 69, 71; *Lead Morning Call*, 20 Jan. 1898.

34. Fielder, *Treasure of Homestake Gold*, pp. 168–70; Smith, *Staking a Claim*, p. 96; Richmond L. Clow, *Chasing the Glitter: Black Hills Milling, 1874–1959*, Historical Preservation Series, no. 2 (Pierre: South Dakota State Historical Society Press, 2002), p. 133. Homestake first tried cyanide processing in 1892, but Merrill's process worked best.

35. *Lead Evening Call*, 8 Mar. 1900; Grier to Edward Clark, 10 Mar. 1900, PAHP.

36. *Lead Evening Call*, 21 Mar. 1900.

37. *Lead City Daily Tribune*, 28 May 1901. *See also* Nickless, "Phoebe Apperson Hearst," pp. 103–23.

38. Phoebe Apperson Hearst to Clara Anthony, 7 June 1901, PAHP.

39. Cash, *Working the Homestake*, p. 74; William M. Grier, *The Griers*, p. 80.

40. *Lead Evening Call*, 7, 21 Apr. 1897, 12 Oct. 1899; *Lead Morning Call*, 1 June, 27 July 1897; Donald D. Toms, *The Flavor of Lead: An Ethnic History* (Lead, S.Dak.: Lead Historic Preservation Society, 1997), p. 63.

41. *Lead Evening Call*, 25 Mar. 1897.

42. The LCMU formed in 1877, built its first hall in 1878, and formally incorpo-

rated in 1880. Cash, *Working the Homestake*, pp. 37–38; Fielder, *Treasure of Homestake Gold*, pp. 198, 200; *Lead Evening Call*, 5 Sept. 1896.

43. George P. Baldwin, *The Black Hills Illustrated: A Terse Description of Conditions Past and Present of America's Greatest Mineral Belt* (Lead, S.Dak.: Black Hills Mining Men's Association, 1904), p. 128.

44. *The Homestake Veterans Association* (Lead, S.Dak.: Homestake Mining Association, [1951]), pp. [5–6]; *Lead Evening Call*, 5 Sept. 1896; *Lead Daily Call*, 8 Oct. 1906, 6 Dec. 1909, 3 Aug. 1914. Members also took issue with an assessment of between two and five dollars per month to pay for operating Union Hall. When hall revenues made the assessment unnecessary, membership increased. *Lead City Daily Tribune*, 29 Apr. 1901.

45. Wyman, *Hard Rock Epic*, pp. 203–5, 207–12.

46. *Lead Daily Call*, 11 Dec. 1906. *See also*, 10, 13 Dec. 1906; *Deadwood Lantern*, 6 Dec. 1906.

47. *Lead Daily Call*, 24, 31 Dec. 1906, 5 June 1907. The process was not smooth, however, and included a five-month-long strike among many employees at other mines. Historian David B. Miller suggested that the Homestake action granting the eight-hour day stung small mine owners. Clearly, Grier did what he believed best for the Homestake. Miller, "The Homestake Lockout of 1909–1910: A Small Mine's Perspective," *South Dakota History* 27 (Fall 1997): 157.

48. *Lead Daily Call*, 26, 28 Mar., 3, 8, 22 Apr., 31 May, 5 Oct. 1907.

49. Ibid., 5 Oct. 1907. *See also* 14 May, 3 Oct. 1907.

50. Ibid., 7 Sept. 1909. *See also* 1 Sept., 27 Dec. 1909.

51. Ibid., 11, 25 Oct. 1909; Fielder, *Treasure of Homestake Gold*, p. 201.

52. [Edward H. Clark] to Richard A. Clark, Nov. 1909, MS 58, File 11, Box 37, PAHP.

53. *Lead Daily Call*, 17 Nov. 1909. See also 10 Nov. 1909.

54. *Deadwood Lantern*, 18 Nov. 1909.

55. *Lead Daily Call*, 19 Nov. 1909; J. V. N. Dorr, "South Dakota," *Engineering and Mining Journal* 89 (8 Jan. 1910): 92; Cash, *Working the Homestake*, pp. 84–85.

56. *Lead Daily Call*, 29 Nov., 7 Dec. 1909; *Deadwood Lantern*, 29 Jan. 1910.

57. *Lead Daily Call*, 29 Nov. 1909.

58. Ibid., 7, 8 Dec. 1909.

59. Ibid., 30 Nov. 1909.

60. Ibid., 27 Nov. 1909. An article in the 13 January 1910 issue of the *Lantern* suggests that Grier may have evicted a "peaceable Russian family," but Grier later stated emphatically that the "Homestake Co. has never issued an order revoking a permit" (*Industrial Relations: Final Reports and Testimony*, 4:3575).

61. Cash, *Working the Homestake*, p. 92. David Miller, "Homestake Lockout," p. 157, noted that while the lockout caused the smaller mines financial hardship, they ultimately benefited from Homestake's breaking of union control. The other mines instituting the non-union pledge employed approximately eight hundred workers. *Engineering and Mining Journal* 89 (22 Jan. 1910): 243, (11 June 1910): 1243–44; *Industrial Relations: Final Reports and Testimony*, 4:3619–20.

62. *Deadwood Lantern*, 30 Dec. 1909. *See also Lead Daily Call*, 30 Nov., 6, 9, 15 Dec. 1909, 6 Jan. 1910; Grier to Edward Clark, 28 Dec. 1909, MS 57, File 4, Box 37, PAHP.

63. *Deadwood Lantern*, 20 Jan. 1910.

64. Cash, *Working the Homestake*, pp. 94–95; *Industrial Relations: Final Reports and Testimony*, 4:3562–63; Fielder, *Treasure of Homestake Gold*, pp. 204–5; *Lead Daily Call*, 6, 8, 10, 13 Jan., 9 Feb. 1910.

65. *Lead Daily Call*, 13 Jan. 1910.

66. Cash, *Working the Homestake*, pp. 92–93, 97; E. F. Irwin to Grier, 2 Nov. 1910, 14 Feb. 1911, Grier File, HMCR; *Lead Daily Call*, 12 Jan. 1910.

67. Fielder, *Treasure of Homestake Gold*, pp. 207–8; *Lead Daily Call*, 1 Aug. 1910; Grier to Robert A. Kinzie, 23 Nov. 1911, and R. W. Bonney to Grier, n.d., Grier File, HMCR.

68. For a history of the building to 1984, *see* Donald D. Toms and William J. Stone, *The Homestake Opera House and Recreation Building: "The Jewel of the Black Hills"* (Lead, S.Dak.: Lead City Fine Arts Association, 1985).

69. William M. Grier, *The Griers*, pp. 72–73; Richard Blackstone to Shattuck & Hussey, 3 July 1912, Homestake Opera House Construction File No. 2, HMCR; Edward Clark to Phoebe Hearst, 10 Oct. 1912, MS 38, File 11, Box 17, PAHP; *Lead Daily Call*, 29 Sept. 1914; Probate of the Will of Thomas Johnston Grier, Fourth Judicial Circuit Court, Lawrence County, S.Dak., No. 1654, Lawrence County Courthouse.

70. Gary M. Fink, ed., *Biographical Dictionary of American Labor* (Westport, Conn.: Greenwood Press, 1984), pp. 161–62, 242–43, 351, 442–43. The testimony collected in Lead appears in *Industrial Relations: Final Reports and Testimony*, 4:3537–3679.

71. *Industrial Relations: Final Reports and Testimony*, 4:3655. When Grier ran notice in the *Lead Daily Call* that troublemakers who supported the WFM during the lockout "would lose their improvements," he meant not only miners but also businesses with structures on land the Homestake owned under the 1892 agreement with the city. *Lead Daily Call*, 27 Nov. 1909.

72. *Industrial Relations: Final Reports and Testimony*, 4:3543–3655; *Lead Daily Call*, 3, 6 Aug. 1914.

73. *Lead Daily Call*, 1 Sept. 1914.

74. Ibid., 23 Sept. 1914. *See also* Edward H. Clark to Phoebe Apperson Hearst, 23 Sept. 1914, MS 38, File 11, Box 17, PAHP.

75. *Lead Daily Call*, 23 Sept. 1914.

76. Ibid., 24, 26, 28, 29 Sept. 1914; Fielder, *Treasure of Homestake Gold*, p. 215. Grier left an estate of $238,310, which would be approximately $4 million today. Edward H. Clark to Phoebe Apperson Hearst, 4 Nov. 1914, MS 37, File 5, Box 37, PAHP.

77. Cash, *Working the Homestake*, p. 26; Clark to Hearst, 4 Nov. 1914.

Edward Louis Senn

A CRUSADER ON THE LAST FRONTIERS

Denise Karst Pearce

When the underground rings of lawless old Deadwood said to E. L. Senn, a newspaper king of the frontier, "Shut up or get out!" he fired back as he once had done to the cattle rustlers, "YOU get out! That's what I'm here for—to run you out." And being a religious man he ordered them in biblical scareheads to "Get thee behind me, Satan."[1]

The Black Hills of South Dakota have an intriguing past filled with colorful characters and places. Wild Bill Hickok, Calamity Jane, Preacher Smith, and Deadwood Dick all have their places in the history of the region. Although largely forgotten today, Edward Louis ("E. L.") Senn also played a significant part in shaping the Dakota frontier. Senn, however, was more than just a character of Old West folklore. In each of his various roles as teacher, homesteader, journalist, prohibitionist, and author, Senn resolved to better the lives of his fellow Dakotans. A fiery crusader with deep moral convictions and an unbreakable spirit, he imagined a prairie governed by justice, a land of opportunity for families, and a Deadwood freed from the vices of drinking, gambling, and prostitution. Defeated on more than one occasion, he refused to relent, maintaining that "one man and God make a majority in any fight."[2]

Senn was born 22 December 1865 in Clinton, Iowa, the

This essay originally appeared in *South Dakota History* 29 (Spring 1999): 1–22.

youngest of three children born to Christian and Louisa Glass Senn.[3] After his parents divorced in 1871, his father disappeared, and his mother soon married Henry Gerold. In 1876, Senn's brother Albert left home for the Colorado gold fields, and the rest of the family moved to Morrison, Illinois, in 1879. Four years later, his mother, stepfather, and sister Lillian traveled to Brule County, near Kimball, in Dakota Territory. Senn stayed behind, graduating from Morrison's high school in 1883 and then teaching school in Deer Grove, Illinois, for approximately one year.[4]

By late summer 1884, his "mother's frequent pleas" brought Senn to Dakota Territory, but he quickly found his new home to be "too small for all of us."[5] Henry Gerold left the shanty later that year, and Senn became the head of his frontier family. To support the clan, he farmed during the summer and taught school in the winter. After their mother died in 1886, Senn's siblings, deciding that the homestead was worthless, turned all legal rights to the claim over to their younger brother, who stayed to farm and teach school for another year before leaving to attend the Normal School in Valparaiso, Indiana.[6]

Returning to Brule County in the summer of 1888, E. L. Senn sold the homestead and traveled to central Charles Mix County to teach in various frontier schools. When he discovered that the area lacked organized religious services, he established a Sunday School program for local children and was soon drafted to preach weekly sermons to his fellow frontiersmen.[7] Senn eventually bought a squatter's claim on the abandoned Fort Randall military reserve, anticipating that the area would be formally opened to settlers. Despite the hardships of living in an area with no railroads, few doctors, and primitive schools, Senn later described his years in the "Lower Military" as some of the most pleasant of his life. He even found time to form a baseball club with his fellow homesteaders, among whom he found "many fine, fairly well educated people."[8] During the early 1890s, however, the need to replenish his exhausted funds drew Senn back to central Charles Mix County, where he again found employment in the classroom.

In the settlement of Bloomington, the family of George Norbeck, the preacher at the local Norwegian Lutheran church, opened their home to the prairie schoolteacher. Senn had become acquainted with Norbeck during South Dakota's statehood campaign, and Norbeck presided over the Law Enforcement League, a prohibitionist organization for which Senn served as secretary. During his stay with the family,

The editorial career of Edward L. Senn, pictured with his wife Christa Stull Senn, spanned nearly three decades. Patricia Senn Dewald, Bowdle, S.Dak.

Senn and Norbeck's eldest son, Peter, forged a lifelong bond of mutual admiration.[9] Peter Norbeck, who would go on to become governor and United States senator, allied with Senn on volatile political issues ranging from state prohibition enforcement to Senn's own crusade to eliminate vice in Deadwood. Norbeck contributed generously to Senn's Deadwood campaign yet declined his friend's offer of full repayment. "Never mind," he told Senn, "I wont [*sic*] carry the account to the next world."[10]

While in central Charles Mix County, Senn frequently visited the home of Charles and Phoebe Elizabeth Stull, with whom he had resided during the spring of 1889 while teaching school in Platte. Christa, the Stulls' daughter, had been one of Senn's pupils and became "a favorite not only in school, but also at home."[11] Upon returning and finding that his former student had grown up considerably, Senn asked for her hand in marriage. Although he was broke and in debt, Christa Stull married him on 14 January 1894, and the couple welcomed their first son, Albert Edward, into the family on 11 November 1894.[12]

Senn continued to teach school and again tried his luck at farming during the early years of his marriage. His wife gave birth to two more children, Edward Louis and Lillian, before Senn moved his family across the Missouri River in 1901. Ready to conquer a new frontier, he filed on a quarter-section tract in Lyman County near the town of Iona. He then purchased one hundred cattle, erected cattle sheds, and built a small home on the site.[13]

While ranching in Lyman County, Senn also began his first weekly newspaper—the *Pioneer*. Initially produced in a corner of the family's primitive shanty, the *Pioneer* was small in size (four pages of four columns each) but large in purpose: Senn intended his publication to unite homesteaders in combating the cattle rustlers who terrorized area ranchers like himself. Through the pages of the *Pioneer*, which he described as "all home print with a few advertisements from Oacoma and Chamberlain business men," Senn sought to "give publicity to conditions and arouse honest settlers to action."[14] The rustlers, however, refused to let the bald-headed little editor break their chain of lawlessness and burned his ranch home to the ground, unaware that Senn had moved his print shop and his family to a shanty in Iona. Having escaped unharmed, the editor continued to publish his message of protest. Senn's efforts eventually helped to break up one of the largest cattle-rustling rings in the area.[15]

Senn also became active in local politics during the early 1900s, founding the Citizen's Ticket Party, whose members worked to elect honest, law-abiding men to public positions. The *Pioneer* was instrumental in promoting the party's efforts to combat rustling and enforce prohibition. In 1903, Senn started his second publication, the *Lyman County Record*, in Dirkstown. After the birth of the couple's fourth child, Bernice, in 1904, Senn moved his family and the *Pioneer* to Oacoma.[16]

The move and his subsequent association with Harry Hunter, an agent for the Chicago, Milwaukee, St. Paul & Pacific Railroad, gave Senn the opportunity to pursue his career as a newspaperman. The railroad was expanding its line from Chamberlain to Rapid City and had plotted town sites along the proposed track. Hunter, who was in charge of selling lots to individual settlers, reached a lucrative deal with Senn. The railroad would give Senn a choice lot in each town, and he would establish a frontier newspaper office on the site. In return, Senn would advertise, at no cost to the railroad, the town lots it had for sale.[17]

Thus began Senn's frontier newspaper empire. He became known as

The sparse furnishings of the Caton Advertiser *office, which Senn may have owned for a time, typified the newspapers of the Dakota frontier. State Archives Collection, South Dakota State Historical Society*

the "Final Proof King" of South Dakota, for the primary source of income for his papers was the "final proof" notices settlers were required to publish in compliance with the Homestead Act of 1862. Under the act, the United States government would grant a "free" 160-acre tract of public land to anyone who resided on it for five years, made specified improvements, and paid a modest processing fee.[18] Before the government would grant a homesteader title to the land, he or she was required to publish for five consecutive weeks in the newspaper nearest the claim the names of witnesses who would attest that the individual had fulfilled the act's requirements. For each final proof published, the homesteader paid the newspaper five dollars. Anyone contesting a settler's notice paid a publication fee as well.[19]

Senn used these federal regulations in tandem with his railroad arrangement to expand his chain of final-proof papers between 1905 and

1908. Taking the old equipment from his early newspapers, Senn was able "to establish new papers at frontier points covering most of [an] area." Other entrepreneurs tried the same scheme, but few were able to accumulate more than two or three papers. "I had the inside track," Senn reported, "and kept my string profitable by purchasing some established by others. As final proof fields became less profitable, two or more were combined, thus expanding the areas for those remaining." Senn admitted in his memoirs that he could not recall the names or locations of all his frontier newspapers, which eventually totaled approximately thirty-five.[20] Senn's former employee and long-time friend Edith Eudora Kohl later wrote that Senn moved his newspapers "across the prairies like checkers across the board."[21]

Kohl, who later chronicled her experiences on the South Dakota frontier in her 1938 novel *Land of the Burnt Thigh*, met Senn when she took over one of his frontier print shops. Arriving on the Lower Brule Indian Reservation in 1907 as homesteaders, Kohl and her sister, Ida Mary Ammons, quickly realized that they needed extra income to survive on the relentless prairie. Despite her lack of printing experience, Kohl boldly asked Senn, whom folks claimed was as "heartless as a Wall Street corporation," for ten dollars a week to take over the *McClure Press*.[22] Although the sum was two dollars a week more than the previous printer had received, Senn apparently admired Kohl's temerity. "I don't know whether you are worth $2 a week more than Myrtle or not," he told her, "but anybody that has the nerve you exhibit in asking for it no doubt deserves it. Moreover, I like to flatter such youthful vanity."[23] Heartless or not, Senn needed someone to continue the *McClure Press*, for printers, with or without experience, were the lifeblood of his "monopoly out here on the raw prairie."[24]

As their working relationship and friendship developed, Kohl learned that the reputation of the Final Proof King was perhaps undeserved. After a particularly frustrating morning, Kohl unleashed her fury over the antique press she had inherited with the print shop. Armed with the nerve and vanity that Senn so admired, she traveled to Presho to confront the editor and demand a new press. "To my surprise, he asked no questions," she wrote in *Land of the Burnt Thigh*. "His kindness so melted my exasperation with the press that I was at a loss to know how to begin the fighting talk I had come to make." Kohl did not have to fight. Despite the financial problems Senn was apparently having at the time, Kohl gained a new press as well as the respect of the "ruthless"

Final Proof King.[25] In a 1947 article entitled "Frontier Crusader," however, Kohl allowed readers a glimpse at the fiery personality that enabled Senn to stand up for his beliefs. During the publisher's early days as editor of the *Pioneer*, Kohl recalled, "a gang leader strode in with a gun in his hand and kicked over the ink bucket." In response, the agile Senn grabbed a six-shooter and ordered the intruder to "get your cattle rustlers out of here or I'll smear this whole county with printers' ink!"[26]

An important event that Kohl reported on and later depicted in *Land of the Burnt Thigh* also played a role in the newspaperman's next move. As Kohl vividly described, the Rosebud land lottery of 1908 drew thousands of people to south-central South Dakota to register for a drawing for land that the government had removed from the Rosebud Indian Reservation and was now opening to non-Indian settlers. Senn himself registered and drew a lucky number, awarding him the opportunity to choose the location of his fourth homestead. In the spring of 1909, he moved his family to their new home in Tripp County.[27]

Around the same time, Senn acquired his first daily newspaper, the *Deadwood Daily Telegram*. With the purchase of the *Telegram*, Senn enlarged the scope of his business by establishing a "ready print" department, which furnished "patent insides" for about twenty newspapers in western South Dakota in addition to his own thirty-five weeklies. While this expansion demanded that he spend much of his time in Deadwood, Senn traveled occasionally to his Tripp County homestead, where his family spent much of the year. During the winter, they joined him in Deadwood, where his children attended school and where his fifth child, Ruth, was born in December of 1911. In 1912, after Senn sold his homestead improvements and relinquished his filing to the government, his family made Deadwood their permanent home.[28]

When Senn took over the *Telegram* in 1909, Deadwood had changed little since its founding during the Black Hills gold rush of 1876. Saloons operated at all hours of the night, bawdy houses advertised openly and freely, and gambling halls emptied the pockets of patrons. Many of Deadwood's most powerful businessmen, Senn found, directed their resources toward maintaining the lawless atmosphere. Using financial pressure, they exerted a strong hold on local law-enforcement authorities and on much of the city's population, one-third of which made a portion of its living from some form of vice.[29]

After assessing the deplorable moral situation in Deadwood, Senn wasted little time in calling for change. "Yea, verily, 'To labor is to pray,'"

THE PIONEER.

VOL. III NO. 18.   IONA, LYMAN COUNTY, SOUTH DAKOTA, THURSDAY, MAY 19, 1904.   OFFICIAL COUNTY ....

JACK SULLY

Died With His Boots On

The death of cattle rustler Jack Sully headlined the front page of the 19 May 1904 edition of the Iona Pioneer, the newspaper that launched Senn's career as Final Proof King. State Archives Collection, South Dakota State Historical Society

he began a scathing editorial on 21 December 1909. "There are many good people in Deadwood who offer prayers for a betterment of civic and social conditions here. If they would back their prayers with more work, they would be more regarded, and more effective." In particular, Senn chided those individuals who failed to act for fear of hurting business. "It is ineffectual for citizens who believe in civic righteousness to keep it to themselves or express [it] only to those who feel the same," he concluded. "To make it effective they must make it known to others, and must assist and encourage those whose official duty it is to enforce the laws."[30]

Senn urged those who favored decency to join forces and elect city officers who did the same. He demanded that local officials follow and enforce the laws of the state. Finally, he warned the owners of illicit businesses that their control over Deadwood would soon end. In a January 1911 editorial, he compared his fight to General Ulysses S. Grant's campaign against Vicksburg, writing, "If storming the citadels of vice in Deadwood will not avail, a siege will be instituted, and shot and shell will be poured over the walls until devastation will be such that the decent people of the city can walk in and take complete possession."[31]

Although many South Dakotans appreciated Senn's clean-up campaign, those on the home front did not respond kindly to his efforts. Within a few months, Senn had illuminated Deadwood's dirtiest and most deeply hidden secrets, and some of the town's most influential businessmen were far from appreciative. The owners of several prominent concerns boycotted Senn's publication, refusing to advertise their goods or services in the *Telegram* and, according to Senn, coercing other businesses into doing the same.[32]

The moral support that poured into Senn's office from around the state, however, was overwhelming. Fellow newspaper editors publicly praised his efforts and urged him to continue his noble fight. The former editor of a local mining magazine, who undoubtedly knew Senn's opposition, was especially emphatic in his condemnation of those whose "cloak of pretense" hid "hearts as black as the pit, and minds as putrid as a sewer." He continued: "These and such as these will oppose by boycott or bullet anybody and anything that tends toward righteousness, reform and right living. They are so thoroughly inoculated with the virus of the shameless that present day demands of society are unobserved and unwelcome." Punctuating his indictment of the greedy and the morally indifferent with exclamations of "Shame! . . . Shame! . . . Shame!" he concluded: "Continue as you have begun, Brother Senn. As certain as there is a God above us you will succeed in your contentions for a purer, cleaner, respectable and respected Deadwood."[33] Outside supporters also bought advertising space in the *Telegram*, even if they had nothing to advertise. Nevertheless, Senn was forced to sell off portions of his weekly newspaper chain to finance the *Telegram*.[34]

Despite the debilitating boycott and his dwindling funds, Senn remained confident that most Deadwood residents desired the changes he advocated. Measuring success in terms of "small victories" over the lawless element, the editor was pleased to report that, by early 1911, three gambling halls had been shut down and their gaming activities forced out of public view. Furthermore, most saloons were complying with ordinances restricting after-hours sales of liquor. Finally, the *Telegram's* appeals to the men of Deadwood "to respect themselves and their wives, daughters and sisters" appeared to have reduced business in Deadwood's red-light district.[35]

As the power of Senn's press grew, his most virulent enemies turned to violence. One Saturday night in July 1911, P. N. Carr, the owner of the Mansion, a popular bawdy house and frequent target of Senn's editorials, brutally attacked the editor, kicking him repeatedly and breaking several of his ribs. News of the attack on Senn spread rapidly throughout the state. Various newspaper editors condemned the assault but predicted that it would serve to awaken Deadwood's slumbering public conscience.[36] Unfortunately, Senn reported in a *Telegram* editorial, the incident "did not cause as much stir in Deadwood for a day as a recent footrace has caused for a week." Even the county state's attorney was indifferent. He refused to press charges against Carr and, according to Senn, implied that the editor "might have expected what he got, . . . and that if he didn't quit he probably would get worse." If the public conscience had been awakened, Senn concluded, "it quickly went to sleep again."[37]

October 1911 brought further violence against Senn and the *Telegram*. Early on a Sunday morning, intruders broke into his print shop and set fire to his equipment. "Just how the better element of Deadwood can stand by and see these things done without interfering we can not understand," commented the editor of the *Parker Press Leader*. "Possibly there is no better class." Senn, however, defended his silent supporters, writing, "The same forces which have made the road so

*Despite personal danger and financial hardship, Senn campaigned
as editor of the* Deadwood Daily Telegram *to expose the city's
dark side. Patricia Senn Dewald, Bowdle, S.Dak.*

To Senn, it was not prostitutes like Irene Love who kept the vice business viable in 1910s Deadwood, but normal citizens who kept silent about the matter. Throughout the decade, he used the Telegram *to try to rouse them to action. Adams Museum, Deadwood, S.Dak.*

rough for the *Telegram* do not hesitate to seek to deprive of employment or injure business of any who are caught giving assistance to the *Telegram.*"[38] Senn realized that while he needed the support of Deadwood's "decent" class, they needed their jobs. He could only hope that this silent majority would soon realize its power.

Senn's scathing editorials and daily sermons on morality appeared to help quiet the gambling rooms and saloons, but prostitution was not as easily removed from the Deadwood way of life. Toward the end of 1913, Senn began a full-fledged war against the city's three remaining houses of prostitution: the Mansion, the Rome, and the Topic. One editorial described local madam Fannie Hill as a "purveyor of the honor of women and a panderer to the lust of men. She owns a lot of such girls, body, clothes and soul. She is permitted to offer them for sale nightly to debauch Deadwood men. And she is permitted to parade them on the streets of Deadwood the same as other 'business interests.'" Senn went on to condemn the city authorities who collected one hundred dollars a month in license fees from brothel owners and thereby legitimatized the enterprises in violation of state law. He concluded by placing the ultimate responsibility for the town's moral character in the hands of the average citizen. "Is it not time," he wrote, "for the people of Deadwood who believe in decency and obedience to law to insist that officials close the three remaining bawdy houses in this city, and take steps to do it themselves if the officials will not do their sworn duty?"[39]

Senn later expanded on the idea of public moral accountability, calling the people of Deadwood "partners in three bawdy houses on Main street." In the editor's view, the city treasury was "a joint purse of the people of the city. All who pay taxes benefit from payments made to it, to the extent in which it reduces their taxes." Those who did not object to the use of the tainted profits were voluntary "silent partners" in the immoral businesses. For those who ignored their moral duty to protest the city's practice, eternal penalties awaited. "When their final accounting is made to the great Judge," Senn warned, "those who profess allegiance to the cause of Christianity and righteousness, may expect to find charged against them in the book of life, their silent partnership in the bawdy house business of Deadwood."[40]

Senn himself went before the city council to demand that the practice of licensing the brothels stop and that state law prohibiting such establishments be strictly enforced. Senn then sent a copy of his comments to the county state's attorney asking for cooperation in prosecuting these "resorts." Both the city council and the state's attorney ignored Senn's requests, and open prostitution, along with the editor's efforts to eliminate it, carried on for many more years.[41]

Senn's morality campaign suffered another setback in February of 1914, when Nathan E. Franklin announced his candidacy for mayor of Deadwood. "Czar Franklin," as Senn would later refer to him,[42] wielded a great deal of influence as president of Deadwood's First National Bank and had used it, Senn claimed, "in every way against the cleaning up of the bawdy houses and other lawlessness." Senn was certain that, if elected, Franklin would "stand for a more wide open town than has the present city administration." As he had done in previous elections, the editor challenged decent, law-abiding citizens to step forward in the contest "between those who believe laws should be obeyed and those who do not" and to support "those who think more of the virtue and welfare of the youth of this city than they do of the dollars that come to them from toleration of vice."[43]

Despite Senn's campaign, voters elected Franklin mayor in the spring of 1914, and the editor lost no time in attributing an increase in immoral activities to the leniency of his administration. Senn reported that under Deadwood's former mayor, William E. Adams, the saloons had generally operated in a legal, orderly fashion. Under Franklin's guard, he asserted, an increasing number had reverted to ignoring both state and municipal operating restrictions. Slot machines were re-appearing, and back-room gambling had resumed, much as Senn had expected.[44]

Near the end of 1914, Senn once again suffered a personal attack at the hands of his enemies. On a Saturday night in early October, a Deadwood policeman assaulted and beat the editor as he walked down a Deadwood street. The action apparently came in response to Senn's comments about the officer's involvement in another case.[45] Calling the attack "one of the most cowardly in the history of the state," the editor of the *Mitchell Clarion* went on to claim that "such assaults only go to prove that what Senn has said about Deadwood is more than true." The Mitchell editor predicted that negative publicity from the attacks on Senn would "do much toward cleaning up the city."[46]

The *Clarion's* predictions proved far from accurate, however. In fact, later that month Senn reported that Mayor Franklin was allowing the city to become "the dumping ground for Lead and other Black Hills cities which are crowding out their undesirables of both sexes." The mayor of Lead, unlike Franklin, had clamped down on vice, restricting bawdy houses, limiting alcohol sales, and banning gambling. "Possibly when all the refuse in the Black Hills has been dumped into Dead-wood," Senn speculated, "the condition here may become so nauseating that decent citizens will find their nerve and join with the rest of the state in demanding a clean-up."[47]

Despite Senn's efforts to unseat Franklin, Deadwood voters again elected him mayor in the spring of 1916. Conditions quickly went from bad to worse, according to editor Senn. The bawdy houses' supply of in-mates steadily increased, saloons operated back rooms all night long, and slot machines made their way back into Deadwood's bars. "These violations," Senn claimed, "are known to the city and county authorities, as they are not blind, and only a blind man could help seeing them."

If drinking could be stopped, Senn reasoned, other evils would soon collapse, too. Adams Museum, Deadwood, S.Dak.

Again, the editor reported, local authorities failed to take an active stance against vice. Nor did South Dakota's attorney general seem concerned with the blatant disregard of state laws.[48] Franklin's reelection appeared to have been a major victory for Senn's enemies, but the editor refused to accept defeat.

Toward the end of 1916, Senn began to focus his efforts on the prohibition movement that was spreading across the state. In an October editorial, the editor identified alcohol as the vice ultimately responsible for prostitution. "It is generally conceded by investigators of the 'social evil,'" Senn asserted, "that drink is directly responsible for the downfall of a large majority of fallen girls; and that the sale and use of intoxicating liquors is a necessity for successful commercial prostitution." Banning liquor and closing saloons would therefore effectively battle the "white slavers" and their vast network of vice. "Most women who have entered into a life of shame must have liquor to deaden their mental and physical sensibilities," Senn claimed, "and most men who patronize houses of prostitution, would not do so unless under the influence of liquor."[49] Senn's rhetoric may have had an effect, for in November 1916, a majority of Deadwood voters joined the rest of South Dakota in endorsing statewide prohibition. A rejuvenated Senn confidently proclaimed, "In less than two years Deadwood will overthrow the corrupt and lawless influences which have dominated its elections and prevented enforcement of laws against prostitution, gambling, and other evils."[50]

Several historical accounts indicate that Senn's crusade was ultimately successful. Watson Parker, author of *Deadwood: The Golden*

Years, reported that Deadwood's "respectable inhabitants . . . in time gained the upper hand and to all intents and purposes cleaned up the town."[51] Senn was also rewarded personally when President Calvin Coolidge appointed him prohibition director for South Dakota in 1925. As the state's chief enforcement officer in the war against liquor, Senn and fifteen deputies worked from headquarters in Sioux Falls to combat bootlegging and speakeasies until 1933, when Congress repealed the Eighteenth Amendment.[52] Bob Lee, editor of *Gold, Gals, Guns, Guts*, called Senn's appointment the end of an "uphill battle . . . against sin" but noted that the editor "lived to see the gambling halls, the saloons, and the girls back in business" when prohibition ended.[53]

After his stint as prohibition director, Senn divided his time between Deadwood, where his son Albert had taken over operation of the *Telegram*, and Pomona, California, where he maintained a home for several years.[54] He spent his remaining years pursuing his passion—writing—although on a less-intense level than he had done as a newspaper editor. During the late 1930s, he wrote and published three pamphlets about early Deadwood's most famous characters: Wild Bill Hickok, Calamity Jane, Preacher Smith, and Deadwood Dick. As Senn aged and his health deteriorated, his old friend Edith Kohl urged him to record his unique frontier adventures. "You must have time to leave to the w[or]ld your knowledge and experience in the building of our West," she wrote in 1948. "No one else has that invaluable knowledge to give." She even sent copies of the articles she had written about him to some of her "motion picture friends in the big studios telling them . . . to contact you if they are at all interested."[55]

After being confined to bed for an extended rest, Senn was finally able to complete three book manuscripts and start a fourth before he died.[56] In his autobiographical "Half a Century on the Last Frontiers," Senn summarized his life's work. "The first half of my half century on the last frontiers," he wrote, "was devoted to constructive work, building up successive area[s] opened up for settlement, by personal labor and use of the string of 35 weekly newspapers I had established or purchased as the frontier advanced." He characterized his second quarter century as being "devoted chiefly to destructive work, in tearing down the false, foul social conditions established in Deadwood and other mining camps."[57] Black Hills author Helen Rezatto later concluded, "Whatever he was—evangelist or hypocrite, impartial judge or prejudiced observer—people who knew this firebrand of South Dakota journalism would probably agree on one point: Edward Senn was a man who had the strength of his convictions."[58] In 1954, Senn's colleagues honored him posthumously by inducting him into the South Dakota Newspaper Hall of Fame.[59]

Senn was nearly eighty-six years old when he died in his Deadwood home on 19 November 1951. He was buried in Deadwood's Mount Moriah Cemetery, where his wife, Christa, was later buried at his side. In reflecting on his experiences, he had once commented to Edith Kohl: "I wanted to carry a torch, no matter how dim, for all the frontier newspapers to follow in making the west a good and safe place to live and raise children. Lawlessness cannot stand in the light of publicity."[60] Senn had carried that torch fearlessly and proudly throughout his career. Whether combating cattle rustlers from a corner of his homestead shanty or fighting vice in Deadwood from his Main Street print shop, the editor demonstrated how one man could fight many.

NOTES

1. Edith Eudora Kohl, "Frontier Crusader," *Rocky Mountain Empire Magazine*, 11 Nov. 1947, p. 5.

2. Quoted ibid.

3. Research into the life of my great-great grandfather, Edward Louis Senn, presented a number of difficulties. While several Black Hills area authors and historians mention him in their publications, most ignore him altogether. Despite these limitations, I had the benefit of a great deal of firsthand information. Much of the material in this article comes from two unpublished manuscripts Senn compiled before his death in 1951: "Half a Century on the Last Frontiers," from which the title of this article is derived, and "Regeneration of Deadwood." Many biographical facts presented here (dates of births, deaths, marriages, and the like) come from a family history titled "Our Family since 1826," compiled by my great-grandmother, Julia Hansen Senn. These items as well as the correspondence cited below remain in the hands of Senn family descendants, who have graciously consented to their use here.

4. Julia Hansen Senn, "Our Family since 1826," Senn Line section, Christian Senn entry.

5. Senn to Julia Hansen Senn and Patricia Senn Dewald, 28 Dec. 1947.

6. Ibid; Senn, "Half a Century on the Last Frontiers," chap. 14. This unpaginated manuscript, which Senn completed in 1945, focuses on his early years in South Dakota. It consists of sixty-nine chapters of two to six pages each.

7. Ibid., chaps. 14, 15.

8. Ibid., chap. 17.

9. Ibid., chap. 28.

10. Quoted ibid., chap. 16.

11. Ibid.

12. Julia Hansen Senn, "Our Family since 1826," Senn Line section, Edward Louis Senn entry.

13. Ibid.; Senn, "Half a Century," chap. 36.

14. Senn, "Half a Century," chap. 38.

15. Ibid., chap. 45.

16. Ibid., chaps. 39, 49, 51.

17. Ibid., chap. 53.

18. Later legislation expanded the acreage a settler could claim. Homesteaders also had the option of purchasing the land for $1.25 per acre after residing on it for six months. Howard R. Lamar, ed., *The New Encyclopedia of the American West* (New Haven, Conn.: Yale University Press, 1998), pp. 492–93.

19. Edith Eudora Kohl, *Land of the Burnt Thigh* (1938; reprint ed., Saint Paul: Minnesota Historical Society Press, 1986), p. 37.

20. Senn, "Half a Century," chap. 53.

21. Kohl, "Frontier Crusader," p. 5.

22. Kohl, *Land of the Burnt Thigh*, p. 39.

23. Quoted ibid., p. 40.

24. Ibid., p. 39.

25. Ibid., pp. 78–79, 81.

26. Quoted in Kohl, "Frontier Crusader," p. 5.

27. Senn, "Half a Century," chap. 57. In writing his account of this chapter in his life, Senn paid Kohl a tribute of his respect, quoting, with her permission, her account of the 1908 lottery (chap. 55).

28. Ibid., chap. 58.

29. E. L. Senn, "Regeneration of Deadwood," 3, 7 Feb. 1911. This unpaginated manuscript is primarily a collection of excerpts, arranged by date, from the *Deadwood Daily Telegram* and press comments from other South Dakota newspapers, along with several "Author's Notes" by Senn. *See also* Watson Parker, *Deadwood: The Golden Years* (Lincoln: University of Nebraska Press, 1981), pp. 212–13.

30. Senn, "Regeneration of Deadwood," 21 Dec. 1909.

31. Ibid., 27 Jan. 1911.

32. Ibid., 24 July 1911.

33. Ibid., 6 Feb. 1911.

34. Ibid., 24 July 1911.

35. Ibid., 3 Feb. 1911.

36. Ibid., 13, 24, 29 July 1911.

37. Ibid., 29 July 1911.

38. Ibid., 28 Oct. 1911.

39. Ibid., 1 Nov. 1913.

40. Ibid., 14 July 1914.

41. Ibid., 7 Oct. 1913.

42. Ibid., 19 June 1914.

43. Ibid., 28 Feb. 1914.

44. Ibid., 25 July 1914.

45. *Deadwood Daily Telegram*, 5 Oct. 1914.

46. Senn, "Regeneration of Deadwood," 15 Oct. 1914.

47. Ibid., 29 Oct. 1914.

48. Ibid., 3 June 1916. *See also* the Oct. 1947 author's note appended to the 10 June 1916 clipping.

49. Ibid., 6 Oct. 1916.

50. Ibid., 21 Nov. 1916.

51. Parker, *Deadwood*, p. 213.

52. Helen Rezatto, *Mount Moriah: "Kill a Man—Start a Cemetery"* (Aberdeen, S.Dak.: North Plains Press, 1980), p. 216.

53. Bob Lee, ed., *Gold, Gals, Guns, Guts: A History of Deadwood, Lead, and Spearfish, 1874-1976* (Pierre: South Dakota State Historical Society Press, 2004), p. 246.

54. *Deadwood Pioneer-Times*, 19 Nov. 1951.

55. Kohl to Senn, ca. 5 Mar. 1948.

56. *Deadwood Pioneer-Times*, 19 Nov. 1951. Senn's correspondence includes several letters written to and from Caxton Press in Caldwell, Idaho, between May and December 1947, but his manuscripts were never published.

57. Senn, "Half a Century," chap. 68.

58. Rezatto, *Mount Moriah*, pp. 217–18.

59. *Sioux Falls Daily Argus-Leader*, 2 Oct. 1954.

60. Quoted in Kohl, "Frontier Crusader," p. 5.

Claire Patterson

A CCC RECRUIT LOOKS BACK ON
A BLACK HILLS EXPERIENCE

edited by George A. Larson

INTRODUCTION

The Great Depression that gripped the United States for
a decade following the stock market crash of 29 October
1929 was years in the making. After the fighting of World
War I ended and wartime price controls were removed,
the United States economy ran at full steam. Beginning
in the 1920s, inflation and overproduction began cutting
into farm income in states like South Dakota, while the
national economy thrust forward. Much of the new prosperity was based on speculation, however, and the 1929
collapse of the stock market pushed the country into a
long period of economic depression that spread to other
major economies of the world, as well. Suddenly, millions of Americans became unemployed as the effects of
the depression rippled throughout the country. Voters
responded to the crisis by ousting Republican office-
holders and electing Democrat Franklin D. Roosevelt as
president in November 1932. Roosevelt quickly presented
the American people with his "New Deal," a wide array
of innovative programs designed to tackle the effects of
the depression and revitalize the nation. It would take
another global conflict, however—World War II—for the
country to emerge completely from the hard times that
beset the nation in the 1930s.[1]

This account
originally
appeared in
*South Dakota
History* 35
(Winter 2005):
335-46.

Young CCC recruits gather among their army cots in the barracks they built at Camp Pine Creek, west of Mount Rushmore. State Archives Collection, South Dakota State Historical Society

Among the most popular and successful New Deal programs were those that put the unemployed to work on any number of public improvement projects around the country. The Emergency Conservation Work Act, which Congress passed and Roosevelt signed on 31 March 1933, led to the creation of the Civilian Conservation Corps (CCC) and gave thousands of unemployed men temporary jobs in projects relating to forest and soil conservation. President Roosevelt called for two hundred fifty thousand men from families who were on relief to sign up for CCC work on state and federal lands by July 1933.

To help solve the logistical problem of moving the thousands of recruits, many of whom lived in the East and were assigned to work areas in the West, the United States Army was brought in to assist with mobilization, using the railroad system and trucks to move enlistees to their work camps. The United States Department of Agriculture and the Department of the Interior were responsible for determining and overseeing the work projects, which ranged from tree thinning and planting to land terracing and dam building. Through its local and state relief offices, the United States Department of Labor recruited and enrolled men for the CCC. Director Robert Fechner, whom Roosevelt appointed on 5 April 1933, headed this unprecedented administrative arrangement. By the end of 1935, 2,650 CCC work camps were operating in the United States, housing 505,782 recruits. Counting army personnel, work-detail supervisors, educators, and administrators, the total came to over six hundred thousand.[2]

The CCC not only provided men with immediate jobs on worthwhile projects but also benefited the families and local economies of those who enrolled. Each CCC recruit received wages of thirty dollars per month, of which twenty-five dollars had to be sent home. This arrangement returned $72 million to local economies short on cash. In addition, each CCC work camp itself pumped an average of five thousand dollars monthly into the economy of the area through purchases of food and basic supplies. Local men with experience in manual labor were also hired to instruct recruits, many of whom came from cities and had never worked outdoors.[3]

Enrollees in the CCC were required to be between the ages of eighteen and twenty-five years, although the enlistment age later dropped to seventeen. They were also to be unmarried and come from a family on relief. Veterans of any age and marital status who were on relief were allowed, and the age requirement did not apply to the local men who served as instructors. In addition to paid work and three square meals a day, the CCC provided many recruits with valuable education. In the camps, an estimated forty thousand men were taught to read and write. This education, conducted during free time, included vocational training that gave the recruits a better chance of obtaining employment once their enlistment periods were completed. The CCC also ultimately enrolled eighty thousand American Indians, twenty five thousand older men, and two hundred fifty thousand veterans in the project.[4]

At its peak in South Dakota, the CCC operated thirty-three camps, although the average at any given time was nineteen. By the time the program ended in 1942, a total of 32,471 personnel had been employed. In addition to the day-to-day work done on resource conservation projects, the largest single CCC project completed in the state was Lake of the Pines Dam, creating Sheridan Lake in the Black Hills. The CCC had a great economic impact on South Dakota, returning an estimated $6.2 million to the families of workers enrolled in the program.[5]

Among the hundreds of thousands of recruits who joined the CCC was Claire Patterson, who eventually retired in Keystone, South Dakota.

The following account is based on an interview conducted at his home on 23 November 2004, in which he related the story of his personal experiences in the CCC. He graciously granted permission for its publication here.

Claire Patterson's Account

I was born in Custer County, South Dakota, in a small town called Folsom on 6 March 1923. When I was very young, my parents moved from Folsom to the southeastern part of South Dakota, to a small town called Mission Hill. When I turned seventeen in 1940, I talked my parents into letting me join the CCC for three months, although I stayed in the organization longer. My folks had to sign the CCC enrollment papers. I went by train to Sioux Falls, and from there, I took another train to Rapid City. At Rapid City, I boarded a narrow-gauge railroad line running west. This narrow-gauge line no longer exists, as with many others once operating in the Black Hills. This railroad was referred to as the Crouch Line. It was very crooked and weaved around hills and obstacles. It went through an area now called Johnson Siding. I eventually ended up in a small town called Mystic. CCC trucks were waiting for me and the rest of the one hundred CCC recruits on the train. Most of us were from eastern South Dakota. We all enlisted at about the same time. We were driven to a CCC side camp called Black Fox, supported by the larger Camp Roubaix.

At Black Fox, we lived in tents with wooden floors. The tents were canvas stretched over a wooden frame. They were quite comfortable, especially with the raised wooden floors, and able to hold eight men. These tents were home for us in the camp into the middle of October 1940. We arrived in the side camp in March 1940, near the end of the month. It was supported and run by the United States Army from Fort Meade, where our officers and camp doctors came from. For the first few days in camp, it was as if we were in army basic training. We were given army physicals, shots, clothing, and other supplies.

On the first work day in camp, I chopped wood. Within one week, we were taught how to fight forest fires, especially which tools to use on the various types and sizes of fires that might break out in the Black Hills. This amounted to seven to ten days of training, during which we built a fire line around our camp area, three to four feet wide. This line

A CCC recruit poses in front of one of the eight-man tents at Black Fox, a side camp of Camp Roubaix. The Roubaix Eagles may be one of the sports teams that most camps fielded. George A. Larson, Rapid City, S.Dak.

was more of a trail than what today is called a firebreak. Later, we were driven in trucks into the Black Hills to cut firewood, using two-man crosscut saws and double-edged axes (for trimming the branches off downed trees). We received considerable instruction on how to safely swing a double-headed ax, which weighed from three to four pounds. When we carried this ax to and from our work sites, the edges were covered with a rubber protector.

The people who were training us were recruited from the local area of the Black Hills and served as our camp foremen. There were usually six foremen assigned to each camp. Each assigned foreman took out his own work detail into the surrounding area. In a CCC camp of approximately two hundred men, work groups consisted of twenty to thirty men. With a work group of twenty men, only one truck was needed to haul men to the work site and back to camp. On one such detail I was on, we had a force of six to eight men assigned to build water troughs for cattle feeding in the forest areas during spring, summer, and into the early fall.

We would locate a large dead and dry tree, approximately thirty inches in diameter, cut it down, and then cut it into a workable length of six to eight feet. Two of us began working, standing back to back, using a flat-bladed ax to flatten one side of the log for stability so it could be positioned on the ground when completed and not roll or move when filled with water. Once this was finished, we rolled the log onto the flat side, allowing us to begin to hollow out the top side of the log. Again, we worked back to back, moving from the center to the end of the log, hollowing it out to form a water trough. This process usually took us from two to three days. We constructed these troughs close to a natural spring. We would run a metal pipe downhill from the water source to the water trough. This would fill up the wooden trough, allowing cattle to drink when grazing on government land. Early in November, we would return to these natural springs, disconnect the metal water-feed pipe, and roll the trough over onto small support logs to keep it off the ground and prevent water from freezing inside during the winter, which could crack the wood. For me, this was one of the most interesting projects I worked on while in the CCC.

One of the other primary projects we worked on was large-scale tree planting in areas that had been burned by fire or damaged due to erosion. In the fall of 1940, I was one of sixty to seventy men assigned to one area, moving in one line, planting young trees. We planted Douglas fir trees, which are not native to the Black Hills, but were planted as an experiment in reforestation. We used the "slip" method to plant trees. We each carried a canvas water bag with the top cut off to hold the plantings. The trees came in bundles of one hundred, six to eight inches tall. The slip method required us to use a three-inch-wide ax spade, which we drove into the ground, pulling the handle back to create a space to drop in one of the Douglas fir trees. Withdrawing the ax and using the heel of our boot, we stomped the tree into a vertical position. We then moved on to the next tree spot and repeated the process. We planted Douglas fir trees for approximately two months. With sixty to seventy of us planting an average of five hundred trees a day, we estimated a total of thirty-five thousand each day.[6]

On another project, during the winter, we thinned trees to promote strong, healthy growth and reduce fire danger during hot and dry weather. We were taught how to go into a thick stand of trees and use proper techniques to thin them to the correct number of healthy trees per 125 square feet in order to maximize straight growth. We each took an area and moved three steps forward and three steps to either side, with the goal of clearing an area of approximately 125 square feet. No matter what size the tree, if it had a crotch, the tree was cut down. If it

Once a week, the recruits at Camp Narrows in Custer State Park took their mattresses out for airing. State Archives Collection, South Dakota State Historical Society

had a dead spike top, it was cut down. The remaining trees selected not to be cut had to be perfectly healthy. The trees we had cut down were further cut to manageable lengths, hauled to a centralized location, and stacked in a teepee arrangement, ready to be burned once sufficient snow had fallen in the winter to keep fire from spreading to standing trees. I spent many days in the winter burning these slash piles.

We stayed at the side camp until 15 October 1940, moving into the main camp at Roubaix for winter operations. At this camp, we lived in permanent wooden barracks, with electricity and stoves for heat. Each building was heated by two square metal stoves, with a slide-opening top for the wood, one at each end of the barracks. On a rotating basis, two men in each barracks were assigned to keep the fires going at night or when we were in camp during cold weather. There was no running water in the barracks, so if the temperature did fall below freezing, there was no damage. The shower and lavatory were in a separate building and continuously heated by wood stoves. Everything in the camp was fueled by wood.

We were issued clothes while assigned to the CCC. One set of clothes was similar to the United States Army's tan uniforms. For the winter and cold weather, we had heavy jackets, shirts, and wool caps with pull-down ear flaps for protection against high wind chills when working outside. We wore blue denims on work details, and, when back in camp, we took a shower and changed into the tan uniforms. We wore black scarves for ties and stood inspection, followed by the day's retreat ceremony. We then marched into the mess hall—the tan uniform with the black scarf was our admission. We had good food while in the CCC.

Some of those in the camp were either selected or volunteered to be cooks, serving for two to three months as assistants under the primary cooks. I volunteered for this duty. While we were on cooking detail, we worked three days with two days off, worked two days and three days off, with every other weekend getting three days off. I eventually ended up as a cook, first class, in the CCC, referred to as a "45," meaning I received forty-five dollars per month. Initially, I was a "36," receiving thirty-six dollars per month. . . . Because we had to send twenty-five dollars home each month, money was always in short supply and had to be stretched as far as possible. Because the CCC provided all our basic needs, it was not too difficult for me to stay within the limited funds each month, and the raise while on cooking detail helped. Almost everyone in the camp was into smoking during their free time, including me. However, we could not afford prepackaged cigarettes. We would go to the camp store and buy a carton of Bull Durham, containing twenty to twenty-four tobacco pouches, for one dollar. We then rolled our own cigarettes.

When I was working as a cook, we served a lot of hamburger, which we ground from hindquarters of beef. The meat was stored in a large walk-in cooler along with other fresh food items requiring refrigeration, due to the bulk nature of the food supplies needed to feed all those in camp three meals each day. All the meat was delivered in quarter sections, which we cut to meet that day's requirements. For two meals (lunch and supper) each day, we served mashed potatoes. As one might estimate, we went through large quantities of potatoes every week, which had to be peeled, cleaned, boiled, and mashed. Meals served for lunch and supper would include a salad and some type of dessert— canned fruit or ice cream. We did not have a cafeteria-style setup but one that can best be described as family-style eating. For family style, all the food would be set on each table. Our mess helpers would set up the table first, with each plate positioned upside down, coffee cup on

The mess hall at Camp Custer shows the early "family-style"
dining arrangements used in the CCC. State Archives
Collection, South Dakota State Historical Society

top of the plate, and silverware on either side. The cooks would dish up
large bowls of beef, potatoes, gravy, salad, and fruit (if ice cream was
not going to be served) from large one-gallon tin cans, which the mess
helpers placed on each table. Every table had to be set up completely
before the camp members were allowed to march inside and be fed.

After all the tables were set with food, the camp's CCC personnel
would march into the mess hall with groups of eight assigned to a specific table, taking position behind the long bench on that side of the
table. The mess sergeant blew his whistle and everyone sat down, turning over their plates and filling them from the food in the bowls. When
one of the serving bowls was empty, someone at the table would hold up
the empty bowl so one of the mess helpers could retrieve it and take it to
the kitchen to be filled and brought back to the table. After a long workday, those in the mess hall had a large appetite. If we served ice cream,
no fruit was served, and we waited until the tables were cleared by the
mess helpers, leaving a spoon for each man on the table. A mess helper
pushed a wheeled cart with piles of bowls, passing out eight per table,

followed by others with ice cream in paper containers, from which two scoops were dished into each bowl.

For breakfast, we had individual boxes of cereal, one set at each plate, with a bowl on top of the plate and a one-pint glass bottle of milk that had a cardboard pull-opening cap. Quite often, instead of cold cereal, we served hot oatmeal from large serving bowls on the table, along with a pint glass bottle of milk. Later in mess hall operations, we set up a cafeteria-style serving operation, with aluminum trays and silverware picked up by each person going through the serving line. Mess helpers dished out individual servings of food onto the tray, receiving various food items as the person moved down or through the serving line. We began this serving style in October 1941. Someone always wanted an extra serving, used to the previous family-style dining we used.

In 1940, we were tasked to build a forest-fire lookout tower at the top of Flag Mountain. This construction was a going to be a difficult project because the closest we could haul building materials up the mountain (because of the steep grade) was two hundred to three hundred feet. The lookout tower's lower base was built out of local stone, cut on location. The top part of the tower was built of wood. Our CCC engineers designed, and we built, a simple but efficient delivery system to move materials the remaining distance up to the top of the mountain, the two to three hundred feet up the steepest part of the grade. The rock cutters prepared the stones to the required size below the final tower site, as determined by the engineers for a specific section of the tower's base. The cut stone was loaded into a metal bucket, two to two-and-one-half feet in diameter. The metal bucket was attached to a steel cable from the work preparation area to the tower's construction location. The bucket could hold up to one hundred pounds. A pulley was attached to a tree at the lower part of the slope and to the framework of the tower above. Two of us were assigned to put on leather harnesses, which each had a small steel cable leading to the larger cable. At the top of the grade, after placing tension on the harness lines, we walked downhill, pulling the loaded bucket to the top. If there was stone in the bucket, it would be taken out, unloaded, and a flagman would signal us to walk back up the hill, allowing the empty bucket to go back down the slope to be reloaded. This process was repeated over and over to move the cut stone to the tower construction site, as well as sand and mortar mix to cement the stones. The cement was mixed at the top of the grade. This method was the only efficient way to move the cut stone, sand, and mortar to the top of the mountain, where the lookout tower was located near what became Deerfield Lake. At that time, the lake was part of the master construction plans for the Black Hills, with construction of a dam planned later. Lumber was carried to the top of the hill to finish the lookout tower. The lookout tower no longer remains, but it was a project I vividly remember.

In late October 1941, we moved out of Camp Roubaix to Camp Galena, whose real CCC name was Park Creek. Once into camp, our purpose was to dismantle it for closure. By December 1941, employment opportunities in the United States were more plentiful as the country created jobs for war industries supporting Lend Lease, as well as increased orders for rearmament of America's military.[7] It was only considered a matter of time before the United States entered the war in Europe against Germany and Italy, on the side of England.

In some areas, such as South Dakota, jobs were still scarce because it took time for the trickle-down effect to get into the state. It was picking up, although, according to letters from my parents. I was assigned to dispose of excess kitchen equipment in the camp and telephoned Fort Meade to determine if they were interested. They agreed to receive the equipment. I still had to maintain meals at the camp, so equipment had to be shipped out in our CCC trucks in phases. I was cooking on Sunday morning, 7 December 1941, when the Japanese attacked Pearl Harbor. We had a small portable radio and were listening to music when a flash bulletin came on announcing that the Japanese had attacked. I did not know where Pearl Harbor was located. Someone finally told me it was in Hawaii, in the Pacific west of California, and that it was a large United States Navy installation.

It did not take long for a military detachment from Fort Meade to come into the camp to start giving us close-order military drill and other instructions. We found out the United States Army was getting ready to transfer the CCC members in the camp into the army. I grabbed my hat and told them I was done with the CCC and wanted to be discharged, which was my right under the enlistment terms, since I had served my initial enlistment. I was able to get a ride in one of the remaining CCC trucks to Rapid City. In Rapid City, I was given an honorable discharge from the CCC and a one-way train ticket home. I got off the train at Yankton, and then people gave me rides into Mission Hill. This ended my experience with the CCC in South Dakota, a part of my life I remember very well.

NOTES

1. For background on the Great Depression nationally, *see* Robert S. McElvaine, *The Great Depression: America, 1929–1941* (New York: Times Books, 1984). For information on the depression in South Dakota, *see* Herbert S. Schell, *History of South Dakota*, 4th ed., rev. John E. Miller (Pierre: South Dakota State Historical Society Press, 2004), pp. 281–97.

2. National Association of Civilian Conservation Corps Alumni, "Roosevelt's Tree Army: A Brief History of the Civilian Conservation Corps," idahoptv.org/OUTDOORS/shows/ccc/history/treearmy.html.

3. Ibid.

4. Ibid.; Kenneth E. Hendrickson, Jr., "The Civilian Conservation Corps in South Dakota," *South Dakota History* 11 (Winter 1980): 5.

5. Hendrickson, "Civilian Conservation Corps," p. 18; Schell, *History of South Dakota*, p. 293: Lyle A. Derscheid, *The Civilian Conservation Corps in South Dakota (1933–1942)* (Brookings: South Dakota State University Foundation Press, 1986), pp. 29–30; Perry H. Merrill, *Roosevelt's Forest Army: A History of the Civilian Conservation Corps, 1933–1942* (Montpelier, Vt.: By the Author, 1981), pp. 174–75.

6. According to the United States Forest Service office in Spearfish, the area of this experimental Douglas fir tree planting was located north of Wren Flats, off Nemo road. Today, the trees are healthy and add variety to the native tree species of the Black Hills.

7. The Lend-Lease program, authorized in March 1941, allowed the United States to supply the Allied Powers with war materiel without participating in the war directly.

9

Alfred Hitchcock and the Faces of Mount Rushmore

"EXPEDIENT EXAGGERATIONS" AND THE
FILMING OF *NORTH BY NORTHWEST*

Todd David Epp

This essay originally appeared in *South Dakota History* 23 (Fall 1993): 181–96.

"Ah, Maggie, in the world of advertising, there's no such thing as a lie, there's only the expedient exaggeration. You ought to know that!" said Cary Grant as Roger Thornhill, protagonist in Alfred Hitchcock's *North by Northwest* (1959). The National Park Service would have done well to have reached the same conclusion before it dealt with Alfred Hitchcock, Metro-Goldwyn-Mayer (MGM), and the world of movie-making. Plenty of "expedient exaggerations" surrounded the filming of scenes for Hitchcock's acclaimed thriller *North by Northwest* at Mount Rushmore in 1958. While the controversy the Mount Rushmore scenes caused appears humorous today, it was, at the time, a serious matter for officials of the National Park Service and the Department of the Interior and for South Dakota's United States senator Karl E. Mundt. The reason for the controversy lay in one simple fact: master film director Alfred Hitchcock had long wanted to film a movie involving the Shrine of Democracy, but the Park Service had concerns about the memorial's potential "desecration." Like Gutzon Borglum, the artistic genius who had preceded him into the South Dakota wilderness and whose creation he longed to use as a backdrop, Hitchcock would not let the federal government or its minions stop him from achieving his dream.

South Dakotans first learned of Hitchcock's intent to film at the site from a 15 May 1958 Associated Press report datelined Hollywood and printed in the *Rapid City Daily Journal*: "Alfred Hitchcock says he expects to realize his long ambition—filming a chase over the Mount Rushmore Monument. He may be spoofing, but you never can tell about Hitchcock. After all, he has made use of the Statue of Liberty, and tilted liner Normandie, and other landmarks in his long and distinguished production of movie thrills."[1] In the past, the filmmaker had occasionally told colleagues about his dream to shoot at the memorial. "I've always wanted to do a chase sequence across the faces of Mount Rushmore," the master of suspense is reported to have said in 1957.[2] Several years earlier, he had remarked: "I want to have one scene of a man hanging onto Lincoln's eyebrows. That's all the picture I have so far."[3] During the summer of 1958, Hitchcock's Rushmore dream took form. From 28 July to 1 August, MGM location manager Charles Coleman visited Mount Rushmore, accompanied by Larry Owen of the Rapid City Chamber of Commerce. While there, Coleman talked with National Park Service officials about the idea of shooting scenes at the memorial.[4]

In setting the stage for the controversy that followed, it is important to understand the complicated plot of the movie, which one Hitchcock scholar has summarized as "a comic thriller about mistaken identity, political depravity, sexual blackmail, and ubiquitous role-playing."[5] Even leading man Cary Grant complained to Hitchcock about the complexity, remarking, "We've already done a third of the picture and I still can't make head or tail of it."[6] Grant plays Roger Thornhill, a New York City advertising executive abducted by Communist spies who have mistaken him for a fictitious CIA agent. Thornhill escapes, only to witness the murder of a United Nations official and be accused of committing the crime. The film chronicles his cross-country flight from both the police and the Communist agents (James Mason, Martin Landau, and others), which takes him from New York to Chicago to Indiana and, finally, to South Dakota. Along the way, Thornhill falls in love with the icy blonde CIA spy, Eve Kendall (Eva Marie Saint). The drama culminates at Mount Rushmore, with Kendall and Thornhill scrambling about the presidential faces to elude the enemy agents.[7]

While Hitchcock and screen writer Ernest Lehman conjured a complicated but ultimately satisfying spy thriller, they seasoned the movie with a few geographical liberties. In the finished film, a Frank Lloyd

Mount Rushmore, its visitors' facilities, and the surrounding woods serve as the backdrop for the climax of Alfred Hitchcock's complicated thriller North by Northwest. *State Archives Collection, South Dakota State Historical Society*

Wright-like house and the mythical "Cedar City," complete with an airport, perch at Mount Rushmore's summit. During the movie's climax, Thornhill, Kendall, and their pursuers simply drive or fly to the top of the Shrine of Democracy and then run willy-nilly about the four presidents' heads.[8]

The issue of "chasing about" Mount Rushmore is critical to understanding both the movie and the resulting controversy. One simply does not chase about or even climb up Mount Rushmore without proper gear—and permission from the National Park Service.[9] In 1958, representatives of Metro-Goldwyn-Mayer and the Park Service had signed an agreement concerning Hitchcock's filming at the memorial. In return for permission to use the site, the filmmakers promised that no scenes of violence would be filmed "near the sculpture [or] on the talus slopes below the sculpture." The agreement further prohibited the de-

Upon arriving at the Rapid City airport, director Alfred Hitchcock paused to pose for reporters as the memorial's "fifth face." Rapid City Journal, *Rapid City, S.Dak.*

piction of violence on "any simulation or mock-up of the sculpture or talus slope." The same restrictions applied to all public-use areas of the memorial, real or simulated.[10] The filmmakers, at least in their early correspondence, assured government officials that the site would be "treated with the utmost respect. None of our characters would tread upon the faces or heads of the Sculpture," wrote Hitchcock's location manager.[11]

Shortly before the shooting at Mount Rushmore was scheduled to begin, a reporter asked the director about the chase scene. Hitchcock, ever the showman, handed the journalist a napkin with the presidents' heads drawn on it and a dotted line purporting to show the chase path. The Rapid City newspaper printed the story and a picture of the napkin. Citing "patent desecration," the Department of the Interior (the Park Service's parent agency), summarily revoked Hitchcock's original permit and prohibited the filming of live actors in conjunction with either the real or mock-up faces. It later reissued a permit allowing the use of a Mount Rushmore mockup on the condition that the presidents' faces be shown below the chin line in scenes involving live actors.[12]

According to James Popovich, chief interpreter at Mount Rushmore National Memorial, Hitchcock was "terribly mad when we told him

*Cary Grant and Eva Marie Saint strolled through downtown
Rapid City the evening before the filming at Mount Rushmore
began.* Rapid City Journal, *Rapid City, S.Dak.*

he couldn't shoot on the faces. He almost pulled the movie."[13] Once
he arrived in Rapid City on 15 September, however, Hitchcock became
a model of citizenship and reassured South Dakotans of his good in-
tentions. "It's a good thing for the world to see the big monuments we
have. This is a part of America," the filmmaker expounded. "When they
say we'll do something on Lincoln's nose, this is very bad. We wouldn't
dream of it. In fact, it would defeat the purpose for which we are using
Mount Rushmore in the film."[14]

Shooting at Mount Rushmore, which had been scheduled to take
two days, took place on 16 September 1958. According to the local press,
the "beautiful" weather and the "cooperativeness" of Black Hills residents impressed both MGM officials and Hitchcock. In his log for the
day, the memorial superintendent stated that the crew had been "well
organized and in spite of the crowds, equipment and extras on hand,
everything went smoothly and the shooting was finished a day ahead

of schedule." While the monthly report of the chief ranger echoed the superintendent's opinion, it also foreshadowed more conflict to come. "This production did not pose any difficulty protection-wise. The movie company was very cooperative," stated the official. "However, considerable adverse publicity did bring in several written complaints. MGM at this writing is making several still shots of the sculptures. Permission was granted for these still shots only after receiving verbal confirmation from the Regional Office."[15]

Altogether, the crew lensed three scenes at Mount Rushmore: Eva Marie Saint's staged shooting of Grant in the memorial's cafeteria, the parking lot scene in which rangers haul away Grant's "dead" body in a station wagon, and a number of views of the memorial from various terraces. Ironically, the way in which some of these general views and the still shots of the stone faces were used contributed to much of the subsequent controversy surrounding the film. Technically, Hitchcock would keep half of his word to the National Park Service. While he did not film any chase scenes on the real memorial, he eventually shot them on a studio mock-up or against a background composed of the still shots. At the close of the on-site filming in September 1958, the *Rapid City Daily Journal* innocently reported, "A replica of the national memorial will be reproduced full scale at Culver City for additional closeup scenes."[16]

"Closeup scenes" was just an "expedient exaggeration" for the climactic death struggle between "good guys" Grant and Saint and "bad guys" Mason and Landau. The National Park Service and the Department of the Interior would object to the use of these scenes in the finished film, claiming their violence desecrated the national memorial.

Nearly a year after the filming at Mount Rushmore ended, press reports confirmed that the Park Service's early suspicions about Hitchcock's sincerity regarding the agreement were about to be borne out. The press was reacting enthusiastically to the use of Mount Rushmore as a locale in the soon-to-be-released film, and the director appeared happy to foster yet another "expedient exaggeration"—the illusion that the movie's climax occurred on the *real* Mount Rushmore. Critic Alice Hughes of *Hollywood Variety* called the Black Hills location "probably the boldest terrain ever chosen on which to bring about the exhilarating, murderous finale. One shouldn't reveal the amazing locale, but the temptation is too great. Six presidents' [*sic*] heads and faces carved out of the stony peaks of Mount Rushmore, South Dakota, by the sculp-

Grant, Saint, and "bad guy" James Mason posed for tourist cameras during a break in the filming. Academy of Motion Picture Arts and Sciences, Beverly Hills, Calif., and Turner Entertainment Co., Atlanta, Ga.

tor Gutzon Borglum, provide the breathtaking background where the hero and heroine and the two foreign villains grapple for life." Hughes mistakenly reported, "This is no studio mock-up; the actual national monument serves as the scene in those last terrifying moments of sliding down the neck and chest of George Washington and the craggy features of Abraham Lincoln."[17]

Louella Parsons of the *Los Angeles Examiner* gushed: "I like James

In a ruse that angered government officials, Hitchcock directed the filming of the movie's climactic scene against a studio mock-up to give the illusion that Grant and Saint were actually at the memorial. Academy of Motion Picture Arts and Sciences, Beverly Hills, Calif., and Turner Entertainment Co., Atlanta, Ga.

Mason when he's being ornery. That suave British voice can be so deadly when he's a villain. Alfred Hitchcock must agree because it is Mason who will terrorize and chase Cary Grant and Eva Marie Saint all over the granite presidential faces on Mount Rushmore." In what must have been the last straw for National Park Service officials, she concluded, "Wouldn't you know Alfred Hitchcock gets Cary Grant to commit movie murder in 'North by Northwest' by having him push [an enemy agent] off Lincoln's nose."[18]

Hoodwinked by Hitchcock and MGM, government officials decided to fight back, although the effort proved to be too little, too late. On 28 July 1959, Acting Interior Secretary Elmer F. Bennett wrote a heated letter to MGM president Joseph E. Vogel: "In accepting these terms [no scenes of violence on the memorial or mock-up], MGM promised to adhere to them. Then MGM, without notifying the other party to the agreement, proceeded to fake scenes which expressly violate the studio's pact. The phony studio shots leave the average customer with the idea that the scenes of violence were staged on the memorial itself."[19]

With the press spreading enthusiastic but erroneous rumors, the Park Service and the Interior Department conceded that little could be done to correct the misconception. Bennett therefore asked Vogel to remove from the movie the credit stating, "We gratefully acknowledge the cooperation of the United State[s] Department of the Interior and the National Park Service in the actual filming of scenes at Mount Rushmore National Memorial, South Dakota." According to Bennett, moviegoers would "doubtless receive the wrong impression that the Department and Park Service cooperated in filming the scenes of violence at the end of the film." Bennett then warned Vogel, "Future permit applications in the National Park Service areas will receive closer scrutiny than heretofore."[20] In 1957, the Park Service had rejected the request of another filmmaker to stage a similar "game of cops and robbers" at Mount Rushmore.[21]

Though beaten by Hitchcock and MGM in this instance, the Interior Department attempted to change the film industry's code of ethics and thus prevent "similar violations in the future." In a letter to Eric Johnston, president of the Motion Picture Association of America (MPAA), Bennett suggested that the MPAA "consider the appropriateness" of a clause concerning filming in national parks. While he reiterated his warning that "the experience gained in this instance will lead in the future to closer restrictions in such permits," Bennett closed on a conciliatory note, offering to cooperate in the writing of such a clause.[22]

Kenneth Clark, MPAA vice-president, responded to Bennett's letter with a healthy dose of Hollywood pseudo-charm: "There must have been an unfortunate misunderstanding because I am confident that Metro-Goldwyn-Mayer would always live up to any agreement that is made. It is regretful that such a misunderstanding has developed and I want to express the hope that it will not in any way impair the fine relationships that have always existed between your Department and motion picture companies belonging to our Association." Clark went on to pooh-pooh the idea of placing a clause in the industry's code concerning filming in national parks. "The Production Code is concerned with the moral content of films [and] would not be appropriate" for dealing with the concerns of the Park Service. He continued: "I know it does not take such a clause in the Code to assure you of the continued har-

Pictured here at the time he opposed the distribution of The Plow That Broke the Plains, *Senator Karl Mundt vowed to take dramatic action after Park Service officials alerted him to the "deliberate desecration" of Mount Rushmore in* North by Northwest. *State Archives Collection, South Dakota State Historical Society*

monious cooperation of our member companies. You can be sure too that this is the attitude of our Association." Completely sweeping the matter under the cinematic rug, Clark concluded, "Let us know when any of us here can be helpful to the Department."[23]

In the eyes of the film industry, Clark's reply may have been the end of the matter. However, to the Park Service and the Interior Department, it was not quite the last take. The "Feds" had a secret weapon—South Dakota's senior United States senator, Karl E. Mundt. A member of the powerful foreign-relations and appropriations committees, Mundt got things done for South Dakota. Perhaps he could make the filmmakers see the government's point, as he had done in a similar situation in 1939.

Two months into his first term as a United States representative, Mundt had attended an Izaak Walton League meeting in Silver Spring, Maryland, where he viewed the government-produced documentary *The Plow That Broke the Plains.* The film depicted the causes, some accurate and some inaccurate, of the Dust Bowl in the nation's heartland. Angered by its depiction of the Dakotas as "a country of high winds and sun, without rivers, without streams, with little rain," Mundt used his first speech on the House floor to rail against the film.[24] He also worked with a number of organizations within South Dakota to get the film pulled from distribution, even though ten million viewers had already watched it over the previous two years. Nonetheless, Mundt was proud of having put a halt to this bad publicity for the state and referred to this success in his 1940 campaign.[25] Thus, twenty years later, the senator was again willing to oppose a motion picture that portrayed his home state in what he thought was an unfavorable light.

On 13 August 1959, Park Service director Conrad L. Wirth sent Mundt copies of the ongoing correspondence concerning the Hitchcock film. By this time, former Rushmore superintendent Charles Humberger and current chief ranger Leon Evans had reviewed the movie at the Elks Theater in Rapid City. They, too, objected to the chase scenes and agreed with their superiors that "the terms of the application for filming the production were not adhered to."[26] Wirth related this information to Mundt, stating, "It is an act of deliberate desecration of a great National Memorial to even imply that a game of cops and robbers, for the sole purpose of producing movie thrills, has been played over the sculptured faces of our most honored Presidents." Wirth, who had also written to Senator Francis Case, Representative George McGovern, and Representative E. Y. Berry, informed Mundt that he was supplying the senator with the information "in case the controversy is brought to your attention by some other source."[27]

Mundt reacted quickly and vehemently. Two days later, he responded to Wirth, "As you may well imagine, I have received a great number of complaints concerning the motion picture *North by Northwest* and the acts of desecration simulated in that picture."[28] The senator vowed to take dramatic action, just as he had done twenty years earlier with *The Plow That Broke the Plains*. "I agree that the Department should make every possible effort to have that picture recalled and corrected," he told the Park Service director, "and if that is not done I think the Department should seriously consider the whole procedure by which they permit future picture applications in the National Park Service area." In a postscript, Mundt told Wirth that he planned to submit the Park Service correspondence for the *Congressional Record* early the next week "so that the general public will know accurately the attitude of the Department of the Interior and the National Park Service." He concluded, "I shall probably include it in a talk on the Senate floor on Monday afternoon, August 17."[29]

Wirth responded to Mundt on 20 August with a four-page letter and more extracts of letters, reviews, and news stories about *North by Northwest*. The Park Service director recommended that if Mundt decided to speak in the Senate about the Park Service's problems with the movie, he "should make a very firm statement to the effect that the desecration was the result of a studio mockup" and not the use of the actual memorial. Wirth ended his letter with an important bit of information. "I have been informed by a local representative of the Company," he wrote, "that the credit line to which the Secretary objected has now been removed from this picture."[30] This statement apparently cooled the senator's ardor over the affair. The next week, Mundt wrote to thank Wirth for the information, adding, "I particularly appreciate having the material made available to me and it is possible that at some other time I will prepare a speech and put it into the *Record* for you."[31]

The senator may have realized that by August 1959 it was too late for anyone to do much of anything about the movie—except buy tickets and see it. MGM had released *North by Northwest* in New York on 6 August to favorable reviews. A. H. Weiler, writing for the *New York Times,* called the movie "a suspenseful and delightful Cook's Tour of some of the more photogenic spots in these United States." He found the Mount Rushmore climax "a bit overdrawn," however.[32]

After all the intrigue—both on screen and off—what is the legacy of the filming of *North by Northwest* at Mount Rushmore? The most obvious legacy is the movie itself. Hitchcock directed a great film that exploits a great location. His biographer, Donald Spoto, notes that the director had "a special fascination in planning and filming the most outrageous human deed in unforgettable and visually arresting ways, the better to impress his audience with the almost chimerical nature of the act of murder." Neil Sinyard, another Hitchcock scholar, adds that the director's depiction of bizarre acts committed against benign backgrounds reached its height in *North by Northwest,* a film in which "a hotel lobby is the setting for kidnapping, the United Nations building for murder, and the stone face of Mount Rushmore for perilous pursuit."[33] A more recent reviewer calls *North by Northwest* "possibly Hitchcock's most likable film if only because it is an over-size bag of his best old tricks."[34]

Part of Hitchcock's success as a director was due to his "obsession with order and controlling every last detail of his film," traits he carried to legendary lengths.[35] This attention to detail, coupled with his long-held desire to film at Mount Rushmore, combined to make the climax of *North by Northwest* one of the greatest episodes in his long and illustrious film career. As Spoto notes, "The last ten minutes of the film comprise one of the most famous set pieces in Hitchcock's career—the realization of a longtime desire. He had at last celebrated the giant, impassive faces."[36] Thus, despite his protestations to the contrary, it appears that the director probably had no intention of obeying any portion of the Park Service agreement that stood in the way of his goal.

A second legacy of *North by Northwest* is the greater renown the film brought to the memorial. The passage of time and the film's achievement of "classic" status have disproved the fears of government officials. Aside from preventing Hitchcock from doing any shooting at Mount Rushmore, the Park Service could probably have done little more to prevent what some considered at the time its "desecration." While park rangers were able to keep an eye on Hitchcock at Mount Rushmore, they had no control over him on a Hollywood back lot. Theirs was a lost cause from the beginning. By the time Interior Department brass enlisted Senator Mundt's aid, the film was ready for distribution. The controversy only served to fan the hype—and the ticket sales—for the film.

Gutzon Borglum the sculptor may have winced at seeing Cary Grant and Eva Marie Saint climbing over even a mock-up of his Shrine of Democracy. However, Borglum the showman probably would have smiled. "It's just my opinion," said Nicole Swigart, a seasonal interpreter at Mount Rushmore, "but Borglum probably would've liked how the Memorial was shown in *North by Northwest*. He liked publicity."[37] The sculptor may even have sympathized with Hitchcock in his dilemma, for Borglum experienced similar frustrations with government officials in carving Mount Rushmore. Further, as an avid movie-goer who sometimes saw the same film three or four times, Borglum could have appreciated Hitchcock's artistic abilities.[38]

According to chief interpreter Popovich, "In the years following the movie, Mount Rushmore park rangers removed more visitors from the secured areas than in any previous years."[39] Today, the movie continues to draw visitors to the memorial. "Even after all these years," Swigart said, "there's still publicity from the film. It still brings people in

Sculptor Gutzon Borglum, shown here at work on the likeness of President Lincoln in the late 1930s, might have enjoyed the publicity that Hitchcock's film brought to the memorial. State Archives Collection, South Dakota State Historical Society

with questions." Just minutes after she made this comment, a tourist entered the sculptor's studio at the memorial. Almost as if on cue, the older gentleman asked, "Was *North by Northwest* filmed here?" Fifty years have elapsed since Hitchcock worked his "expedient exaggerations" with Mount Rushmore. Yet, this simple question from a tourist is probably the most fitting tribute to *North by Northwest* and its lasting impact on South Dakota's Shrine of Democracy.

NOTES

This article grew out of research the author did as producer of a television documentary entitled *Mount Rushmore's Dreamers, Drillers, and Presidents*, which aired on South Dakota Public Television in 1992. The author is indebted to Pearl Hein of the Karl E. Mundt Historical and Educational Foundation; Jim Popovich, chief interpreter at Mount Rushmore National Memorial; Tami Freitag, associate producer at South Dakota Public Television; and Mary Kallsen, a graduate student in history at the University of South Dakota, for their assistance.

1. *Rapid City Daily Journal*, 15 May 1958.

2. Donald Spoto, *The Dark Side of Genius: The Life of Alfred Hitchcock* (Boston: Little, Brown & Co., 1983), p. 392.

3. Ibid., p. 333.

4. Superintendent's Narrative Reports, July, Aug. 1958, Mount Rushmore National Memorial Archives, Keystone, S.Dak. (hereafter cited Rushmore Archives).

5. Spoto, *Dark Side of Genius*, p. 406.

6. Neil Sinyard, *The Films of Alfred Hitchcock* (New York: Gallery Books, 1986), p. 95. According to John Eastman, *Retakes: Behind the Scenes of 500 Classic Movies* (New York: Ballantine Books, 1989), the director deliberately withheld vital details from the cast to make the actors' confusion evident in their performances (p. 236).

7. In discussing the plot of *North by Northwest* with a local reporter, Hitchcock commented on the difficulty of making a spy movie in the post-World War II period. "'How can you tell who a spy is these days?' he sighed. 'They no longer sport cloaks and daggers. They might be the nuclear physicists or the wives of millionaires'" (quoted in *Rapid City Daily Journal*, 15 May 1958). The plot of *North by Northwest* reflects the Cold War era, which witnessed the McCarthy hearings, the Alger Hiss affair, and any number of other incidents pitting the free world against communism.

8. According to Nicole Swigart, a seasonal interpreter for the National Park Service at Mount Rushmore, the house depicted in the film is actually located in Boulder, Colorado. Swigart says visitors often inquire about the house, including

one movie fan from England who was reenacting Grant's cross-country chase. Interview with Swigart, Mount Rushmore National Memorial, 11 Aug. 1991.

9. Hitchcock biographer Donald Spoto notes that placing the actors on the actual memorial was physically impossible *(Dark Side of Genius*, p. 407). In my two ascents of Mount Rushmore, I have peeked over the edge a number of times and even "bellied up" to the edge as far as I dared to go. The drop from the top to the faces is sheer. Sliding down the granite edges would shred both clothing and skin.

10. Excerpt of Agreement between MGM and National Park Service, contained in Elmer F. Bennett (acting secretary of the interior) to Joseph E. Vogel (MGM president), 28 July 1959, Box 152, File 7, Record Group 182–185, Karl E. Mundt Historical and Educational Foundation Archives, Dakota State University, Madison, S.Dak. (hereafter cited Mundt Archives).

11. Charles Coleman to National Park Service, 8 Aug. 1958, contained in Conrad Wirth to Sen. Karl E. Mundt, 20 Aug. 1959, ibid.

12. Spoto, *Dark Side of Genius*, p. 407.

13. Interview with Popovich, Mount Rushmore National Memorial, 10 Sept. 1991.

14. *Rapid City Daily Journal*, 15 Sept. 1958.

15. Ibid., 17 Sept. 1958; Superintendent's Narrative Report, Sept. 1958, and Chief Ranger's Monthly Report, Sept. 1958, Rushmore Archives.

16. *Rapid City Daily Journal*, 17 Sept. 1958.

17. Undated clippings, contained in Wirth to Mundt, 20 Aug. 1959.

18. Ibid.

19. Bennett to Vogel, 28 July 1959.

20. Ibid.

21. Wirth to Mundt, 20 Aug. 1959. In his letter, Wirth alludes to a request that the National Park Service had turned down at another park: "A television producer finally gave up a planned series supposedly to portray the life of a ranger in another National Park because he could not produce a script which maintained both the dignity of the Park and the ranger. It had to be blood, thunder and gun slinging or else it could not be sold." Apparently, the motivations of the television business in the 1950s were much the same as they are today.

22. Bennett to Johnston, 28 July 1959, Box 152, Mundt Archives. This correspondence included a copy of Bennett's 28 July letter to Vogel.

23. Clark to Bennett, 3 Aug. 1959, ibid.

24. Scott N. Heidepriem, *A Fair Chance for a Free People: Biography of Karl E. Mundt, United States Senator* (Madison, S.Dak.: Karl E. Mundt Historical & Educational Foundation, 1988), p. 31.

25. Ibid., pp. 31–32. *See also* Larry Pressler, *U.S. Senators from the Prairie* (Vermillion, S.Dak.: University of South Dakota Press, 1982), pp. 131–39.

26. Superintendent's Narrative Report, Aug. 1959, Rushmore Archives.

27. Wirth to Mundt, 13 Aug. 1959, Box 152, Mundt Archives.

28. Mundt to Wirth, 15 Aug. 1959, ibid. While the Mundt Archives contain extensive correspondence about Mount Rushmore through the years—from complaints about poor toilet facilities to comments on a sound-and-light show—no other letters complaining about the movie, aside from those of the Park Service and the Interior Department, could be found in the files.

29. Ibid.

30. Wirth to Mundt, 20 Aug. 1959.

31. Mundt to Wirth, 25 Aug. 1959, Box 152, Mundt Archives.

32. George Amberg, *The New York Times Film Reviews: A One-Volume Selection, 1913–1970* (New York: Arno Press, 1971), p. 325–26.

33. Spoto, *Dark Side of Genius*, p. 331; Sinyard, *Films of Alfred Hitchcock*, p. 104.

34. Leslie Halliwell, *Filmgoer's and Video Viewer's Companion*, 9th ed. (New York: Harper & Row, 1988), p. 829.

35. Ann Lloyd and David Robinson, eds., *Movies of the Fifties* (London: Orbis Publishing, 1982), p. 173.

36. Spoto, *Dark Side of Genius*, p. 408.

37. Interview with Swigart.

38. Ibid. For more information about Gutzon Borglum and the creation of Mount Rushmore, *see* Rex Alan Smith, *The Carving of Mount Rushmore* (New York: Abbeville Press, 1985); Howard Shaff and Audrey Karl Shaff, *Six Wars at a Time: The Life and Times of Gutzon Borglum, Sculptor of Mount Rushmore* (Sioux Falls, S.Dak.: Center for Western Studies, Augustana College, 1985); and Gilbert C. Fite, *Mount Rushmore* (Norman: University of Oklahoma Press, 1952).

39. Popovich to the author, 11 Sept. 1991.

10

Donald and Christina Bolin

JIM CREEK JOURNAL

REMEMBERING A BLACK HILLS SUMMER

Donald W. Bolin

EDITOR'S NOTE: In 1971, Donald W. Bolin, along with his wife Christina Bolin, his sister Betty Sexton, and her husband Donald, purchased a thirty-acre parcel of land in the Black Hills of South Dakota. Schoolteachers from Columbus, Ohio, the Bolins had been spending their summers near Spearfish since the early 1960s. They bought their property near Nemo with the plan of moving there upon retiring. Situated northwest of Rapid City, the small "ranch" was divided by a scenic trout stream called Jim Creek.

The Bolins arrived to spend their first summer on Jim Creek in the aftermath of the Rapid City flood of 1972. On the night of 9–10 June, heavy rain in the upper reaches of the Black Hills swelled streams and broke the Canyon Lake Dam above Rapid City, killing 238 people and injuring hundreds more. As a result, the Bolins' first days at their new summer home were filled with sobering sights and problems to be faced and resolved. Soon, however, they found opportunities to enjoy the scenery and solitude that had led them to make the parcel in the Jim Creek Valley their second home.

Presented here are three chapters of Donald

This journal originally appeared in *South Dakota History* 33 (Summer 2003): 120–54.

Bolin's "Jim Creek Journal," which he began as a reminiscence in 1972. In addition to his account of the aftermath of the flood, the author preserves for us a record of how one man felt about the tensions and struggles that preoccupied Americans in the wake of the 1960s and during the divisive campaign leading up to the presidential election of 1972. Bolin's entries are presented essentially as he wrote them. In the few places where material has been omitted, the omission is indicated by ellipses.

Donald Bolin's Journal

Shopping in the Hills
In July 1971, after returning to Spearfish from a trip to Cody, Wyoming, my sister Betty, her husband Donald, my wife Chris, and I applied our energies to finding a place in the Black Hills where we might spend our summers in peaceful happiness and someday, eventually, live our final years in tranquil and productive retirement. In the beginning we were agreed to settle for any place that offered acreage, isolation, and trout fishing; but like other human beings in search of contentment, we discovered that the more we looked, the more refined and sophisticated our demands became. Even in the midst of civilized society, the abrasiveness of life may develop anxieties without dulling sensitivities.

The first place we examined was located near Custer. It proved to be an old mining claim of twenty-one acres, consisting of, perhaps, one acre of level land and the remainder in hilly woods. Along the front edge of the flat area ran a spring small enough for a man to step across, which didn't meet our requirement of a trout stream. The owner, a gas-station attendant in Rapid City, had bought the claim for taxes, after which he slapped on it an almost prohibitive price tag. Still, the size of the place would have provided sufficient elbow room for us, and the isolation would have made traffic jams on freeways a hazy memory at best. Even the necessity of having to travel two miles or so to fish French Creek would not have made life on that piece of land altogether intolerable, . . . but we soon realized that not just any place would do. . . .

One day we drove to Nemo to talk with Tony Martin, the owner of a dude ranch called the 4-T. We had heard that Tony was selling plots on Box Elder Creek. What we found spread out along the creek didn't exactly kindle our enthusiasm. Thirteen acres had been divided into twenty-five plots, each plot measuring approximately one-half acre. Most of the plots carried creek frontage, a feature that in no way counterbalanced our impression of being transplanted in the outskirts of some overburdened city. The idea reminded us of a development project designed to destroy the very wilderness we sought. Needless to say, we refused to consider a partnership in a conspiracy against nature. Just before we drove away, though, Tony said, "Say, you might stop at Claude Crisman's place about four miles down the road. I hear he wants to sell his thirty-acre ranch."

The Crisman ranch lay nestled a mile from the road in a gorgeous valley surrounded on all sides, except for five acres of private owner-ship, by national forest reserve. When we drove down to the ranch house on a dirt road that must have been maintained specifically to discourage trespassers, the entire area resembled one of those quiet, sleepy farms mentioned in "Rip Van Winkle." We introduced ourselves to Claude and Sylvia Crisman, who had once ranched in the Badlands and were now in their sixties, expressing to them our interest in their place. It was, indeed, a place to stimulate interest. A small stream, sing-ing melodiously as the clear water hurried toward Box Elder Creek, divided the land into two distinct parts. On one side of the stream lay fifteen acres of green meadow, presided over by a barn and generous with clover. On the other side stood fifteen acres of ponderosa pines and Black Hills spruce trees, persuasive in their stunning beauty. Above swayed that unbelievable sky of pale turquoise that never ceases to tear me up. Surely, in such a setting any man could discover a new world without having to cross an ocean. . . .

On 29 July 1971, after making a few telephone calls to Donald and Betty in Columbus, we bought the Crisman ranch. The Crismans were contracted to continue living there for a period of five years, since re-tirement for the four of us lay nine years away. In addition, it was agreed that during the summers of those five intervening years we would have access to three rustic cabins conveniently located there. Whatever ar-rangements we might be willing to make at the end of that five-year period simply could not be forseen at that time.

After the legal transaction had been completed, Chris and I returned to Columbus to prepare ourselves for the oncoming school year. In the fall, winter, and spring, however far away from us in actual miles, that gorgeous stream, Jim Creek, would flow through our thoughts like a

A dirt trail leads past the Bolins' Black Hills retreat.
The log cabin in the foreground is where the owners spent
their summers. Donald W. Bolin, Columbus, Ohio

tonic, carrying with it all the healing powers of the Hot Springs of Arkansas.

—30 September 1972

The Meaning of Jim Creek
Before returning to Columbus, Chris and I spent our last day in the Black Hills browsing around the ranch. The Crismans were hauling to the barn some hay from land they had leased in Nemo Valley, leaving the ranch exclusively to us. We who are accustomed to the stifling confinement of, if not enchained by the wretched need for, phone booths, suburban shopping centers, and freeways had never fully realized the release of fancy that thirty acres of elbow room make possible. We hiked leisurely through the woods where wild roses, fleabane, and sunflowers ran like wayward children everywhere. We made plans as to how, someday, selective cutting in our woods might bring about maximum

benefit in tree growth and minimum evidence of human interference. We followed Jim Creek downstream, where in pools phantom signs betrayed all those polka-dot darlings. To enhance our appreciation, we imagined the strategic placement of log dams. Through observation, we absorbed minute details; through sensation, we recorded memorable impressions. In short, we remembered all over our land because forgetting scowls at us as the strongest enemy of a contented mind. It is a long time from summer to summer.

It became obvious to us that our ranch would be more than an investment for absentee landowners, more than a summer hideaway for civilized refugees, even more than a home for prospective retirees. Far less concerned with involvement in the nation than desertion from it, we had sought a relatively safe refuge from which we might view the rest of the country, if we chose, as a beaver looks upon the surroundings from its secure underwater home. Since the nation had decided to permit crime without meting out any appreciable penalty to the criminal, we would use Jim Creek as a beaver home. If the Walden Pond area had been invaded by muggers from any of our large cultural cities, I think Thoreau might have found resignation unnecessary only if he had armed himself for a total war. I rather suspect he would have altered his views, the transcendentalism notwithstanding, and resigned in the face of futility, perhaps writing a treatise on the glaring shortcomings of a free society.

Had the purchase of Jim Creek been solely our impatient reaction to the loss of safety, we might just as well have stayed in the city and armed ourselves to fight side by side with other Americans victimized by the same deprivation. For is it not true that Americans everywhere are deprived of the one thing that a republic should be equipped to provide, namely, safety? I suppose Jim Creek itself could easily serve as the setting for a mugging, however much safer the Black Hills are than, say, New York City. So, other factors really caused Jim Creek to stand like a fort in the wilderness, visible through the illusions, inspirational above the clamors, and friendly in spite of the hostilities.

It is no well-guarded secret that the quality of our national life has deteriorated into a mishmash of crowded living conditions. We must get permission from our neighbor to blow our nose for fear of nudging him in the ribs with our elbows. As pedestrians, we once had to look both ways before crossing. Now, we dare not cross at all, or the newspaper will honor us in the obituary. If overpopulation does not annoy us, innumerable by-products, appearing in the form of social illnesses, certainly do. . . . As for natural real estate, we need a magnifying glass to scan the dwindling map. Even if we were to convert cemeteries into development projects, we still could not avoid the graveyards of crowded conditions. All our efforts to understand this social chaos have put us on a treadmill with a loss of equilibrium and an annihilation of purpose.

Jim Creek loomed as our answer to a shrinking land supply with which to house and feed an expanding population. The rest of the nation would have to seek its own answer. At Jim Creek we would escape almost entirely from air pollution. The color of the sky there seems to deny that factories and automobiles exist at all. In addition, we were blessed by the absence of polluted water, for at that altitude of approximately five thousand feet there are so few people to pollute anything. Cold springs, clean and clear, feed our stream, making it safe. Surrounded by national forest reserve and a plentiful wildlife, Jim Creek stood as a retreat from society, if you will, a private withdrawal, free from the excessive outrages of a nation that will not discipline itself. I think Jim Creek, above all else, symbolized for us a return to basics wherein equilibrium and purpose would be assured through our mutually good interchanges with nature.

We were not prepared to abandon on the doorsteps of society all the children of modern technology and research. When the nose is running and a virus makes a mockery of good health, the prospect of recovery is enhanced through the magic of a doctor's credentials, not a shaman's incantations. We would take with us, therefore, the cure without being weakened by any of the disease. For Jim Creek was not, in any sense of the expression, an escape from precepts; it was more a long-overdue return to sanity, a worthwhile confrontation with essentials, an entirely new rediscovery of life.

Summer, 1972
We did not learn of the Rapid City flood until 10 June, the day after it happened. Not only are we located nineteen miles northwest of Rapid City, a considerable distance away from the center of the disaster area, but we are also a thousand feet higher than Rapid City. The possibility that our own ranch might be ravaged did not, at first, occur to us.

We had spent the winter months in pleasant reverie, imagining long hikes up Jim Creek Canyon and interminable fishing excursions along

Box Elder Creek. That nature always remains in control, we never for a moment doubted; but that she would unleash her fury in the direction of Jim Creek, for whatever reason, we did not, in our wildest dreaming, allow. As news reports began to dominate the airways, the truth that our place was vulnerable slowly revealed itself to us, however reluctant we may have been to believe it. The cold air of truth never fails to sober a man from the dizziness of his false thinking.

The flood caused a temporary discontinuation of telephone service from Rapid City. The Crismans, therefore, could not contact us. For all we knew, though, they may have been wiped out. While we were awaiting a call from them, we tried to establish some kind of communication with friends in the Black Hills. We called Ruth Williams at Sturgis and Rita Martin at the 4-T in Nemo, but neither could give us much information about our ranch. Frankly, both women were preoccupied with their own personal concerns. Ruth, for example, grimly faced the unenviable job of consoling her sister, whose sixty-thousand-dollar home in Rapid City had been a total loss. Rita was helping make arrangements with Tony to shore up the 4-T, which had sustained extensive damage. Rita did tell us that, although Box Elder Creek had swelled its banks, drowning one man in the Nemo Valley, she thought our place suffered few losses. The Crismans, she said, were safe.

Three or four days passed before we heard from the Crismans, who finally managed to contact us from Rapid City. Yes, the ranch had been damaged but not severely. The ranch house and barn were untouched, but at the height of the torrential downpour the creek water had swelled to within thirty feet of the house. Our well, which had once stood between the house and the creek, disappeared. Along with it, a considerable amount of fence, as yet unknown because unmeasured, washed away. In addition, innumerable ponderosa pines and spruce trees, which had stood on either side of the creek, were uprooted and carried downstream. Considering the vast destruction of the flood, described by the media in graphic detail, we felt our own losses to be minimal. If Zeus had been sitting on a thunderhead directly above Jim Creek, taking especially careful precautions not to destroy us, he could not have been more generous; for we learned that in the vicinity of Bogus Jim Creek, located not far south of us, fourteen inches of rain fell between the afternoon of 9 June and the morning of 10 June.

Chris and I arrived in the Hills on 28 June, not knowing fully what to anticipate. As a safeguard against one of the predictables, we had taken

typhoid shots in Columbus. Except for adaptability of mind and body, there was no safeguard against any of the unpredictables.

Rapid City had been transformed into a hubbub of mechanized activity, but the massive destruction still lay in evidence all around. It was our hope to be able to take the Nemo Road to Jim Creek, a trip of only nineteen miles. Upon inquiry, however, we found the Nemo Road closed as a result of eight or nine bridges having been washed out. To get to Nemo, we had to drive west on Route 40 past the Canyon Lake area, which so resembled a bombed city that I was not tempted to take any pictures. We do not preserve in photographs the destruction nature does to our cities when it reminds us so painfully of the greater destruction we are capable of doing to ourselves. From Route 40 we turned north on U.S. Highway 385 and drove to Nemo by the back way, so to speak. At Nemo we drove from the 4-T to Jim Creek without much difficulty, although the road had been washed out and hastily repaired at Estes Creek near a dude ranch called the Ox Yoke. The trip from Rapid City to Jim Creek covered about forty-eight miles.

The three cabins, which for want of a better word I have already described as rustic, stood luxuriously on Jim Creek (now that I have had time to feel for greater accuracy), plush in their rusticity. There was a two-room log cabin, built in the 1930s by Mr. Voice, who owns the five-acre plot of land adjacent to ours. There was a two-room rectangular

Among the Bolins' "comforts of inconvenience" was the outhouse, shown here in the process of being painted. Donald W. Bolin, Columbus, Ohio

frame cabin, which had had red tar-paper siding put on it. Then there was a smaller cabin, square in shape, covered in dark tar-paper siding. This small cabin once served as a washhouse for Mr. Voice when he lived in the log cabin during the Great Depression.

We unpacked the car and set up housekeeping in the log cabin, which was furnished with a refrigerator, a propane gas stove, a kitchen table, a wood-burning stove, a couch, two dressers, and two beds. Four chairs of dubious strength and questionable appearance sat ready to accept any tired bodies willing to trust them. For our bathroom we used an old outhouse, which, because of its dilapidated appearance, must have dated back to the turn of the century. Never before did we realize that having access to so few material niceties made possible so much physical comfort. As Chris appropriately described our situation, "The comforts of inconvenience surround us."

Having put away our equipment and tidied up the cabin, we walked over the land, reacquainting ourselves with old familiar scenes: the green forest and hills surrounding us, the pasture thick with grass, the lush woods, and the eternal Jim Creek. After an absence of one year, we yearned to be there, enriched by our own understanding and fulfilled through our own appreciation. The beauty of the land is a miracle, confirmed each summer by the marvel of nature's power to renew. We do not question the power of the sun any more than we deny the mag-

Newly exposed rock and uprooted trees line the banks in this view of Jim Creek. The ranch house is located up the bank to the left. Donald W. Bolin, Columbus, Ohio

nificence of its setting. Both are integral parts of a scheme from which we could not extricate ourselves even if we dared. Nor do we accept the splendor of a stream of water without giving to nature the power, in fact, the right to make whatever changes she must make. Standing on the banks of Jim Creek and examining not the damage but the re-creation of the flood, we could not help feeling that nature had given us a new Jim Creek, unlike the one we left a year ago. Nature may damage the works of man, embarrassing his economics; but herself she always re-creates and revitalizes, glorifying those ineffable processes that man too often disregards.

Where there had before been grassy banks leading down to the water's edge, now there were boulders and, in many instances, beds of solid rock. The surface dirt had utterly disappeared under the tremendous force of the current. Rock exposure extended perhaps twenty or thirty feet from either side of the stream. The water had washed out nearly all movable things in its path, including trees. At places where the stream turned sharply in its course, gigantic deposits of dirt and rocks had occurred, making the channel distinctly narrower than before. Our new Jim Creek, for all its flooding, looked rugged, primitive, even antediluvian. Had Moses been delegated to lead us across it, parting the water to make a way, we would not have been liberated into a world more fully alive with wonders.

Claude and Sylvia Crisman could not conceal the effect of having been shaken by their experience. When the water continued to rise early in the morning on 10 June, they feared for the safety of the ranch house because the stream swelled to within thirty feet of the foundation. If the water had risen perhaps one more foot, . . . but fortunately it did not. The sight of all that water, moving swiftly and uncontrollably, must certainly have been disturbing. Claude told me that while standing on the bank, he saw hundreds of trees float downstream. In addition boxes, debris, and miscellany went surging downstream, either to be buried or to surface, quite by chance, as the water receded. Later in the summer down on Box Elder Creek, Donald found a shovel and crowbar. They had been hurled from God knows where upstream. I myself found two metal fence posts still in good condition. Mr. Voice had placed near the stream a beautiful red fire engine, made by his own hands, for the protection of his house. In looking at a photograph of this machinery afterward, I guessed it to weigh no less than one thousand pounds, for one part consisted of an automobile engine. Not only did his apparatus disappear, but it also neglected to reappear, although I did find buried in the rocks on our ranch a section of the hose. Claude said the deafening roar of the stream so affected the dogs, Chinook and Ding, that they scurried under the house and came out only after the most persuasive argument. Chinook, in particular, who during spring had spent considerable time in the stream trying to catch trout, no longer went near the water. Any spectator not shaken, at least temporarily, by such an experience would have to be a religious fanatic, a fatalist, or a perfect physical specimen with nerves of stone. . . .

The Crismans have a son named Eddy, who was living in a trailer somewhere near Rapid City. Eddy managed to escort his family to safety, but he could not save his home. Thirty feet of water passed over the trailer, carrying it out of existence. Only a few pieces were ever found.

As soon as the water receded, shock goaded the Crismans into action. They spent several days in Rapid City, helping to look for flood victims.

They searched the banks, investigated piles of dirt and rocks, and examined trash and brush wrapped around trees. They scoured the low levels, probing and uncovering. They played the kind of hunt in which finding the quarry wounds the hunter. Claude inflicted himself with one body, that of a baby.

Upon settling down at Jim Creek, we concerned ourselves with making water available. Since the flood had washed out the well, we needed water badly. For two or three days, I carried from the stream enough water for washing dishes and taking sponge baths. Then Claude, Sylvia, and I set up a pump in the stream, an arrangement that made water available for Chris and me at a hydrant about forty feet from the log cabin. It also made water available in the chicken house and the barn. The Crismans, of course, had access to stream water inside the ranch house. Getting drinking water proved to be an entirely different matter. Until the new well was dug, the pump installed, and the lines laid out late in July, we were forced to haul our drinking water in gallon jugs from Brownsville on Highway 385, eighteen miles away.

One day Claude and I measured the length of barbed-wire fence that the flood had torn out and washed away. We stepped off the distance, walking parallel to the stream, although in three places the fence crossed over. Claude had strung up wire in order to rest one pasture while the animals were grazing in another. We estimated the loss to be roughly 1,650 feet, or one hundred rods. Poet Robert Frost observes accurately that something in nature does not like a wall, a commentary on the extent, I think, to which a barrier must be alien to the scheme. Nature flattens, not erects.

On a July morning the temperature at Jim Creek generally fluctuates between fifty and sixty-five degrees. At nine o'clock the temperature begins to climb. If the sky is clear, the thermometer may reach eighty, even eighty-five degrees by noon. At seven or eight o'clock in the morning, however, the cool air, brisk and invigorating, makes the act of crawling out from under warm blankets a ritual not easy to forget. To take the chill from the cabin, we built a fire every morning. On our front porch stood a wood box, which we kept full of pine cones and pine logs. In the spring Claude had sawed up pine trees into a huge pile of logs. By getting a permit from the ranger, he could claim for firewood the trees that were down in the forest. The pine cones we had gathered ourselves. In a matter of moments, Chris or I had glowing in the pot-bellied stove a grinning invitation to meet the day on its own terms.

The evenings are no different. As soon as the sun disappears over the hills, bringing down darkness, the temperature drops abruptly. At that time we always interrupted what we happened to be doing to build a fire.

There is, in fact, nothing like a fire to kindle the spirits, and no kindling is better suited to build a fire than pine cones and pine logs. At the burst of a match the pine cones enlighten; later, the pine logs illuminate. When pine trees dominate a forest, there are not likely to be cold or dark spirits in a nearby cabin, for pine is the fuel of life.

One morning after having been at Jim Creek three or four days, I decided to try for the first time my skill with the spinning rod. After all, we considered trout fishing one of the attractive features at our ranch. Nearby flowed the creek, not big by customary standards but adequate for ordinary circumstances. A half mile downstream roared Box Elder Creek, into which our Jim Creek emptied. Unlike the smaller Jim Creek, Box Elder moved along boldly. Robust and aggressive, it tumbled headlong down the Nemo Valley, a real challenge to a man not afraid to float his hat. In either stream, surrounded by unbelievable scenery, a fisherman could lose the city and gain his soul, feeling that he had struck a good bargain in the exchange. . . .

Having put on my waders, I picked up the rest of my gear and headed for Jim Creek, determined not to be diverted from the main stream of my thoughts by tactless campaign tactics, violent non-violent demonstrations, and decisive supreme court indecisions. Though I chose a spinning rod instead of a fly rod, no A.C.L.U. chapter would appeal to the Division of Wildlife on the grounds that Fly Tying, Inc., of Justice, U.S.A., should be given equal kill time. For once, at least, I could act without being endangered by criminals operating openly under the protection of indulgent politicians, who, in their attempt to curb crime, pass slipshod, stopgap legislation. In spite of all the personal sacrednesses defiled by national permissiveness, one holy act by virtuous men still remains, namely, communing with nature on a trout stream.

The flood had left several trees lying across the stream. In one instance the water had undermined the roots of a clump of six spruce trees. These trees lay where they had fallen, presumably after the water had receded. The roots were still clinging feebly to the earth in a hole where once there had been a solid foundation for support. In another instance a big ponderosa pine lay parallel with the stream, maybe fifteen feet from it. I found no evidence that this giant pine had ever stood on our land. Many of the trees bordering the south side of the stream had been badly undermined by the flood, but they stood tall and proud, hugging the good earth. When they would fall, if indeed they were ever destined to do so, I could not foretell.

Jim Creek was noticeably bigger than it had been a year ago, for which gift the fisherman is always grateful. True, I had seen the stream in 1971 during late August when the water level is generally low everywhere, especially in the Hills. Although the water level is considerably higher in late June and early July, still the stream seemed to contain more water than it should. For some reason the flood had actually increased the amount of water, a fact that puzzled me until I later learned from Claude that new springs upstream had been opened up.

The sun was just beginning to light up the sky in a typically magnificent turquoise display when I stepped into the water at about nine-thirty. No one who sees a South Dakota sky on a bright day fails to be affected by it. Somehow, events go better, as if benevolent influences prevail, corroborating Ralph Waldo Emerson's observation that nature does everything well. I turned upstream, facing a pool in the middle of which lay the clump of six spruce trees. My spinning rod contained a Panther Martin lure attached to four-pound-test monofilament line. On my first cast I caught a nine-inch brook trout, at that moment the most beautiful animal in the world. After netting my brookie, I killed it with a blow on the head from a pocket knife I carry expressly for that purpose. A trout the fisherman intends to keep should be spared the indignity of having to flop out of water embarrassingly. Only an uninformed novice or a vicious sadist would subject so beautiful a spirit to such inhuman treatment as a slow death outside its natural habitat. Having put my brookie in the creel, I stood there in the water, wrapped in wonder. The experience was, oh, so lovely.

I moved downstream but continued to fish upstream. In this manner I covered about three hundred yards, a distance that took me just beyond the boundary line of the ranch. Box Elder would entice me to it another day, but this day I was held sufficiently enthralled by Jim Creek. Working my way downstream, pool by pool, I exhausted all possibilities and assimilated all benefits. There rose in my mind a question as to which caught more, the spinning rod or my spinning eyes. Eventually, I returned to the cabin with four brook trout and one rainbow, but who would ever know the number of captured sky glimpses and landscapes, perfect and sublime?

On the evening of 3 July, Donald and Betty, tired yet spirited, came driving in from Columbus, Ohio. Following them were my brother Mike and his wife Elizabeth (known to us as "Butch"), both of whom had decided to test their endurance in the face of what they suspected might be the inhospitality of Jim Creek. If life there proved pleasant and comfortable, they would count their blessings; if it turned out to be rough and primitive, they had agreed to make the most out of a bad situation. In comparison with, say, Howard Johnson's Motor Inn, our lifestyle at Jim Creek probably would have qualified us for national sympathy if not governmental welfare assistance. We could not, however, compare favorably with combat conditions before casting aside soft mattresses, warm stoves, and hot meals. For Mike, a former soldier who once shared severities of the march with Patton's Third Army, any style of life superior to K-rations in a foxhole might tend to grade out as tourist class. Still, I was positive Mike and Butch would happily accept us as we were, namely, in a condition somewhere between a fashionable motor court and a harsh bivouac.

"Hey, Butch Baby," I said, pointing to the outhouse, "there's your boudoir. If you have any complaints, see your chaplain."

"No complaints, Donny," she said. "I'm just curious as to where the maid is."

"She's been given a long summer vacation," Chris said, "compliments of the house."

Donald and Betty unpacked their car and set up housekeeping in the log cabin with us since the cabin is spacious enough, a second bed having been installed by the Crismans for their hunters, providing sleeping accommodations for four. While they busied themselves, Mike and Butch took to the red cabin, setting up their own home quarters. Although they would have to carry water to the cabin, a handy two-burner hot plate permitted them to heat it for brewing coffee and taking sponge baths. All similarity with life on the front suddenly faded. Even the meals for all six of us were to be cooked and served in our log cabin. Sometimes, we must learn to be thankful when our endurance is not tested.

After the four arrivals had rested for a couple of days, Mike, Donald, and I set about piping water into the log cabin. The carrying of water, though from a hydrant only forty feet away, seemed an inconvenience we did not feel it necessary to continue living with, particularly in the light of our great cooking needs. In our cabin where the cooking was

to be done, inside water could scarcely be called a luxury. We attached to the hydrant a garden hose, ran it under the cabin and up through the floor, and finally connected it to an old, worn, but usable sink. The plumbing required several hours of work, primarily because of the rusted condition of the connections; but at the end of our labor, we had access to stream water by the twist of a faucet.

Having completed that job, we next set about piping our used water away from the cabin. The necessity for an adequate drainage system loomed as a stark fact, for the lack of any system at all proved as unnecessary an inconvenience as the carrying of water into the cabin. We had been catching the used water in a bucket under the sink, hauling it outside, and dumping it into the septic tank. After connecting a plastic pipe to the sink, we merely ran our drain down through the floor. Luckily, the pipe flowed downhill all the way from the floor to the septic tank. In a single day we had eliminated two nagging inconveniences that Mr. Voice for years had accepted as integral parts of his daily routine in that log cabin.

One day Claude was advising Chris and me about the location of the well to be drilled.

"I witched this place behind the house with a bar. Seems like a pretty good vein all right," he said, motioning toward the yard.

*Posing in front of the red guest cabin are (from left) Don Sexton,
friend Ray Miller, Mike Bolin, Elizabeth ("Butch") Bolin, Christina
Bolin, and Don Bolin. Donald W. Bolin, Columbus, Ohio*

The ranch house stands on a high bank about thirty feet above the
stream bed. The land moves away from the bank at a gradually elevated
incline so that the place he referred to as a good drilling site would, we
hoped, be safe from future floods.

When Claude spoke about witching for water in the yard, Chris
beamed, her eyes becoming two 1964 Kennedy half dollars. Whenever
a conversation touches upon such topics as divination, prognostica-
tion, ESP, reincarnation, or glossolalia, nothing else matters. She riv-
ets her attention to each word. Whereas baseball fans worship Babe
Ruth, opera buffs adore Enrico Caruso, and literature devotees idol-
ize William Shakespeare, so Chris admires psychics Edgar Cayce and
Jeanne Dixon. Lustrous with burning interest, she delights in talking

about subjects related to the occult, subjects I sometimes facetiously call "spook-a-boo."

"A bar?" Chris asked.

"Yea," Claude answered, "Chet Amen was here, oh, a week ago and used a chokecherry branch. Some fellows use one thing; some, another. I use a bar, a metal bar. But Chet and me both hit the same vein. Wait a minute. I'll show you."

He disappeared behind the house. When he returned a few seconds later, he held a piece of iron or steel. It looked like a three-foot crowbar straightened out. Holding the bar parallel with the ground, he walked over the area designated by him as the most likely site for our well. The front end of the bar tipped downward. As he continued to walk, the bar again resumed its horizontal position.

"See," he said, "just like before. Amen hit that same vein. Good water there."

"Give me that bar," Chris said.

She balanced the bar in her right hand, as Claude had done, and walked across the yard. When she reached the designated area, sure enough, downward the front end of the bar tipped. An additional two or three steps brought the bar to its original position.

"There's no water down there," I said to Claude and Chris. "There's nothing but a big magnet under the ground. Give me that bar."

"Here," said Chris, handing it to me, "but since you don't believe, miracles will not be revealed. You have to believe to be able to find." She spoke with too great an air of the jocular for me to take her seriously.

I balanced the bar in my right hand, as Claude and Chris both had done, and walked across the yard. Nothing happened. I may have felt like Moses but only for a single moment. I saw no burning bush. I found no tablet. To walk across ground beneath which cold, clear water flows and not to be able to receive promises through a metal bar, especially when others have already tapped the ineffable, is downright embarrassing. If Claude and Chris had not undermined the solemnity of the moment with the levity of their remarks, I would have been disgusted. I so wanted to find water.

Claude took the bar again and without hesitation found water. Then Chris took the bar again, and she too found water. I took the bar again and found nothing. Though not disgusting, it was shamefully frustrating.

Afterward, Chris and I used an occasion to test our powers of divination again. Mike, Donald, and I had driven to the home of Chet Amen to find out when he could start drilling our well. Chet lives about halfway between Nemo and Brownsville on a hill overlooking a beautiful valley, most of which is owned by his father-in-law. Chet told us the day we could expect him. Since our stay in the Hills was limited, he gave the job of drilling on our place the highest priority. On that scheduled day he came driving his rig slowly down our road over the chuckholes, bumps, and rocks. What a welcome sight he was! The first thing he did after parking was to invade Mr. Voice's place to find a chokecherry fork, for the flood had washed away most of our chokecherry bushes.

"I was here a while back and found a good vein that probably comes right down Voice's place," he said, "and on through yours."

"We know," Chris said. "Claude told us."

Chet cut his chokecherry fork and hurried to the yard behind our ranch house. He held the fork in front of him while walking back and forth across the yard. In the course of his walking, the fork dipped, designating pretty much the same area Claude had indicated as being the best drilling site. The difference was that Chet, by his pattern of walking, charted the direction in which the vein of water was flowing.

"Give me that chokecherry fork," Chris said.

This time, however, when Chris walked across the yard holding the fork, unlike before, nothing happened. She was following the script I thought had been written exclusively for me.

"What's wrong?" she asked Chet. "I could make Claude's metal bar work for me."

"A magnet doesn't attract a chokecherry fork," I said.

"I don't know," Chet said. "Let's see if both of us can make it work." He took in his left hand one side of the fork, while Chris took in her right hand the other side. Under his direction they walked across the yard together. When they reached the designated area, the fork started to dip.

"Do you feel the force pulling it downward?" he asked. "Yes," she said.

"Now it's my turn. Give me that chokecherry fork," I said in an old familiar vein.

Needless to say, when I walked across the yard holding the fork, just as before, nothing happened. Not even when Chet's influential presence comprised one half of the attempt would any change take place in

the position of that chokecherry fork. My career as a water witcher or diviner came to an end abruptly and decisively. . . .

When Chet started drilling our well, we felt relieved to know that eventually one of our basic problems would be solved. Soon, drinking water, having flowed only from our thoughts, would once more flow from a well deep in the earth. Nor would we ever forget what not having access to a well was like. The value of good drinking water can scarcely be appraised by one whose thirst is always quenched after a trip to the well or sink. Refuse to provide the means by which good water is made easily available, and one learns very quickly the economics of supply and demand. Drinking water had understandably become for us an extremely valuable commodity because we had but a limited supply, a grisly fact that glared at us constantly and gnawed away at our consciousness. We were habitually checking our needs against our reserves. True enough, we never miss the water till the well runs dry.

From its appearance, the rig used by Chet in drilling our well seemed an ancient one, but the principle upon which it operated is still used to drill most wells in the Black Hills. Most wells are, in fact, not really drilled at all; they are pounded out. The rig consisted of a series of geared spools of steel cable. Attached to the end of the cable was a circular steel shaft about five inches in diameter and about sixteen feet in length. Different kinds of bits could be put on the working end of the shaft, giving it a length of twenty feet and a weight of one thousand six hundred or one thousand seven hundred pounds. This shaft, weighing nearly a ton, could be lifted by the rig to a desired height and allowed to drop, causing it to crash into the earth. As long as the shaft pounded into dirt, progress was unimpeded. The well hole descended quickly enough, and wear on the bit was slight. As soon as the shaft hit rock, though, the descent of the hole slowed down considerably, and the bit required constant attention. Needless to say, "drilling" a well anywhere in the Black Hills grates on the emotions because of the vast amount of hard rock lying underground there.

I have since considered the humor of designating a well hole as having been pounded out instead of drilled. Even so, Chet informed me that a well could actually be drilled but that the high cost of the machinery makes such an operation almost impossible.

Having decided upon the exact site for our well, Chet started pounding out the hole. It was a suitable spot, high and dry, thirty-five feet from the ranch house. At first, the shaft cut through the soft surface dirt very easily. Within a short time the hole had descended fifteen feet, at which depth disappointment began to harden like concrete because the shaft cut into rock that Chet called granite. He said it was as hard as any rock he had ever cut into. For five days he pounded away at rock, finally penetrating to a depth of forty feet. Even at that depth only a trickle of water greeted our eyes in the mirror that from time to time he would hold over the hole. Aside from these disappointing developments, though, an even greater disappointment presented itself. The bit he had been using required the welding of new cutting edges every two feet or so. As a direct result of this time-consuming obstacle, the hole at forty feet was so crooked that on the upstroke the shaft would hang up on the jagged edges of the rock.

Chet feared for the loss of his rig, which on two or three occasions gave us all cause for alarm. It became increasingly apparent that he would lose this initial effort. Not even after blasting out the bottom with dynamite twice could he open up the hole enough for the shaft to move freely. When he first saw the problem, he ordered a new carbide bit from Pittsburgh, but it did not arrive in time. After five days Chet wisely but reluctantly abandoned the hole.

Perhaps it was a lesson obtained from so much utter failure having preceded the second effort that produced successful results without a single hitch or delay. If, as in Emerson's words, nothing worthwhile was ever achieved without enthusiasm, Chet was destined to succeed. Feeling that his honor depended upon the outcome, he attacked the job with a vicious vigor. Having witched the yard again, he decided upon a spot this time ninety feet from the ranch house. I helped him set up the rig, no easy undertaking. With the new bit recently arrived from Pittsburgh, he started pounding out the new hole. At nineteen feet he struck some water, another trickle as before. At twenty-eight feet, however, he struck a flow of water that corresponded with our sanguine expectations. Joy overflowed at the rate of six gallons per minute. Acting under his advice, we had him take the hole to a depth of sixty feet.

Donald and Betty and Mike and Butch could not share in the delight of our success because they left for Columbus on the very day Chet started pounding out the second hole, but the emotional reaction of Chris and me more than offset any reduced response caused by their absence. We had every reason to feel justified in enjoying what Chris had appropriately called "our glory hole." Frankly, no miner ever looked into the earth with a wider smile or a fuller heart.

Although the diameter of the well hole measured only about twelve inches, the dropping of plastic casing to the bottom, a job requiring the utmost in skill and patience, was but routine. Having then sealed the well with concrete seven feet from the surface to protect our water from runoff, Chet concluded the operation, completely redeeming himself. After two weeks he had given us what we needed most, what lay mysteriously hidden in nature quivering to be taken, and what, without his old rig, advice, and labor, we surely would have been forced to do without, namely, a well full of cold, clear drinking water. The work of installing the pump and digging a ditch for laying the electric wiring and the water line would fall to the plumber.

During the time that Chet spent getting us our well, we helped him whenever he needed help. I, in particular, must have seemed like a self-appointed boss, for I was often walking around the rig, picking up tools and keeping a check on the progress of the operation. Because much of the time the work consisted of nothing more than Chet's standing over the hole, guiding the shaft as it pounded away at the earth, there wasn't anything for us to do but watch. On such occasions we six would take off hiking or fishing. From the moment of our arrival at Jim Creek, we intended to enjoy as frequently as possible the natural endowments of the land.

Even before Chet had come driving his rig down our road, we one day hiked down Jim Creek to Box Elder Creek. Only I, in fishing alone a few days before, had passed below the boundary line of our property; but none of us, in spite of this fact, knew what Jim Creek really looked like between our line and Box Elder.

The day itself waxed beautiful beyond telling, for the bright, golden sunshine made a dazzling spectacle of every object it touched. The sky spread above us a canopy of pale blue, gigantic in its impact upon the emotions. I was convinced then (and still am now) that one of the beauties of Jim Creek lies in its great capacity to evoke delightful and memorable responses. In such a splendid setting, of course, no visibility gap exists at all. How can anyone, under normal conditions, deny truth verified by his own eyes?

Our fishing rods remained in the cabins that day, for in hiking we did not seek so specific an objective as fishing. If we must always undertake a hike with an object in mind, let the eyes and ears be receptive to miracles. Then we find ourselves necessarily moved by any object.

Whatever sights and sounds may be perceived in the city are sometimes overshadowed and subdued by society's indifference in either protecting or preserving them. Even if a beautiful scene or some haunting music were to stimulate us on Main Street, we would more than likely respond like Pavlov's dog, only to hurry with unparalleled speed to our next appointment. Too many bells ring in our heads, blurring the visions and distorting the harmonies. On Jim Creek there were no ringing distractions to prevent a full appreciation of the bluebird and its song.

This reference to the bluebird, by the way, is literal, not figurative. How could the genius of Jim Creek fail to produce an actual embodiment of the one perfect spirit that has for so long stood symbolically as the ultimate in man's happiness? Claude had nailed high on the porch of the ranch house a bird box. Chris and I were quite surprised but thoroughly pleased to find two bluebirds nesting there. Before that unexpected pleasure, I don't remember having seen a bluebird since living in New Boston, Ohio, in the early 1940s. We spent a part of one evening sitting on the porch with Claude and Sylvia and watching Mom and Dad fly home with grasshoppers for their children.

The hike down Jim Creek, a journey of maybe half a mile, confirmed our expectations, for pleasures lie steadfast and secure when they are anticipated. What we found proved to be, at least in places, a canyon. The high, barren walls of cliffs looked down upon us from both sides of the stream. Wherever the cliffs played out, heavily timbered bluffs succeeded them. Jim Creek, an apparently ancient stream, had carved out of the hills through which it flowed a landscape at once rugged and picturesque.

On four or five occasions we forded the stream very carefully since at that time early in July there flowed a strong current of water. We stayed with Jim Creek all the way to Box Elder and absorbed every pleasure. We absorbed the flowers that grew in patches under pine trees and spruce trees or in open meadows beneath the radiant sky: Rocky Mountain iris, blue verbena, the meadow rose, white prairie aster, western salsify, and Missouri goldenrod. At the confluence of Jim Creek and Box Elder, we absorbed the scenery, in spite of devastation wrought by the flood. Evidence of the destruction lay everywhere. Piled logs were scattered about, and limbs were jammed here and there. Trees that stood near the water held the telltale debris wrapped around their trunks. In contrast with a traffic scene on the freeway, however, what we saw emerged as a picture-postcard view, lovely and inspirational. At the confluence a huge pool formed, suitable in challenging the skill of fisherman, artist, or poet. I had seen Box Elder often in Nemo, but never had I seen it this far downstream from close-up. Indeed, the hike along Jim Creek to Box Elder proved to be more than we had bargained for, and we absorbed all that the excursion offered.

In walking half a mile along a city street, one risks his life; and since the aesthetic by-products of such a walk are scarcely worth the effort, he would do well to stay at home and read the statistics rather than become part of them. In hiking half a mile down Jim Creek, one risks his life being given back to him; and, since such a gift makes the effort necessary, one can do no less than resurrect himself at the opportunity. A rebirth along Jim Creek is worth the hiking to experience.

Still prior to Chet's arrival, Donald and Mike one day took the car and went fishing down on Box Elder. Meanwhile, Butch and I sought Jim Creek, where I began teaching her how to use the spinning rod. We headed toward Box Elder, moving from pool to pool, first fishing upstream, then downstream. A beginner in the use of spinning equipment, Butch did not at the start get the knack of casting a lure; but the more she cast, the more skill she acquired. By the time we reached Box Elder, she was casting with some proficiency and accuracy. Although she didn't catch a trout, her creel spilled over with catches of joy and contentment.

In demonstrating to her different kinds of casts, I caught three nine-inch brookies in Jim Creek. At the confluence in the huge pool, I nested a beautiful thirteen-inch rainbow. When it jumped, I was disappointed that time did not pause, if only to assure me of one additional gasp.

Upon returning to the cabins, we learned that Donald and Mike, who had fished Box Elder upstream from us, caught some fine browns and rainbows. Needless to say, we soon enjoyed one of the most sumptuous of fisherman's meals: a green salad, a baked potato with sour cream, fried trout wrapped in bacon strips and served with a lemon wedge, fruit salad, bread, and coffee.

One morning Claude said to me in the yard, "Did you hear the ruckus last night?"

"If you mean the dogs," I said, "I did. I hear them barking every night about twelve o'clock chasing critters in the meadow."

"No," Claude said, "I mean about three o'clock in the morning."

"I didn't hear anything then. I was sound asleep."

Claude proceeded to tell me the story of the ruckus. Sylvia had put four setting hens in a small dilapidated shed used solely for that purpose. Although the shed was closed up, a big buck raccoon somehow got inside and killed two of the hens. The noise made by the hens aroused Chinook and Ding. They immediately staged an angry howl in trying to find a way to get inside the shed. Having ripped off one of the side boards, they rushed the raccoon, after which a real tooth-and-claw struggle took place. Finally, following a fierce fight, the dogs killed the raccoon.

This episode places in a clear light our attitude toward animals. I submit that we value animals, wild or tame, to the extent that they do not interfere with our own economics or life-supporting interests. That we raise chickens for the same reason a raccoon attacks them in the night is beside the point. The fact that a raccoon also likes the taste of chicken makes him a competitor and, therefore, an unwanted and suspicious adversary. The great undoing of the raccoon is that he did not long ago become a vegetarian. . . .

For three or four nights following the ruckus, Charley, the Crismans' peacock, roosted fifty feet or higher in the top of a ponderosa pine. He knew instinctively, without benefit of books, that the occasion must be fortified with action, not waiting for others to act.

Shortly after Chet's arrival, everyone except me went hiking up Jim Creek Canyon. Standing in the yard behind the ranch house, one can see farther *up* Jim Creek than *down* it. For this reason, we knew that a canyon lay upstream without our ever having hiked in that direction. I did not go along on that hike because Chet needed my help at the rig.

So it was that we fished and explored whenever the opportunities presented themselves. In fact, when Chet set off the first charge of dynamite in an attempt to open up the first hole, a loud package of six sticks, Mike and I were fishing down on Box Elder better than a mile away. We heard the explosion but apparently not nearly so well as the animals there on the ranch. The dogs retired under the house again and threatened to boycott our human society. Only after a long period of time did they venture once more into a world filled with too much water and too much noise. A duck that Sylvia had setting in what looked, appropriately enough, like a doghouse, left the nest and refused to return to it. The two surviving hens from the shed had already abandoned their nests as a result of the ruckus. Thus, the raccoon and Chet had succeeded admirably in turning some of the ranch animals in the direction they may not prefer but sometimes know best—away from us.

On the day Chet started pounding out the second hole, Chris and I closed up the first hole with rocks. Anyone with a working imagination knows that many rocks would be required to fill up a forty-foot hole one foot in diameter. We drove Chet's pickup through the meadow to the edge of the stream. Using pick and shovel, we loaded buckets of rocks into the bed of the truck. Five-gallon buckets were best suited for this job. We both would fill the buckets, after which I would carry them a short distance to the pickup. The job wore out both of us physically since we worked all morning.

When we had nearly completed our labor, Chet appeared on the scene in a state of some excitement.

"Have you seen Chinook?" he asked.

"No," we said, "Why?"

"He's got a mouthful of quills," Chet said.

"Bad?" Chris asked.

"I'm afraid so. He's really suffering."

I first saw Chinook when he came walking across the meadow looking for us. He was in no particularly big hurry. At a distance he seemed to be carrying in his mouth a loaf of bread, but upon examination, I saw sticking from around his mouth thirty-five or forty porcupine quills. Who can presume to say what passes through a dog's mind during such a time of misery? I would guess that he simply might seek some relief from the same people who feed him. Since the Crismans had several days earlier taken to the road for a trip to Alaska, Chris and I had been feeding all the ranch animals. I would guess, therefore, that he sought relief from us. At any rate, he came meandering toward us like a long-lost pet, devoid of all enthusiasm. Although I did not hear him whimper or whine, he gave every indication of being in the throes of excruciating pain.

Chris and I took the pickup to the first hole, gaping and conspicuous. After back bending with shovels for twenty minutes, she and I, assisted by Chet, had filled that abyss with rocks. Afterward, the three of us turned our full attention to Chinook.

"How good are you with pliers?" Chet asked me.

"Not very," I said, "but if you can hold him, surely I can play Androcles. You, Chrissie, sing to him. Talk to him. Tell him about the silver lining. Convince him that to bite any of us would be unsportsmanlike."

The ensuing scene, judged by any fair standard, might have seemed hilarious had it not been for the pitiful condition of the major actor in that yard play. Aside from the fact that Chinook's agony was the direct result of his not having learned a valuable lesson from a previous encounter with a porcupine, his behavior entitled him to the utmost in sympathy. Poor Chinook so wanted to be free from those wretched quills that he cooperated in every way possible. He allowed himself to be put in the vise of a bear hug from behind by Chet, the best arrangement for the safety of all concerned. Using the pliers in a manner which, I admit, would not have recommended me for an award in finesse, I managed to extract two or three quills before Chinook, through brute strength, broke away. Each time I pulled out a quill, the blood squirted, Chinook yelped, and a wrestling match followed. Chet wrapped the cooperative Chinook in a blanket and held him fast while both lay in a bundle on the ground. The result was no different. We even tied him to the fence with belts and ropes. Our success proved to be no better. It became apparent that Chinook's great strength made utterly useless any effort on our part to help him. Once or twice the pain so annoyed him that he threatened to reach for his instinct to set up a defense. Had we continued our clumsy handling of him, admittedly lacking in both tenderness and subtlety, he probably would have bitten one of us. After removing seven or eight quills, I felt that only if he were put to sleep could the job be done safely and, above all else, painlessly. Chrissie's soothing

words to him during this awful ordeal meant not nearly so much as a knockout needle from a vet would have meant.

I asked Dr. Gene Wheeler by telephone to drive to our ranch from his office forty-five miles away in Sturgis. The trip measures less than half that distance when Vanocker Canyon is open, but since flood damage forced a closing of that route, the motorist had to detour by way of Whitewood, Saint Onge, and Deadwood. The doctor wished me to transport Chinook in my car to his office, sparing him the time required for the ninety-mile round trip. I would have acceded to his wish had Chinook been able to convince me that no additional harm might result from his role as cargo on such a long journey. The fear from realizing that a great variety of things could happen, coupled with the shock from knowing that something disastrous probably would happen, led me to a more diplomatic coaxing. That I finally persuaded the doctor to drive so far to provide relief for a suffering dog will forever attest to his dedication and genuineness. By contrast with the predictable response from urban men of mercy, the reaction of Dr. Wheeler could be called an errand of unselfishness or, if you insist, an act of martyrdom. How many doctors working in a big city would drive forty-five miles even to attend a suffering child?

Dr. Wheeler, accompanied by his wife, drove up in front of the ranch house at two o'clock in the afternoon.

"I'm Gene Wheeler," the friendly, personable man said, getting out of his car. "This is my wife Alma."

To get even with the weather, they requested water. Because the day burned hot and dry, the body needed plenty of water. I gave them a good supply of ice water, which they drank while the five of us exchanged pleasantries. Gene, we discovered, had graduated from the University of Minnesota, an athletic rival of Ohio State University, the alma mater of Chris and me. . . .

Meanwhile, Gene was getting acquainted with Chinook. Before you stick a needle into a dog as big as Chinook, you wisely establish a basis for friendship. For lap dogs and toy poodles, medical necessity will suffice in any crisis; for Chinook, you need solid friendship and, if you're extremely cautious, a good insurance policy.

Gene estimated Chinook's weight to be 105 pounds and measured the appropriate dosage for an injection. While Chet held Chinook from behind, using the now-perfected bear hug, Gene gave Chinook the knockout needle, causing the bewildered dog to wonder, perhaps, why he was being given another quill instead of having one taken from him. Chrissie tried to formulate an answer comprehensible and acceptable to the not altogether nonverbal animal. Ten minutes later Chinook collapsed, the bulk of his huge body as limber as a wet chamois cloth.

While Gene removed the remaining quills and patched up Chinook's mouth, he discovered that two of the quills had broken off, the imbedded pieces requiring extensive probing and cutting. In addition, a wound inflicted on Chinook's neck in the winter by either hunter or culprit had become infected and needed to be lanced. Gene did not hesitate to say that calling him away from Sturgis was, in view of Chinook's condition, a wise decision. Looking back in retrospect, he said his coming was, in fact, a necessity. This pronouncement, stated at a time when I was beginning to feel a twinge of guilt for having drawn the good doctor from so far a distance, made me feel much better. Make no mistake about the matter: Gene Wheeler was a real human being, stripped of all pretense and froth.

Before Gene and Alma left our ranch at three o'clock, he gave Chris a spray can of disinfectant together with instructions for using it. Chinook could not have cared less for the price of figs in Calcutta. He slept all afternoon and evening, scarcely moving a muscle. At night when darkness covered the land and dew formed a bed of dampness, Chris and I spread a blanket over our sleepy patient for protection.

At eleven o'clock that night, believe it or not, Ding came out from her refuge under the house where she had spent the afternoon and evening. Standing there beside Chinook, she barked, urging him to get up. At eleven o'clock they had long been accustomed to fun-filled nocturnal adventures, chasing shadows, uprooting denizens of the darkness, and making formidable foes out of silent silhouettes. Chris and I were, at the time, reading in our cabin. Upon hearing the barking, we ran down to the ranch house to investigate. Sure enough, Ding was trying to tell her sidekick, "Wake up, you big palooka, and let's go ratting around." Chinook, for all his unconsciousness, tried desperately to get up on his legs; he actually did take four or five steps before collapsing in a heap at Ding's feet.

After again covering Chinook with the blanket, we locked Ding in the utility room under the house. Then dear Chrissie set the alarm for three o'clock in the morning, at which time she rose (while I admittedly slept) to help Chinook negotiate his leaden legs on their winding way to the utility room also. He had been made unconscious by the knockout needle for over twelve hours.

At noon the next day Chinook came lumbering forward, ready to be undone by whatever perils still lay ahead, though not before first satisfying a most ravenous appetite.

Installing the pump in a well shield and digging a ditch for laying the electric wiring and the water line proved to be a relatively simple matter. We hired a Deadwood plumber named Keller to perform this work. One day during the last week of July, he brought to our ranch his equipment, including a back hoe. In the Black Hills a plumber often runs his own back hoe, especially if he installs well pumps. In so doing, he avoids troublesome delays and costly time losses that would otherwise be forced upon him by the necessity to adjust to another's work schedule. Not having to depend upon a back-hoe operator happily reduces the length of time required by the plumber to do a job and the amount of money the customer needs to pay for it.

Chris and I decided to use plastic pipe instead of copper tubing for the water line. After talking with Keller, we made several other momentous decisions such as the kind of pump to install, the placement of the many different items inside the well shield, and the best protection for the buried lines in terms of the method used in covering them with dirt.

We felt that the ditch for our water pipe should go underground at least six feet to escape the frost line. Keller said that in Deadwood, even at that depth, water had been known to freeze. Still, for all practical purposes, a depth of six feet would be sufficient, according to him.

At the end of a week Keller had completed the job. On 3 August we finally gained access to cold, clean, clear well water at the faucet in our sink. That day will always remain focused in my memory, for as soon as the water became available, I drank seven glasses of it. No better way, at least no more ceremonial way, of christening "our glory hole" seemed fitting.

—20 April 1973

Donald and Christina Bolin enjoyed several more summers at their ranch along Jim Creek. Shortly after they retired in the early 1980s, Christina Bolin's health began to fail, preventing the couple from moving there permanently as they had planned. The Bolins reluctantly sold their property in 1986, after making their last trip to the Black Hills.

Contributors

Donald W. Bolin grew up in New Boston, Ohio. After graduating from high
school in 1944, he served in the United States Army Air Corps as a radio
operator during World War II. Returning home, he attended Ohio State
University and taught high school in Columbus. He has published works of
poetry as well as prose.

Thomas R. Buecker, a native Nebraskan, spent part of his childhood growing
up on a Faulk County ranch. He holds a B.A. from the University of Nebraska Kearney and an M.A. from Chadron State College. He is currently
the curator of the Nebraska State Historical Society's Fort Robinson Museum in Crawford.

Todd David Epp is a partner with Galland Law Firm in Sioux Falls. He has a
B.A. from Washburn University of Topeka, Kansas, a J.D. from Washburn
University School of Law, and an LL.M. from the University of Houston
Law Center. He lives in Harrisburg, South Dakota, with his wife and two
children. His interests include history, writing, blogging, Buddhism, and
the Civil Air Patrol.

Rose Estep Fosha is a historic preservationist with the Federal Emergency
Management Agency. She earned B.A. and M.A. degrees in anthropology
from the University of Kansas at Lawrence. Her interests focus on historical archaeology, with research and field investigations including
nineteenth-century brick manufacturing, sod houses, and the Chinese on
the western frontier.

Eileen French volunteered during the 2003 Deadwood Chinatown excavation.
She has worked at the South Dakota State Historical Society's Archaeological Research Center in Rapid City, cataloging the hundreds of thousands of
excavated artifacts. French continues to research the history of the Chinese
in the Black Hills.

Todd Guenther's ancestors homesteaded in South Dakota in 1873. He is director of the Western American Studies Program at Central Wyoming College.
An archaeologist and historian, Guenther's research interests focus on race
and gender in westward migration and settlement.

Mary Kopco has been the director of the Adams Museum & House in Deadwood, South Dakota, since 1995. The museum was the 2001 recipient of

the South Dakota Governor's Award for History. Kopco is an author and historical consultant.

George A. Larson, Lt. Col., USAF (ret.), lives in Rapid City and is an aviation and military historian. He has published over three hundred magazine articles and five books. The latest, *The Superfortress and Its Final Glory*, describes B-29 operations in the Korean War.

James D. McLaird is professor emeritus of Dakota Wesleyan University, Mitchell, South Dakota, where he taught history for thirty-seven years. He has specialized in western history and myth-making. His major works are *Calamity Jane: The Woman and the Legend* and *Wild Bill Hickok and Calamity Jane: Deadwood Legends*. He has authored, coauthored, or edited more than a dozen articles in *South Dakota History*.

Rex C. Myers received his Ph.D. from the University of Montana and has published numerous books and articles about the American West. He teaches history and geography part-time at Northwest College in Powell, Wyoming.

Denise Karst Pearce graduated from the University of South Dakota in 1997 and the USD School of Law in 2000. Denise and her husband, Marc, live in Lincoln, Nebraska, with their two young daughters, Erica and Keelyn.

Susan L. Richards directs the John Hinckley Library at Northwest College in Powell, Wyoming. She received her Ph.D. from the University of New Hampshire and has published articles on library history, philanthropy, and nineteenth- and early twentieth-century working women.

Maxwell Van Nuys was born in Rapid City and graduated a civil engineer from New York University. After working for the Tennessee Valley Authority, he volunteered with the Army Engineers in Europe in WWII. Back in Rapid City, he served with the Air Force and encouraged his mother, Laura Bower Van Nuys, to write *The Family Band*. After working for the Colorado State Health Department, he retired to Denver.

Edith C. Wong of San Luis Obispo, California, is a great-granddaughter of Wong Fee Lee. With her mother Beatrice, she carries on the passion for genealogy begun by her late father Kam Leung Wong. A third-generation member of the Society of Black Hills Pioneers, she has made several visits to Deadwood and helped to organize the first reunion of Wong Fee Lee descendants, who gathered at the Wing Tsue buildings in 2004.

Index

Page numbers in *italic* indicate illustrations.

Bower, Willis, 179, 195, 210

Bower Family Band, 3–4, 176–220

Bowman, John, 74–75, 94–95n11

Box Elder Creek, 68n106, 297–98, 302, 306, 308, 319, 321

Boyce, Edward, 232

Brick Store. *See* Hearst Mercantile Company

Briggs, Rachel, 103, 122n11

Bright, William, 121n10

Bryan, Jerry, 98n47

Bryant, Clyde, 19

Bryant, Faye, 19

Budd, Kirk, 19

Buffalo (American Indian), 30

Bugle calls, 20, 25, 28, 38, 40, 41, 61n33, 66n87

Bull Neck (Arikara Indian), 21–22

Calamity Jane. *See* Canary, Martha

Calhoun, Frederic S., 38, 67n94

Calhoun, James, 16, 24, 38, 40, 61n39, 63n52, 64n59, 67n94, 68n101

California Joe. *See* Milner, Moses ("California Joe")

Cameron, C. H., 95n15

Campbell, Sarah ("Aunt Sally"), 115

Camp Collier, 95n18

Camp Echo, 30

Canary, Martha ("Calamity Jane"), 5, 72, 80, 84, *85*, 88, 96–97nn36–37, 263

Cannonball River, *20*

Canton, China. *See* Guangzhou, China

Canyon Lake area, 303

Canyon Lake Dam, 7, 296

Captain Kate: The Heroine of Deadwood Gulch, by Leander P. Richardson, 91, *92*

Carr, P. N., 257

Carty, J. R., 86

Castle Creek Valley, 30, *31*, *33*, 65n67

Castle Rock Butte. *See* Slave Butte

Caton Advertiser, *252*

Caucasian League and Miners' Union, 167n16

Cave Hills, 20, 69n113

Caves, 20, 29–30, 61n32, 64n63

Census data: on Chinese individuals, 129, 136–38, 141–43, 145, 147, 165n3

Central City, S.Dak., 107, *110*, 114–15, 118, 226, 228

Champagne party (Black Hills Expedition), 18, 40, *41*

Chance, Josiah, 23–24, 26, 37, 53, 62n41

Chang, Iris, 151, 159

Chapin, Charles, 96–97n36

Charles Mix County, 249–50

Chew Men. *See* Wong Chang See

Cheyenne, Wyo., 73–75, 86

Cheyenne and Black Hills Forwarding Company, 128

Cheyenne Leader, 76

Cheyenne River, 23–24, 43, 68n97, 76

Cheyenne River Ranch, 95n18

Chicago, Milwaukee, St. Paul & Pacific Railroad, 251

Chinatown (Deadwood, S.Dak.), 3, 127, *128*, 129–30, *131*, *134–35*, 139, 166n6; archaeology of, 139

Chinese Exclusion Act (1882), 136, 137, 144, 147, 159–60, *161*, 162–63, 174nn134, 135

Chinese immigrants, 3, 126, 136, 141, 165n2; and business, 159; calendar, 170n66; family histories, 139; foodways, 135; gender roles, 144; marriage, 142; merchants among, 151–52; and mining, 136, 157;

mortuary practices, 151, 154–56, 173n111; music, 152–54; names and titles, 139–40; national character of, 163; and property ownership, 127, 129–30, 141–42; sentiment toward, 129–30, 162–63, 167. *See also* Chinese Exclusion Act

Chinese Masons, 154–55, 157, 172n108

Chinese New Year, 152–53

Chinese Revolution (1911), 164

Citizen's Ticket party, 251

Civilian Conservation Corps (CCC), 5; in Black Hills, 267–78; camp accommodations, *268*, 270, 273; clothing, 273–74; daily routine, 274; foodways, 274–76, *275*; organization of labor, 271; pay and benefits, 267, 274; requirements for enlistment, 269; work projects, 5, 270–73, 276–77

Civilian Conservation Corps (CCC) camps: Black Fox, 270, *271*; Custer, *275*; Galena, 277; Narrows, *273*; Park Creek, 277; Pine Creek, *268*; Roubaix, 270, 273

Civil rights, 121n10. *See also* Race relations

Clair, Elihu F. *See* Clear, Elihu F.

Clarenbach, J. F., 118

Clark, Edward, 226, 243n17

Clark, Kenneth, 287–88

Clear, Elihu F., 37, 43, 58, 66n86, 68n100

Cleveland, Grover, 229

Cold Hand (American Indian), 30

Cold War, 293n7

Cole, H., 115

Coleman, Charles, 280, 282

Colwell, Edmond, 111

Comets, 23, 62n43

Commons, John R., 239

Congressional Committee on Industrial Relations, 239–40

Coolidge, Calvin, 263

Coon Sing, 153–54, 157–58

Coyotes, 75

Crazy Horse Memorial, 8n5

Crisman, Claude, 298, 302, 306–7, 309–13, 318–20, 322

Crisman, Eddy, 306

Crisman, Sylvia, 298, 302, *303*, 306–7, 310, 318, 320–22

Crook, George, 106, 191

Crouch Line, 270

Cunningham, John, 63n51, 69n107

Cuny (logger), 84, 86

Curtis, William E., 12, 16, 22, 30–32, 48, 62n43

Custer, Boston ("Boss"), 40, 67n94

Custer, Elizabeth, 18

Custer, George Armstrong, 2, *11*, *45*, 103, 115, 222; leads Black Hills Expedition, 9–70

Custer, Margaret Emma, 67n94

Custer, Thomas W., 24, 34, 40, 65–66n74

Custer, S.Dak., 5, 76–77, 192

Custer County Stock, Mineral, and Agricultural Fair, 192–95, *193*

Custer Expedition. *See* Black Hills Expedition

Custer's Park, 38, 67n90

Custer State Park, 6

Cyanide process (gold mining), 230, 244n34

Dances, 106

Dandy, George B., 19, 61n30

The Dark City; or, Customs of the Cockneys, by Leander P. Richardson, 91–92

Davis, J. C., 86

Fire prevention: and the CCC: 270–73, 276–77

Fireproofs, 130, 132, 167n17

First Aid and Mine Rescue program (Homestake Mine), 237

First National Bank: Deadwood, S.Dak., 164, 260; Lead, S.Dak., 243n14

Fishing. *See* Trout fishing; Wild game

Flag Mountain lookout tower, 276–77

Flooding: at Vermillion, D.T., 181. *See also* Rapid City Flood

Floral Valley, *29*, 29–30, 64n62

Food and cooking: in CCC, 274–76; among Chinese, 135; Lucretia Marchbanks, 105–8; on the trail, 74–75, 80–81

Forest management: by CCC, 272–73, 278n6. *See also* Fire prevention

Forsyth, George A., 11, 19, 24, 54–55, 66n77, 67n93, 68nn101–2, 69n109, 70n122

Fort Abraham Lincoln, 10, 55, 61n30

Fort Laramie Treaty (1868), 2, 8n1, 10, 58

Fort Meade, 111, 112, 270, 277; military band, 191

Fort Pierre, 186, *189*

Fort Randall military reserve, 249

Fossils, 23, 62n43

Fourth of July, 152, *153*, 190–92, 195, *211*, 212

Franklin, Mrs. William B., 210

Franklin, Nathan E., 260–62

Franklin, William B., 210

Fremont, Elkhorn & Missouri Valley Railroad, 190

French Creek, *42*, 66–67n88, 68n97, *190*, 207, 215

Fruit. *See* Wild fruit

Fruiting Brooke camp, 46

Fundraisers: in Deadwood, 106–7

Funerals, 87–88, 118–19; on Black Hills Expedition, 27–28, 54, 70n121. *See also* Chinese immigrants

Gambling: and Chinese, 137, 157, 162; in Deadwood, 254, 257, 259, 261–63

Game animals. *See* Wild game

Garretson, Austin B., 239–40

Gates, Julius G., 24, 34, 50–51, 55, 66n78

Gayville, D.T., 78

Geary Act. *See* Chinese Exclusion Act

Gender roles, 3, 102, 105. *See also* Chinese culture

Gerold, Henry, 249

Ghost Dance, 195

Gibson, Francis M., 24, 27–28, 40, 63n55

Godfrey, Edward S., 42–43, 47, 67–68n97

Gold: and Black Hills Expedition, 10, 27, 38, 42, 46, 56–57, 67n91, 68n98

Golden Gate Hotel (Deadwood), 106

Gold mining: and Homestake Mine, 221–47. *See also* Miners and mining

Gold rushes: Black Hills, 2, 57–58, 73, 76–78, 100, 103–5, 111, 126, 221–22; California, 102, 121n8, 141

Goose (Arikara Indian), 61n32

Gorder, C. O., 137, 162

Gossage, Alice Bower ("Od"), 177, *179*, 186–90, *188*, 195, *196–97*, 202–6, *206*, 215, *217*

Gossage, Joseph R., 186–90, *187*, 191, 202–6, 215, *220*

Government Farm (near Fort Laramie), 74, 94n8

Grand Central Hotel (Deadwood), 105–6

Grand River, 50, 69n114

Grand River (Ludlow's) Cave, 20, *21*, 61n32

Grant, Cary, 279–80, *283*, 284, *285–86*, 291

Grant, Fred D., 22–24, 28, 40, 43, 61n36, 62n40, 67n91, 69n112

Great Depression, 5; and CCC, 267–78; recovery from, 277

Great Sioux Reservation, 2, 10, 186

Great Sioux War (1876), 58

Gregg, Mrs. Harry, 109

Grier, Mary Jane, 229, 231, 240

Grier, Thomas J.: 4, 221–47, *223*. *See also* Homestake Mining Company

Grinnell, George Bird, 11, 23–24, 64n61

Guangdong, China, 141, 159–60

Guangzhou, China, 141, 143–44, 164–65

Guidinger's Hotel (Beulah, Wyo.), 116

Gunderson, Carl, 179

Guns, 79–80, 82, 86

Haggin, James B. A., 226, 228–30, 241, 243n17

Hale, Owen, 24–25, 40, 63n54

"Half a Century on the Last Frontiers," by E. L. Senn, 263

Hall (judge), 157

Hal Shek, 136, 137, 139, *140*, 143–46, 148–49, 151, 160, *161*, 168n43

Ham, Charles, 135

Hanes, Caroline D., 13

Hanes, Garland, 13–14

Hangings, 84–86

Harney Peak, 38–40, *39*, 42

Hart, Verling K., 24, 30–32, 53, 55, 65n68, 67–68n97, 70n124

Hat Creek, 74–75, 94–95n11

Haw Shoog Gain. *See* Hal Shek

Haynes, F. Jay: photographs by, *128*, 129, *134*

Hearst, George, 4, 222–24, 226

Hearst, Phoebe Apperson, 226–31, 234–35, 239, 241, 243n18

Hearst Free Kindergarten (Lead, S.Dak.), 222, 229–31, 233

Hearst Free Library (Lead, S.Dak.), 222, 229, 233, 237

Hearst Mercantile Co. (Lead, S.Dak.), 222, 224, *225*, 227, 230, 232–33, 235, 242n10

Heart River, 51–53, 55, *56*, 69n114

Helena, Mont., 121n10

Helena (steamboat), *184*

Hermosa, 192–95

Hickok, James Butler ("Wild Bill"), 3, 5, 71–72, 78–82, *79*, 86–88, *89*, 90, 95nn15, 23–24, 96n26, 97–98n44, 103

Hi Hop, 157

Hi Kee, 130, 134, 152, 155–57, 173n108

Hiking, 317–21

Hill, Abe, 111–12

Hill, Fannie, 259

Hill City, 77, *77*, 195

Hinch, John, 86

Hitchcock, Alfred, *282*; *North by Northwest*, 279–86, 290–93, 293n7

Hi Young, 157

Hodgson, Benjamin H. ("Antelope Benj"), 16, 22, 24–26, 30, 40, 46, 50–51, 53–55, 58, 63n49

Hoener (army private), 63n49

Richmond, Va., 13–15, 24

The Road Agents: A Tale of Black Hills Life, by Leander P. Richardson, 90–91

Road-building: on Black Hills Expedition, 47

Roberts, M. C., 118–19

Robertson, William, 63n50

Robinson, C. H., 151

Robinson, Doane, 1

Rocky Ford (Wyo.) Inn, 116

Roller, William, 63n52

Rome (Deadwood bawdy house), 259

Roosevelt, Franklin D., 5, 267–68

Rosa, Joseph G., 96n26

Rosebud Indian Reservation: land lottery, 254

Ross, Horatio N., 42–43, 68n98

Ross, W. G., 139

Running Water, 74

Rushmore, Charles E., 1

Rustic Hotel, 109–11, 114

Rustling, 248, 251, 254

Saint, Eva Marie, 280, *283*, 284, *285–86*, 291

Saint Paul Daily Pioneer, 12, 15, 19

Saint Paul Daily Press, 2, 13, 15, 21, 40–41, 48

Saloons. *See* Drinking

Sam Wah, 157

Sanborn Map Company, 129, *131*, 132, 134

Sanger, Louis H., 34, 38

Sawpit Gulch (Central City, D.T.), 109

Saylor's Creek (battle), 15

Schools and teaching: and Bower family, 177, 179, *180*, 195, 198, 207, 210, *212–13*, 215; in Lead S.Dak., 229; and E. L. Senn, 249–50

Schwarzwald, Sam ("Hoodoo Sam"), 127, 162, 167n28

Scientists: on Black Hills Expedition, 11–12, 56. *See also* specific individuals

Scooptown. *See* Sturgis, D.T.

Scouts. *See* Indian scouts

Scribner's Monthly, 72–73

The Secret Service, the Field, the Dungeon, and the Escape, by Albert D. Richardson, 72

Sen Lee, 162

Senn, Christa Stull, *250*, 264

Senn, Edward Louis ("E. L."), 4, 248–66, *250*, *258*; as anti-vice crusader, 248, 254–63; as newspaperman, 251–66

Settle, A. C., 114

Settlement: of D.T. and S.Dak., 249–54

Seventeenth United States Infantry, 11

Seventh United States Cavalry: 2, 112; and Black Hills Expedition, 9–70

Sexton, Betty, 296–98, 310, *311*, 317

Sexton, Donald, 296–98, 310, *312*, 314, 317, 319–20

Sheridan, Philip H., 10

Sheridan Lake, 269

Shootings: 71, 86–87; on Black Hills Expedition, 25, 37, 63n52

Shu Lin Lau, *140*

Sickness: on Black Hills Expedition, 25, 69n107, 70n121

Silver: and Black Hills Expedition, 38, 42, 66n77

Silver City, D.T., 112

Sinyard, Neil, 290

Sioux Indians. *See* American Indians; Indian scouts

Sitting Bull (Sioux Indian), 69n111

42–43, *45*, 46–47, 49, 50–51, 53–55, 64n61, 68nn100–101, 105
Williams, John W., 24, 27, 64n56
Williams, Ruth, 302
Williams & Son (Deadwood, S.Dak.), 134
Wilson, Robert, 19
Winchell, Newton H., 11, 22–24, 38, 64n57
Wind Cave, 6
Wing Tone. *See* Wong Fee Lee
Wing Touie. *See* Wong Fee Lee
Wing Tsue. *See* Wong Fee Lee
Wing Tsue Bazaar, 3, 127–28, *132*, 133–36, *138*, 142, 146, *148*, 150–52, *156*; meaning of name, 128–29. *See also* Wong Fee Lee
Wirth, Conrad L., 289–90, 294n21
Women. *See* Gender roles
Wo Mung Shing, 129
Wong, Kam Leung, 128–29, 139, 140–41, 166n11, 167n23
Wong, Tung Quang. *See* Wong Tong Quong
Wong Bing Quong, 137–38, 159–60, 162; family of, 138
Wong Bong, 129, 142
Wong Chang See, 145
Wong Coon, 129
Wong Fay Juchs, 136–37, 139, *140*, 148–50, 160–62
Wong Fay King, 136–37, 139, *140*, 148–50, 160–62
Wong Fay Lan, 139, 151, 160–62
Wong Fee Lee, 3, *140*, *161*; and assimilation, 149–50, in census, 129, 136–38, 141; children dead in infancy, 148–49, 151; and Chinese Exclusion Act, 159–60, 162–63, 174n134; as community leader, 152, 155–56, 172–73n108;

in early Deadwood, 127–29; early life of, 141, 169nn50, 52; family, 136–37, 142–51, 160–62, 164; legal troubles of, 156–58; meaning of name, 166n11; as merchant, 151–52; political beliefs of, 164, 175n141; properties owned by, 126–27, 129, 130–35, *133*, 136–37, 139, 141–42, 149, 157, 162, 164, 168n38; as "Wing Tsue," 140–41
Wong Hoi, 162
Wong Hong Quong, 136–39, *140*, 144–47, *146*, 149–50, 160–62, 164
Wong King Que, 136–37, 139, *140*, 145, *146*, 149–50, 160–62
Wong King Sowe, 136–37, 139, *140*, 145, *146*, 149–50, 160–62
Wong Loung Quong, 141, 143
Wong Mow, 160
Wong Nung, 129
Wong Som Quong, 136–39, *140*, 146–50, *146*, 160–62, 164, 167n23, 173n111
Wong Tong Quong, 136–39, 142, *146*, 149–51, 160–62
Wong Wing Hui, 142
Wong Woo Shee, 141
Wong Yick Lai, 160
Wong Yuen Yum, 141
Wong Yun Cherk, 137–38, 145
Wood, William R., 23
World War II, 277
Wo She, 142
Wyoming, 114–15, 121–22n10

Yates, George W., 24, 34, 40, 55, 58, 66n79
Yuet Ha Tang. *See* Tang, Anna

Ziolkowski, Korczak, 8n5